BITTER WATERS

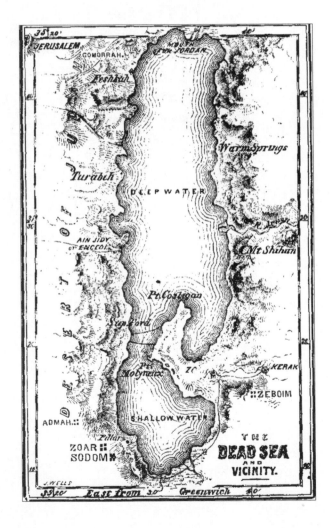

BITTER WATERS

America's Forgotten Naval Mission to the Dead Sea

DAVID HAWARD BAIN

THE OVERLOOK PRESS
New York, NY

First published in hardcover in the United States in 2011 by
The Overlook Press, Peter Mayer Publishers, Inc.

141 Wooster Street
New York, NY 10012
www.overlookpress.com

For bulk and special sales, please contact sales@overlookny.com

PICTURE CREDITS

Title page: facing map of the Dead Sea from *Harper's Magazine*,
January 1855 (Author collection).
With the exception of illustrations credited in captions, all others presented
here are from the 1849 edition of Lynch's *Narrative* (Author collection).

Cataloging-in-Publication Data is available from the Library of Congress

Book design and typeformatting by Bernard Schleifer
Manufactured in the United States of America

ISBN 978-1-59020-352-1

2 4 6 8 10 9 7 5 3 1

For Ellen Levine
for decades of friendship
and counsel

Contents

9

List of Illustrations

Acknowledgments

I AM INDEBTED TO MY LONGTIME AGENT AND FRIEND, ELLEN LEVINE, to whom this book is warmly dedicated. Thanks, too, to her great staff. Deep thanks to Peter Mayer of The Overlook Press; Aaron Schlechter, for his support and elegant editing; Rob Crawford, for his skillful navigation through the publishing process; Jennifer Rappaport, for her copyediting; all the others at The Overlook Press.

My profound thanks to Eve Ness, extraordinary reader and editor, for her professional and personal help, given most generously. Katherine and John Duffy offered invaluable advice and support on yet another book by their son-in-law, who will always be grateful for their careful reading; Mary Smyth Duffy, who died before I began writing this book, was present as it was first envisioned long ago and was its great champion; Mimi and David M. Bain buoyed me with their enthusiasm and boundless curiosity; Lisa, Christopher, and Terry Bain read various stages and were always supportive, as were Marc Santiago and the late William Schwarz, brothers-in-law and faithful readers. Thanks, too, for the support of my Middlebury College colleagues Brett Millier, James Ralph, Paul Monod, Robert Schine, Ron Liebowitz, and John McCardell, as well as thumbs-up from Christopher Shaw, Michael Collier, Robert Cohen, and Jay Parini, often from nearby tables at Carol's Hungry Mind Café, Middlebury, Vermont.

So many librarians, curators, directors, and staff helped me with the research for this book, in large and small ways, that I fear I cannot list them individually, but my gratitude goes out to the staffs of Davis Library at Middlebury College, New York Public Library, National Archives and Records Administration, Library of Congress, Navy Department Library, Naval Historical Center, Naval War College Library, U.S. Naval Academy, U.S. Naval Observatory, Butler Library at Columbia University, Burke Library at Union Theological Seminary, Alderman Library at University of Virginia, Davis Library at University of North Carolina-Chapel Hill, Maryland State Archives, Newport Historical Society, and Mystic Seaport Library. Thanks, also, to Dan Monahan, Superintendent, Green Mount Cemetery in Baltimore, and to John S. Lynch and John S. Lynch II. Finally, legions of unknown but much-appreciated people are behind the information revolution of the past decade (particularly the last five years), scanning many libraries and archives and making them available to researchers on the Internet. When I think of the time and travel necessary for my previous books, and, during this project, what became accessible with a few clicks of the keyboard and the right paths and search terms, I am at once awed and beholden.

—DAVID HAWARD BAIN
Orwell, Vermont
February 2004—February 2011

BITTER WATERS

Introduction

SOMETIMES BOOK IDEAS LURK IN ONE'S HEAD FOR YEARS—EVEN, IN this case, decades.

In early 1985, I signed a preliminary contract with a publisher for *Empire Express: Building the First Transcontinental Railroad*. As I remember it, I had three months to produce a formal proposal and bibliography, after which a full-fledged book contract would follow. I was living in Park Slope, Brooklyn, at the time; my second book, *Sitting in Darkness: Americans in the Philippines*, had been published three or four months before by another firm.

I spent much of that proposing period in happy study at the grand old New York Public Library at Fifth Avenue and 42nd Street. Much of the scholarly research for *Sitting in Darkness* came out of that building; in fact, the inspiration for its past-and-present narrative form had hit me in a beam of light which struck me as I was looking at an old map at a table in the reading room. I sneezed in the light; inspiration struck; and I quickly sketched out an outline that scarcely deviated from the final narrative. Still grateful and pleased in 1985, I settled into the library yet again.

These were the days before computerized catalogs. One went upstairs to the third floor and walked into a cathedral-like, sunlit room whose walls held great banks of golden oak card-catalog drawers, tiers

17

of them running up to balconies with circular staircases. Mysteries lurked in every drawer. The yellowed cards inside were sometimes typewritten, sometimes handwritten in spidery style, and it was a glorious tactile feeling to thumb them. One could not fail to feel a simultaneous connection with the thumbs and the quests of untold thousands of researchers, and with the patient librarians who had held books and pamphlets when they were still bright and fresh, their spines stiff, as the bibliographic data was copied off onto a three-by-five-inch piece of cardboard with a hole punched into the bottom for the brass rod of a catalog drawer.

Older researchers extracted the drawers and made a place at the great tables nearby, but I was younger then and impatient and working under a deadline. I simply stood, pulled out a drawer, thumbed, and copied down dozens of citations. I needed a place to set my notebook, however, so I pulled out nearby drawers as an impromptu work area. Writers who have labored under similar conditions in the old days like to talk about the serendipity of finding resources on cards happened upon by mistake—computer catalogs don't allow for serendipity. As I stood one day at my post, I pulled open the adjacent drawer. Before I could cover it with my notebook the heading cards pulled me away from thought about a railroad threading across the Western plains and mountains. "Exploring Expeditions, United States, 1838–1863," I think it said. These were not Army-sponsored, though, and had nothing to do with the continental United States. These were naval expeditions, and in all my years of reading history I had heard nothing about them—with the exception of Commodore Matthew C. Perry's "opening" of Japan in 1853 (over subsequent years all general readers and most historians I consulted were unaware also).

Just for fun, I copied down several dozen card entries of official reports and forgotten antebellum bestsellers . . . *the River Jordan and the Dead Sea . . . Patagonia and Paraguay . . . the source of the Amazon River . . . the Western Africa coast . . . the North Atlantic and the Arctic . . . the China Sea and Japan . . . the North Pacific and Bering Strait . . .* and

18

said to myself, "There's a future book in this." Of paramount interest to me was the 1848 expedition to the Holy Land, a surprising historical juxtaposition in that era of the California Gold Rush and covered wagons.

The copied citations sat on a shelf over my writing desk as it was moved from my New York City apartment to a dilapidated farmhouse in Shoreham, Vermont, and from Shoreham to a onetime Methodist parsonage in Orwell, Vermont, and the years flipped by like those calendar-montages from old movies. The transcontinental railroad book, *Empire Express*, was done 14 years after I started with a bibliography and a proposal and sore feet from standing for days at the New York Public Library. A 7,000-mile, one-way summer driving trip in 2000, following old pioneer wagon ruts and vanished railroad tracks, resulted in the next book, *The Old Iron Road*. Then it was time to wash the alkali road dust from my mouth and mind, and embark figuratively on a long sea voyage I had prescribed for myself long ago.

I can never refrain from putting this story into context—how strange, how surprising, how inexplicable it is that in the decades before the Civil War, with all that newly opened continental territory to explore and control (especially after the conclusion of the Mexican War won the vast, mysterious Far West in 1846), that the United States would find the energy and resources to look far, far beyond its shores. Certainly the Army and its topographical corps dispatched their many explorers, surveyors, cartographers, and cavalry out past the Missouri River, trying to comprehend what was now the continent-wide United States. The westering impulse of pioneers, homesteaders, and prospectors kept the energy flowing in that direction, an absorbing kind of national self-regard.

But there were sporadic diversions from foreign climes, courtesy of the Navy, and they swept up the peoples' interest and imagination even as their hopes tended westward. Intent as Americans were on focusing on themselves and their swiftly enlarging sense of home, a transformation was taking place that would, after the Civil War and as the Gilded Age boomed and busted and boomed again, open the American imagination to faraway places, to possibilities, to a greater involvement and a quickening competition—for better or worse—with the world beyond our shores.

As my research developed over the years, the personalities of these ambitious, visionary seafarers illuminated their era; not only their ideas and exploits but also their voices, their characters, called out to their contemporaries. In particular Lieutenants William Francis Lynch and Matthew Fontaine Maury—both sons of Virginia, by turns shipmates, friends, and co-conspirators (as they would have cheerfully admitted as young men) in the causes of professionalizing the U.S. Navy, broadening its power and reach, extending human knowledge of science and geography purely for its own sake—seemed to speak clearly to me. Overcoming limitations of their humble backgrounds and self-education, and struggling against their own physical frailty, they prevailed within the service and with their minds and hands succeeded admirably in their goals; they changed history. Maury—the scientist—transformed the way humanity looked at the world, its oceans, its skies. Lynch—the mariner—followed a lifelong urge to explore what he saw as the cradle of humanity's hopes, the Holy Land, applying nineteenth-century science to understand ancient events and the global forces that had shaped that place. Lynch was always of a literary bent; his narrative of his Dead Sea and River Jordan explorations was a runaway bestseller for the time, going through multiple editions and translations. Lynch and Maury were emblematic of their time and place—how ironic, then, that in just a few years with the onset of the Civil War, their loyalty to their native Virginia soil would impel them out of the naval service to which they had devoted their lives, and away from the orbit of the Union whose national interest they had, for decades, championed. Even presidential pardons after the war could not restore their former place or influence. But in the time they did have, previously, those two Virginia friends Lynch and Maury were of immense value to the United States, playing a major role in the Navy.

On reflection, politics being what it has always been, it stands to reason that in those two decades preceding the Civil War, the competitive U.S. Navy would vie for attention and benefit from such figures as Lynch and Maury. It was, after all, at the mercy of isolationist elements in Congress and the press, representing not surprisingly the interior states—what need of a navy to the people of Ohio, Tennessee, or Arkansas? In political terms, dispatching sailing ships and steamers to the Holy Land or the western edge of the Dark Continent or the highest tributaries of the murky Amazon is the equivalent of the modern-day manned space program of NASA. Both captured the public imagination, made further subsidies possible, and gave collateral support to purely scientific discovery. And back before the Civil War, official expedition reports and popularized travel memoirs by commanders and their crews were bestsellers; newspapers, monthly magazines, and crowded lyceum lectures further spread the word. The fact that more than a century and a half separate us from that heady time, that the adventures are sometimes mere footnotes—not conforming to the simple narrative most history-minded people carry with them of explorers, pioneers, tracklayers, and Civil War combatants—does not diminish the vividness of the era or the excitement of plumbing mysterious depths, sighting mysterious shores.

Prelude: Acre, Palestine

THEY SET SAIL SOUTHWARD FROM BEIRUT IN MID-AFTERNOON, propelled down the Mediterranean coast by a fine northwest breeze. Off the port side was the lush maritime plain of ancient Phoenicia, cultivated with gardens, groves, and orchards running up toward the brown foothills of the mountains of Lebanon. There on the coast were its two fabled cities, Sidon and Tyre.

Such a sight would swell the heart of any mariner. Great Sidon was named for its founder, the son of Canaan and grandson of Noah; in antiquity the city was celebrated by Homer as a center for arts and the sciences of navigation, astronomy, geometry, architecture, and philosophy. Now it sat in decline on its peninsula, the harbor lapping beneath a decrepit castle connected to the mainland by a nine-arched bridge. Twenty-five miles down the coastal plain lay Tyre, all of its former glory buried beneath rubble and shifting sands, with only shattered ruins of citadels, castles, palaces, and temples, and monuments to hint at what once was.

There was so much. In ancient days from Phoenicia that bold navy had commanded the entire Mediterranean from Sidon and Tyre to the Pillars of Hercules and out past Gibraltar into the monstrous Atlantic, the mariners touching Britain and sailing around Africa, planting colonies, creating and controlling commerce. And then, inevitably, there was the great decline, invited by Phoenicia's idolatry, its worship of celestial bodies, the feminine principle, love, and base immorality, its rejection of entreaties and prophecies of the followers of Jehovah.

Over the centuries retribution of all manners laid siege outside the cities' gates—the Assyrian king Shalmanezer, Nebuchadnezzar of Babylon, and Macedonia's Alexander the Great, who in victory laid grandeur to waste, scattering tens of thousands of survivors into slavery across his wide empire: the once great commercial people now made items of commerce themselves. Successive waves of civilization broke over those old plains, building up their cities only to be crushed and rebuilt: Egyptian, Assyrian, Roman, Muslim, Crusader, and finally, Ottoman.

A great naval power without the imagination to foresee its own downfall: now, that invited meditation.

In modern times, a young and vibrant nation was subduing its own continent, and, before even that task was completed, its wise and far-thinking administrators were sending feelers of the best intent— for the benefit of scientific knowledge (though quite possibly also commerce of some developing sort). Modern thinking, democracy, and Christianity: those were powerful aids in the Holy Land. Rifles, pistols, bowie knives, and a blunderbuss would not hurt, if trouble threatened. And threaten it might. Scientific knowledge could be terrifying—to the wrong people.

U.S.S. *Supply* pierced the swells of that illimitable sea, Lieutenant William Francis Lynch of Virginia commanding. It was Tuesday, March 28, 1848. Back home in North America, the ink was hardly dry on the Treaty of Guadalupe Hildalgo, which ended the two-year war between the United States and Mexico and transferred 1.2 million square miles of territory, including Texas, New Mexico, Arizona, Nevada, Utah, and California, land of golden promise, to the United States.

It had been the Army's war; opportunities for service and promotions in the Navy were limited. Lieutenant Lynch had repeatedly implored the secretary of the Navy for a ship so he could do his part, but with few openings and no political patronage he had sat out the war on dry land, at half pay, wondering, now in his late forties and having been stalled at a lieutenant's rank for nearly two decades, how much of a future was ahead of him. At low points in the last year he had morosely considered resigning his officer's commission, picking up an Army rifle, and heading out toward Cerro Gordo or Churubusco or Mexico City, where at least something might happen— though that something might be a Mexican bullet or machete (nearly 6,000 Americans had been killed or wounded) or a tropical fever (more than 11,000 died of disease). William Francis Lynch contemplated a career that seemed to have run out of steam, and a personal life that was in ashes. But with the prospect of peacetime came intriguing opportunities, the kind that came once in a lifetime and could alter its trajectory.

Two days before in Beirut, working out some last-minute financial arrangements, Lieutenant Lynch had been introduced to a wealthy Syrian merchant. "When informed of the nature of our undertaking," Lynch would write, "he first said, 'it is madness!' But the moment after, forgetful of the comforts and luxuries around him, he turned to me, and, with his soul beaming in his eyes, exclaimed, 'Oh! How I envy you!'"

It was now midnight, a good time to contemplate the relative lunacy or desirability of the lieutenant's mission. For the love of science and the sake of longtime personal fixation, as well as for the glory of the United States Navy and his own career, William Francis Lynch was about to lead a tiny party of American sailors into the geographical center of the Holy Land, from the Mediterranean shore to the Sea of Galilee. Embarking upon life boats dragged overland by camels, they would sail under the Stars and Stripes across that ancient and ennobled lake to its outlet, the River Jordan, mapping the watercourse's entire lower length through dangerous terrain inhabited by hostile Bedouin tribes. Then, they would continue as the sacred river spilled into its noisome, mineral-choked conclusion, the Dead Sea, where nothing could live beneath its surface, or even, as some reports held, upon its miasmic waves. Their scientific instruments would answer ancient riddles while their arsenal, and their wits, would persevere against antagonists.

Or so one hoped. Others had perished in similar attempts, and not too long before. U.S.S. *Supply* heaved to opposite the bold and precipitous White Cape—Promontorium Album to the great chronicler Pliny, and Ras el-'Abyadh to the Arabs—where, the old commentators said, an awe-inspiring staircase had been carved up the steep white rock from the breaking waves at its base to its summit, 200 feet above, and the ancient coast road. Built for chariots and ox-cart caravans, the road ran north to Beirut, Antioch, Tarsus, and Asia Minor; south, to Joppa, Rhinocoruba, the Nile, and Alexandria; east, past Mount Hermon toward Damascus, Palmyra, Nineveh, Babylon, and Baghdad. Many paths, many destinations, a profusion of stories—Lieutenant Lynch's would commence in the morning.

PART ONE

CHAPTER ONE

From Virginia to Heartache

HIS LIFE HAD BEGUN ON A FARAWAY SHORE—WHERE VIRGINIA'S Elizabeth River and Hampton Roads flowed into lower Chesapeake Bay—at Norfolk, on April 1, 1801. His ancestral home was Ireland; the family emigrated via the Port of Baltimore to America and put down roots at Frederick, Maryland. His father was engaged in business in Norfolk, and little else is known about him and Lynch's mother; William had two brothers, Edward and Eugene.

Norfolk was a city with such abiding maritime traditions that for someone like William Francis Lynch, to grow up on its sand-gritty cobbled streets with its tree-shadowed, brick-fronted houses was to always see one's destiny in the forest of masts bobbing majestically at anchorages that nearly surrounded the city. Every boyish exploration of the peninsula's inlets and marshes, of Norfolk's quarter of commercial streets, outdoor markets, wharves, warehouses, and its warrens of rooming houses, taverns, tattoo parlors, and curio shops, was accomplished with the odor of salt water in the nostrils. Shouldering throngs of merchant seamen and sailors and marines from the nearby naval base would tower over the local boys, lending a whiff of foreign ports, mysterious coasts, demanding seas.

After William's mother died when he was 17, he left home and school. There seemed to be little to hold the family together anyway, for the elder Lynch, if "not devoid of affection," William recalled, "was engrossed by the care of his property." Still "in the garb of mourning," he "embraced the roving, stirring, homeless, comfortless, but attractive life of a sailor."[1]

Signing on as a midshipman, he obtained a berth on U.S.S. *Congress*, the third naval vessel of that name, a 36-gun sailing frigate that had been launched in 1799 from the Portsmouth shipyard and had seen considerable action against privateers and pirates in the Atlantic, the Caribbean, and the Mediterranean, once under the famed Stephen Decatur, and against British shipping in the War of 1812. Now it was fitted for the long voyage to China, the historic first such cruise of an American warship, with the object of "showing the flag" around the world, protecting merchant shipping, and contributing to diplomatic efforts to solidify ties between Washington and Canton in the still unsettled aftermath of Britain's Opium War.

The Navy had no officers' academy comparable to the Army's at West Point, so midshipmen learned at sea. It would be vivid schooling for young Lynch. *Congress* sailed for the Azores, where the midshipman took careful notice in his journal of the culture and mores of Madeira, and then for Rio de Janeiro, where evidence of the active Brazilian slave trade horrified this son of Virginia. Then *Congress* made for the Cape of Good Hope. Java Head and the entrance of the Sunda Strait appeared before them on the 64th day. Stopping briefly over to water at Anjeer, and joining a small mainland-bound convoy of American and British merchant ships, the frigate continued into the China Sea at nearly the height of monsoon season, bearing through a furious typhoon that nearly drove them onto shoals athwart the island of Luzon in the Philippines; at one point the roar of surf was clearly audible. Not until they were nearly in sight of the Ladrons Islands and the city of Canton did the sea subside.

All the way across, *Congress* was a crowded, floating academy for

William Francis Lynch and his young comrades. Midshipmen were officers in training, outranked by all but ordinary sailors, berthed in hammocks down in steerage, on watch much of the day and learning constantly, whether they were supervising sailors on deck or rigging duties, taking gunnery practice, or being tutored by the sailing master in mathematics, navigation, and astronomy, learning what little was understood about tides, currents, and winds. As such, the education was paltry; much of their work was menial, and the natural high spirits of the youths made sustained train of thought difficult.

For several months *Congress* used an anchorage some 80 miles up the shore from Canton, while its crew mapped and sounded coastal waters—Lynch's diary recorded how happily reminiscent of home were the pine forests and gentle, mist-shrouded hills of mainland China—and then the ship spent six weeks pursuing a rumored but elusive open-sea shoal, with the detailed officers and midshipmen suffering long exposure to the sun while sounding the bottom from boats. Probably it was during this time, given the drills and maneuvers, that Lynch badly injured an ankle while helping to launch a cutter from the frigate. The injury would hamper and pain him for years.

Twice, the frigate sailed to Manila. The first voyage was for replenishing stores as well as seeking better medical care for their swelling sick list, where there were "considerate and attentive" Spanish colonial authorities and competent (for the era) doctors and nurses. The second, however, begun as the first leg of the long return cruise home, took *Congress* into disaster. In Manila a galloping cholera epidemic was blamed by superstitious Filipinos on the foreign community; mobs burned out and massacred many Westerners, with the colonial army and police restoring order only after great difficulty. By then, *Congress* had sailed into Manila harbor; its commander had conferred with local authorities about the "sickly airs" they then believed caused cholera; and the ship had filled its tanks with local drinking water. It was infected.

Already resembling a floating hospital, recalled Lynch, with many sailors bedridden with heatstroke, tropical diseases, and injuries, *Congress* sailed hastily south and west across the China Sea but was rapidly overtaken by the contagion they did not understand, which decimated the weaker sailors but reached even the robust. "Of those who assembled at the evening meal," recalled Lynch of those tense days, "sometimes he, whose manly frame and sanguine temperament seemed to defy the pestilence, would be attacked during the night, and the next morning, sewed up in the hammock in which he had long been rocked to sleep, his bodied awaited the rites of sepulture." Seventy men were dead before the ship reached Java Head and the plague abated.[2]

More trouble was ahead. The ship reached the Cape of Good Hope, but gales prevented it from pausing to take on fresh water, and when *Congress* neared the island of St. Helena, the commander seriously erred in bypassing the island and not getting water because he was anxious to make a Western port and wanted to take advantage of generous winds. But then they were becalmed in the middle of the South Atlantic. After a week of growing thirst among the crew, scurvy appeared and pervaded. The suffering began to abate with a copious shower and breezes, which then sent them westward toward succor at Rio de Janeiro. When *Congress* and its crew were replenished, they sailed out of Buenos Aires harbor for the final leg.

Two years away from home—the hard work and tension, the terrible food and too much drink, the storms and unfriendly seas, the fevers and injuries, the numerous deaths—accumulated upon the crew in the ensuing weeks, their anticipation of home port rising, and *Congress* actually quickened as it neared the Chesapeake, propelled by a stiff breeze.

As Lynch recorded in his journal, "My messmates insist upon it that the Norfolk girls have a tow-rope secured to the ship, and that they are hauling us in with a speed proportioned to their impatience."[3] *Congress* reached Hampton Roads and anchored against a sunset. Early the next morning it navigated slowly and majestically through the narrow channel toward the Navy yard past the town of Norfolk, with the entire population turned out on docks and wharves to cheer its return from China. William Francis Lynch would never forget the pride and exhilaration, and he keenly looked forward to his next voyage.

His maritime education continued, with the ships on which he served sailing in and out of history, and with the young man who was being formed developing an interesting set of contradictions.

Bookish and well read, religious and philosophical, Lynch had entered an active, dangerous profession in which there were few in the apprentice ranks who shared his interests or passions, and the others of his age who were common seamen were more often than not, he noted, of a loutish or roguish character.

From Virginia, a state that owed its prosperity and its prominence within the American union to the fruits of slave labor, Lynch was at his core a passionate abolitionist, freely expressing his views in the memoir he penned in middle age and published in 1851, the decade so scored by dissension and violence over slavery that overflowed into conflagration in 1861 with the Civil War. Even on his maiden voyage to China in 1819, the year that the U.S. Congress had declared the slave trade to be piracy (it had been forbidden to American shipping since 1808), young Lynch had been revolted by the cruelties he witnessed in Rio de Janeiro. "The slaves so much exceed the freemen in number," he wrote in his journal, "that the police [are] necessarily very strict, and gangs of the poor wretches are compelled to work in chains. The heart sickens at the sight of hordes of these unfortunates, almost in a state of nudity, like driven cattle, exposed for inspection and sale, and this, too, immediately in front of the palace. What a contrast!"[4]

His second voyage heightened his outrage. The schooner *Shark* left port in August 1821. It was a swift, 200-ton Baltimore clipper, 86 feet long and armed with 12 mounted guns, under the command of Lieutenant Matthew C. Perry, a zealous abolitionist. The mission, after conveying the U.S. minister to the new colony of Liberia, was to interdict slave ships off the African coast. American and British cruisers were hard pressed to make a dent, especially when there were so many other nations who refused to honor the restriction to their commerce. Off the coast of Liberia, they had a memorable encounter when they spied a suspicious ship and gave chase. When "the bow guns were cleared away," Lynch recounted, "and we were calculating how long before they could be brought to bear . . . through the spyglass, we were shocked to perceive that gangs of negroes were brought up, placed at the sweeps, and made to labor for the prolongation of their captivity."

That cruelty spurred them, he said, "to renewed exertion." When the enemy schooner was finally overtaken, it proved to be flying French colors and bound for the French West Indies. "The overpowering smell and the sight presented by her slave-deck, can never be obliterated from the memory," Lynch wrote. "In a space of about 15 by 40 feet, and four feet high, between-decks, one hundred and sixty-three negroes, men, women, and children, were . . . confined," dovetailed head to feet with children forced to lie atop the adults. "Their bodies were so emaciated, and their black skins were so shrunk upon the facial bones, that in their torpor, they resembled so many Egyptian mummies half-awakened into life. A pint of water and half a pint of rice each, was their daily allowance."

Lynch and all the other midshipmen, and indeed all the junior officers, were astounded when Lieutenant Perry examined the slavers' documents and pronounced that he was powerless to stop them or seize their cargo: France had not yet signed the antislavery pact. They urged their commander to do the right thing, but he said he was hampered by diplomatic and legal restrictions. Not even when the younger officers pledged their own purses to offset any fine to which Lieutenant Perry might be held would he act: his hands were tied,

Perry said, and no one felt it more keenly than he. "With feelings which I cannot undertake to express," Lynch wrote, "we saw the schooner fill away and steer to the westward, bearing into life-long captivity the unhappy wretches whom we had inspired with a hope of freedom."

Frustratingly, *Shark* was soon ordered to the West Indies before they could strike a blow against slavery. American naval interdictions along the African coast would continue until the program was abandoned in 1824—with ships flying French or Spanish flags off-limits, few efforts could be successful.[5]

Not only were Lynch's political and moral beliefs about slavery an interesting indication of his contrasting nature. There was also the issue of alcoholic spirits, of course a mainstay in most sailors' lives. By the conclusion of his second long voyage, from America to Africa to the West Indies and then up the Atlantic coast to New York, he had begun to see the habit of hard indulgence with a clear eye.

It was bitterest wintertime, and they worked northward above Cape Hatteras against a nor'easter snowstorm. The crew had become accustomed to tropical seas. As schooner *Shark* neared its destination it was "a pyramid of ice." Moreover, said Lynch, "some of the officers and many of the men were frost-bitten; a few of the latter so severely, that they subsequently lost the use of their feet for life." And there was a moral and also a physiological truth: "The greatest sufferers were those who drank ardent spirits; and those who were strictly temperate, almost to a man escaped. Next to temperance, exercise was the greatest preservative, and he who kept his blood in circulation by constant motion, if it were only marking time, retained the full use of his limbs, while his more indolent watchmates were severely frost-bitten."[6]

A year before in Buenos Aires the inexperienced Lynch, after sampling hard spirits in a big way, found himself with his friends howling at the moon, carousing streets, waking slumberers and shooting out windows of complainers. Now he was seeing the light of cause and effect, and responsibility and sensibility, and trying to improve one's chances of survival. As a mature commander during his life-defining exploit, he would insist that all the men who accompanied him to the Jordan and Dead Sea sign temperance pledges and be of clean and upright character.

Certainly, during Lynch's third sea tour he saw many individuals of an opposite nature: he was posted to the anti-pirate "mosquito flotilla" of Commodore David Porter, plying the waters around St. Thomas, Puerto Rico, Santo Domingo, and Cuba. Against a seemingly endless supply of privateers who had the run of the Caribbean and had had a terrible effect against shipping, the Americans had a grab-bag force of small schooners, a steam ferryboat called *Seagull*, and row-barges named *Mosquito*, *Gnat*, *Midge*, *Sandfly*, and *Gillinipper*. Lynch first served on a schooner before volunteering for one of the little barges, which were powered by sail and oar and served by 2 officers, a coxswain, and 16 seamen.

He was soon fully immersed in more action than he had ever seen, as the squadron was sent to fan out across the seas. Barges, including the one on which Lynch served, sailed straight from Key West to the Cuban pirate stronghold of Sagua la Grande, where at daybreak they mounted a strategic attack on shore batteries and several moored schooners. Quickly, the fight moved to hand-to-hand combat with sword and single-shot pistol; it was long and exceptionally bloody, mostly on the side of the pirates, who were cut down at their guns and on deck, or shot as they attempted to swim away.

Within three days his ship found itself along Cuba's northern coast, in pursuit of one of the most dreaded and remorseless bands of privateers. When they saw they would be overrun, the pirates deliberately grounded their ship and melted into the jungle with the Americans unable to stop them.

So passed two years of service in the Indies, in which Lynch took part in uncountable battles and chases under horrid tropical conditions—short water rations, salt-preserved food, sun-blistered, skin-diseased, and attacked by swarms of mosquitoes and sand fleas that "goaded us," wrote Lynch, "almost to madness. It is wonderful how we stood it; and but for the high state of mental excitement, the most powerful constitution must have succumbed. Whether chasing vessel far to seaward, or dragging our boats up some narrow creek, by the jutting roots or overhanging branches of the mangrove, or pushing them, as we waded, across a wide but shallow lagoon, the toil was unceasing, the exposure baneful, and the privation scarce endurable."[7]

At the end of the first year, Commodore Porter ordered his command to congregate at Key West for recuperation, but no sooner had the Navy force gathered than yellow fever struck. "Of that dreadful period," Lynch wrote, "so painful to think of, it would be laceration to the feelings to attempt a recital." But he gave a glimpse of the "dreadful mortality" that had thinned them: his barge had consisted of 2 officers and 17 men, and after three weeks of the epidemic, only 5 survived.[8]

Lynch and the other lucky ones lived to spend another year chasing pirates. But by the end of the campaign under Commodore Porter, they had pushed the number of captured pirate craft to 65, and the extirpation would be all but complete.

Shipping on the *Brandywine*, a newly launched 44-gun frigate under Commodore Charles Morris, young Lynch went on his fourth tour. He would encounter an inspiring figure out of history, as well as meet one of the most influential friends of his life.

Service during that fall voyage of 24 days from the Chesapeake Bay to the French port of Le Havre was considered to be the most honorable post of the day, for the esteemed guest was Marie Joseph

Paul Yves Roch Gilbert du Motier, the Marquis de Lafayette—General Lafayette, last surviving general of the American Revolution. The marquis, who in his youth with a love of democracy hastened to America to volunteer his life and considerable treasure to the cause, had now by the age of 66 outlived his great friend Washington by two and a half decades. Lafayette had been invited to return to his adopted land by President James Monroe. Accompanied by his son and by his secretary, he sailed in July 1824 for New York on the American ship *Cadmus*, waving away the offer of free passage on a U.S. naval vessel and insisting on paying his party's passage himself.

When he reached America—his ship sailed beneath a rainbow arching over New York harbor from Staten Island to Brooklyn—the resounding reply came from America: *your money's no good here!* Remembered in one of many accounts as "half hero, half god, second only to Washington," Lafayette was engulfed by a cascade of adoration that carried him on a 30-month tour, by special coach and riverboat, of all the 24 states in the Union: down the Eastern seaboard from New York to Georgia; across the southern belt to Louisiana; up a network of interior rivers, Great Lakes, and a momentous canal— the Mississippi, Cumberland, and Ohio; Lakes Ontario and Erie; and the Erie Canal—and then crossing through all of New England (several states twice), before redoubling through the mid-Atlantic states to Washington.[9]

Thirty months of that kind of tour would have killed a lesser man—almost a thousand days of bowing humbly and lovingly before deafening cheers of vast crowds, of embracing old comrades, accepting gifts, kissing infants, dedicating monuments, sweeping mayors' and senators' and generals' wives out on the dance floor, giving hundreds of impromptu speeches and probably thousands of toasts, of downing all that champagne and wine and spirits, of all that rich food. No account of his tour describes any stiffness of the knees or tenderness of the toes (only a slight limp); if the marquis escaped gout it was the miracle of the age.

Or paralysis of the facial muscles from smiling. At most encounters with an old comrade, and most stirring speeches made in his honor, and most tableaux of gratitude—at Providence, 200 little girls in white, strewing flowers in his path; at the Bunker Hill battlefield near Boston, triumphal arches and banners; at Hartford, being presented with his original major general's epaulettes worn during his service, and a sash he had worn at the battle of Brandywine, "spotted with blood from the wound received by him on that memorable occasion"; at Washington's tomb at Mount Vernon in Virginia, kneeling by the sarcophagus—Lafayette wept copiously, as did all around him. At the White House, in multiple farewell embraces with Monroe's successor, President John Quincy Adams, their shoulders were soaked with each other's tears. One always feels better after a good cry; for the marquis, who turned 67 while on his 30-month American tour, that may have been his secret for survival.

The frigate *Brandywine* was riding the swells at the mouth of the Potomac on December 7, 1825, when the young midshipmen excitedly sighted the approaching steamboat *Mount Vernon* with its distinguished passenger. By presidential directive, there were 24 midshipmen aboard rather than the normal complement of 8 or 10 for a vessel of its size. "It was gratifying to the general," recalled Lafayette's secretary, Colonel Auguste Levasseur, "thus to find himself surrounded by these young representatives of the republics he had visited with so much pleasure, not only as their presence recalled spots he loved, but also as some of them, being sons of old revolutionary soldiers, gave him an opportunity of speaking of his former companions in arms; and the young men, on their part, proud of the mission they were engaged in, endeavored to render themselves worthy of it, by strict attention to study, and the performance of their duties."

When *Brandywine* entered the Chesapeake under full sail, it passed beneath a brilliant rainbow, according to every chronicler, which arched from the Maryland shore to Virginia's—just the sign that had greeted Lafayette on his arrival.[10]

Matthew Fontaine Maury, USN. *(Library of Congress)*

Out on the swelling Atlantic, the marquis had disappeared into his cabin for a day or so, suffering from seasickness, but as soon as he got his bearings, Lafayette drew the young officers into conversation frequently, an acknowledgment that the grateful, worshipful Midshipman Lynch would remember his whole life. So, too, would his new friend, and fellow Virginian, named Matthew Fontaine Maury, from Fredericksburg.

On his first voyage, Maury was five years younger than Lynch and had spent part of his childhood in Tennessee—his midshipman's appointment, and likely his assignment to the *Brandywine* was due to the support of his Nashville family's congressman, the Honorable Sam Houston, years before his own emigration to Texas. Maury's older brother John had been the youngest officer of his rank in the Navy and served as flag-captain for Commodore David Porter's fleet in the campaign against the West Indies pirates—but he succumbed to yellow fever on the return voyage to Norfolk in June 1823.[11] Thereafter, any mention from the younger Maury that he was interested in West Point and an Army career sent his father into a rage.

Matthew probably would never have escaped duty on his father's farm were it not for the fact that he seemed to be as accident-prone as his new friend Lynch. In his 12th year he fell a distance of 45 feet from the heights of a tall tree, injuring his back and nearly biting through his tongue. Thereafter, since he was unfit for hard farm labor, his father yielded to the boy's entreaties to continue his studies. He finished his academy schooling in Tennessee before following his brother into the service in 1825, without telling his parents. His strict and still-bereaved father lost his temper at not being consulted and refused to give him as much as a penny toward his rough country journey to the naval port at Norfolk. But young Maury was as determined as he had been precocious in the study of science, and he made it to the coast.[12]

Finally aboard the *Brandywine*, Maury was impatient at the lack of formal instruction afforded the midshipman; while Lynch was prone to whiling away time between duties lost in novels, poetry, history, and travel literature, Maury, in his free time, was glued to whatever scientific volumes he could get his hands on. Even Lafayette noticed young Midshipman Maury's insatiable thirst for knowledge, studying late into the night and during every break as *Brandywine* bore its heroic passenger back to his home. "If I went below only for a moment or two," Maury wrote to a cousin, "and could lay hands upon a dictionary or any book, I would note a sentence, or even a word, that I did not understand, and fix it in my memory to be reflected upon when I went on deck." He inspired Lynch and the other young officers.[13]

Lafayette regaled them with reminiscences during the voyage to Le Havre. In return, their feelings deepened for the old Revolutionary hero. As Lafayette's secretary recalled, "The paternal friendship testified towards them by the general, during the voyage, so completely gained their affection, that they could not separate from him without shedding tears." The midshipmen, whose monthly pay started at $19 per month, combined their purses and ordered an elaborately engraved silver urn from Paris to be sent to Lafayette. As he finally left the frigate, Lafayette assured them that they would always be welcome at his home, and that "at La Grange you are not on a foreign soil."[14]

After depositing the honored passenger at Le Havre, the frigate sailed for the Mediterranean. By the time *Brandywine* arrived at Port Mahon on the island of Minorca for resupply in the last week of December 1825, its large crew of midshipmen was about to be reduced by one: William Francis Lynch, due to illness. The injury to his ankle sustained during his first voyage to China was still acting up and he was unable to perform his duties. The frigate, along with his new friend Maury, sailed on into the Mediterranean without him, while Lynch had to make his way back home on his own; he sailed from Gibraltar on the passenger ship *Mary*, landing in New York in March 1826.[15]

Lynch remained on sick leave during 1826 and 1827, seeking surgery on the bad ankle in Philadelphia and recuperating, and then, finding little improvement, making arrangements for another operation, this to be performed in France. But before sailing in December 1828, he was informed that midshipmen of his service date were to undergo examination for lieutenant's grade. Lynch went to New York to be tested. While he anxiously waited for the results, he returned to active duty in a short, two-month posting as navigator on the sloop of war *Falmouth* as it was prepared for a voyage to the West Indies and the Gulf of Mexico. The long-awaited promotion came through in March 1828.[16]

It was cause for celebration on more than one level: the lieutenant's higher pay enabled him to marry, something he could not previously afford. In June 1828, in New Haven, Connecticut, he married Virginia Shaw, a beautiful and vivacious, high-spirited young woman and seemingly the ideal life partner and mother. She was the daughter of the late esteemed war hero, Naval Commodore John Shaw, distinguished captain of the 12-gun sloop of war *Enterprise*; her mother, a Philadelphia Quaker, died when Virginia was young, and the girl was boarded by her father at a school for young ladies in Jamaica Plain, outside of Boston.[17]

William Francis and Virginia Shaw Lynch settled in Norfolk, both knowing that his chosen career would mean long absences—a hazard to any union. They enjoyed married life for just three months, until the new lieutenant's sea orders arrived: he was to join the sloop of war *Erie* in the West Indies as it operated against the slave trade and protected merchant shipping. When Lynch mounted the gangplank of *Erie* at Norfolk in October 1829, Virginia was pregnant—their daughter, Mary Virginia, was born early the next year—and he surely knew that his participation in any kind of family life was to be limited. He served aboard *Erie* until June 1830. Virginia and the baby girl had gone to live with a sister in New Haven, Connecticut, and he joined them there—again, drawing shore pay—until the next Navy Department envelope arrived. Before too long, another baby was on the way; a son, Francis Edward, was born in 1832.

Lynch's frequent health problems affected his career, but ship duty, he would see in retrospect, would take its toll on their marriage, as would his attractive wife's needy nature. It was a complicated time, and the young lieutenant must have felt pulled by many obligations. In 17 years of marriage, when Lynch was not at sea, they lived in Norfolk, New Haven, and last and longest, in Frederick, Maryland, near his relatives. Virginia and their children resided with family in New Haven or Frederick when her husband was at sea.

During this time Lynch served in Norfolk on the naval receiving ship, training new recruits in 1831, 1832, and early 1833; in the Atlantic on the frigate *Brandywine* for two months in 1834; in the Mediterranean aiding shipping and "showing the flag" in ports aboard the sloop of war *John Adams* and the flagship *Delaware*, for 19 months in 1834 and 1835; in Atlantic coastal cruises on the side-wheeled steamship *Fulton*, aiding ships in distress, conducting ordnance experiments, and training gunnery officers, in late 1837 and early 1838; out of Norfolk commanding the U.S. Steamer *Poinsett* during outfitting and testing repairs, in 1839; in the Mediterranean on the sloop of war *Fairfield* between 1840 and 1842; in New York with the naval rendezvous, in early 1843; in Atlantic waters between Philadelphia and Key West, and then the Gulf of Mexico, commanding the U.S. side-wheeled steamer *Colonel Harney* in efforts to slow timber piracy from public coastal lands, in 1844 and 1845.[18] More active sea duty was certainly wanted and needed, but what he drew was seemingly the best the service could do for him given the small fleet and his own spotty health.

Other obligations pulled him away from family and home even when on leave or awaiting orders. Lynch boarded for several months

William Francis Lynch,
USN, CSN. *(Museum of the
Confederacy)*

at a time in 1836 and 1838 in Philadelphia while seeking surgical
treatments for his ankle and an ailing right eye. For three months and
two cruises in 1838, the lieutenant got himself detailed to ride and
study Britain's impressive new *Great Western*, the large steam-
powered, paddle-wheeled passenger ship that was the first steamship
to provide transatlantic service. He reported in the *Army and Navy
Chronicle* that "for stiffness and buoyancy combined in just proportions, for perfect comparative safety from explosion within, or the bat-
tling elements without; for speed, security and comfort; the *Great
Western* may hereafter be equaled, but can scarcely be surpassed."[19] In
the winter of 1843–44, having been advised by his physician to avoid
cold weather, Lynch extended his already extended leave, left home
and headed for a southern port, and sailed to St. Croix, Virgin Islands.

This last, however, was a melancholy mission for Lynch: his two brothers, Edward and Eugene, had died there of lung diseases within five days of each other, in March 1843; the lieutenant wanted to visit their graves.

Loss followed loss.

His marriage fell apart. The crisis apparently had boiled over the previous year—between when Lieutenant Lynch returned in November 1842 from two years of duty in the Mediterranean, and when, that winter, Edward fell seriously ill and was taken to recuperate in St. Croix by Eugene. Lieutenant Lynch, trying to care for his siblings' families in addition to his own, learned from a New Haven relative that his wife had been flagrantly adulterous while William was away. He was shocked but not surprised; adultery was a career hazard for both parties in a nautical marriage, and even in their earliest days of wedlock, Virginia had seemed flighty and flirtatious enough to arouse her husband's anxieties. His love for her was ardent, though, and he hoped that responsibilities for their two young children would temper her feverish nature. Perhaps in those early years the impropriety to which he objected had been more serious, he would reflect, and he just failed to catch her at it. At any rate, this time while he was at sea and she was living with their children at the New Haven home of relatives, Virginia had been seen going and coming from the rooms of three male boarders in the house, and they from hers. Other men may have enjoyed her attention in that overheated house, according to depositions later collected. There was even a rumor, whether grounded or not, that Virginia may have earlier dallied with one of William's now deceased brothers.[20]

Obviously, it was too late for repair. Lieutenant Lynch took the children, now in their teens. He filed for divorce in Maryland in October 1845. Virginia did not contest his allegations.[21]

Loss followed loss.

In September 1846, while Lynch was stationed at the Pensacola Navy Yard in Florida and filling a correspondence file at the Navy

Department with his entreaties for a Gulf ship and a part in the war with Mexico, his daughter Mary died, aged 17.

The department detached him from Pensacola and granted him three months' leave for mourning, and caring for Francis. The boy was approaching the age when his father went to sea, and Francis showed similar leanings.

CHAPTER TWO

Lighthouses in the Sky

TWENTY-ONE YEARS BEFORE, ON DECEMBER 6, 1825—AS YOUNG Lynch and his good younger friend Maury absorbed a midshipman's duties on that famous cruise with Lafayette—President John Quincy Adams sent his first annual message to the Senate and House of Representatives. It included a stirring call for the advancement of knowledge as fulfilling a "sacred debt" for the hard-won prize of nationhood; the time had passed when America could content itself with receiving knowledge "second-hand" from Europe. America must establish new colleges and universities, he declared, and research laboratories, and astronomical observatories—"light-houses of the skies"— and most certainly, there must be exploration. It must employ its armed forces, especially in peacetime, in the systematic collection of information— not just for defense but for the sake of knowledge itself. The Navy should have an academy of its own, like the Army's West Point. If the nation were not necessarily ready to launch a naval exploring party to circumnavigate the world for the advancement of scientific knowledge, there were, in addition to patrolling coastal waters and navigable rivers, responsibilities to safeguard oceans from piracy and other lawlessness. There was the Pacific coast, not just of America but of Central and South America. And there was the broad Pacific Ocean itself. "The spirit of improvement is abroad upon the earth," President Adams declared. "It stimulates the hearts and sharpens the faculties."[1]

Adams's words did not launch an immediate movement, in Congress or at large. Hardly; his young administration staggered against opposition from strict constructionists, states-rightists, slavers, and stay-the-course isolationists before the curtain of its only term. "Returning light for light" did not fit in with the sentiments of the day. But as far as the notion of an exploring expedition went, others took up the pennant, chiefly an Ohio newspaper editor, Jeremiah N. Reynolds. He had been an active publicist for both private and public exploration. For a few years he had fastened on the Arctic regions, partly lured by the old explorers' chimera of a northwest passage and partly from a temporary infatuation with a popular crank theory making the rounds, regarding a hollow Earth with an Arctic entrance to the globe's interior latitudes. Reynolds began championing—from the lecture platform as well as in numerous government lobbies—the commercial and scientific allure of the South Pacific, from the polar regions to the Sandwich Islands.

Some in Congress heeded—but there was not enough support to push through legislation launching an expedition in 1828, in the waning months of the Adams administration. But by 1836, during the second term of President Andrew Jackson when the well-connected Reynolds was invited to give an evening address in the House of Representatives chamber, he spoke words that stirred many in Congress (not the least of whom was Massachusetts congressman John Quincy Adams, whose presidential words of 1825 found an echo in Reynolds's).[2]

Scientific research ought not to be pursued only if a tangible reward was anticipated, Reynolds intoned. On the contrary, it was an "immutable law of nature" that "utility cannot be computed in advance." Rewards might be virtually guaranteed, but there was a higher justification: "national dignity and honor." It was time to "throw back on Europe, with interest and gratitude, the rays of light we have received from her" and thus "wipe off, with one glorious effort, the taunting imputation so long cast upon the American character." A South Pacific exploring expedition would do much more than reliably chart the ocean—it would

> collect, preserve, and arrange every thing valuable in the whole range of natural history, from the minute madrapore to the huge spermaceti, and accurately to describe that which cannot be preserved; to secure whatever may be hoped for in natural philosophy; to examine vegetation, from the hundred mosses of the rocks, throughout all the classes of shrub, flower, and tree, up to the monarch of the forest; to study man in his physical and mental powers, in his manners, habits, and disposition, and social and political relations; and above all, in the philosophy of his language, to examine the phenomena of winds and tides, of heat and cold, of light and darkness . . . in fine, there should be science enough to bear upon every thing that may present itself for investigation.[3]

There may have been muttering in the chamber from isolationist Jacksonians, but there were plenty of adherents present besides former President Adams, including Senator Samuel Lewis Southard of New Jersey, who had been Adams's secretary of the Navy, and Representatives John Young Mason of Virginia and Isaac Toucey of Connecticut, both future naval secretaries.

Weeks before, Senator Southard had steered an expedition bill out of committee and before the whole Senate, which approved an appropriation of $150,000. Now, in the House, Jeremiah Reynolds's words echoed in their ears and drowned out objections of isolationists like Albert Gallatin Hawes of Kentucky, who denounced the "chimerical and harebrained notion" that would "take the vessels and seamen of the United States, and send them to the South Seas, exposing them to all the diseases, hurricanes, and mishaps of that climate."[4]

On May 9, the House approved the legislation. Within weeks, President Jackson had announced that he was "feeling a lively interest in the Exploring Expedition" and urged "that it should be sent out as soon as possible." The eloquent and persuasive Jeremiah Reynolds must go along—"this the public expect."[5] As leader, Jackson appointed his old comrade-in-arms from the War of 1812, Commodore Thomas ap Catesby Jones (the "ap" in his name was Welsh for "son of," making him the son of Catesby Jones). Jones was a 47-year-old Virginian who had fought piracy in the Gulf of Mexico and signed a treaty with King Kamehameha III of the Sandwich Islands, among his many exploits. President Jackson gave him authority to select expedition personnel.

This did not sit well with Jackson's secretary of the Navy, Mahlon Dickerson. A former New Jersey governor and U.S. senator with inherited wealth and entitlement, he had wanted the vice presidency but had to be satisfied with a cabinet seat. Dickerson, 66, was in poor health, had no experience and little interest in naval affairs, and no administrative talent for decision making or leadership. He was opposed to naval modernization efforts, a naval academy, a national observatory, steam power, and of course to a Pacific exploring expedition. He heartily disliked Jeremiah Reynolds and Commodore Jones, yet was expected to work with them. It should be no surprise that he became the primary impediment for the rest of the Jackson administration, bickering with Jones over every aspect of planning and attempting to inject his own people into the project.[6]

Congress and the president had hoped that the expedition could be launched in the fall of that year, 1836, but delays plagued Jones's mission. By the late fall, at least, Navy shipbuilders had launched several new vessels. Most dramatic was the commander's flagship, the *Macedonian*, a 36-gun frigate refitted from the keel of the ship of the same name captured from the British in the War of 1812, bearing a figurehead of Alexander the Great and equipped with specialized quarters for the expedition's scientists. Also there were two brigs, the *Pioneer* and *Consort*, a small schooner, *Pilot*, and a storeship, *Relief*.

Further repairs and modifications extended the delay through the winter, spring, and summer of 1837, though Jeremiah Reynolds used the time to generally good effect despite Dickerson's dependable interferences, recruiting what would become a distinguished roster of civilian scientists. This corps included a geologist, several zoologists, an artist-naturalist, a conchologist, an entomologist, a philologist, several draftsmen, and a landscape painter. Thanks to Secretary Dickerson, a totally amateur botanist and a "zoologist" with no expertise in zoology were also slipped into the corps. A vexing need for a qualified astronomer, however, went unfilled despite both Reynolds's and Dickerson's vigorous efforts.

Some 500 seamen were selected for the convoy—but the expedition still lacked enough officers, and in Commodore Jones's recruitment he continued to vie against the meddling of Secretary Dickerson, whose tenure lengthened in the spring with the inauguration of President Jackson's hand-picked successor, Martin Van Buren.

One of Jones's earliest requests was the up-and-coming, newly appointed—and newly published—Lieutenant Matthew F. Maury, who had continued to pull himself up by his own intellectual bootstraps.

That he had to always serve as his own schoolmaster was driven home to Maury in that thrilling midshipman voyage where he basked in the glow of General Lafayette and learned to call William Francis Lynch "friend." This continued in subsequent voyages. Maury had seen much of the world, with the Mediterranean Squadron on the *Brandywine*; in the South Atlantic to Rio de Janeiro and Callao, Peru, via Cape Horn on the same vessel, commanded by Commodore Jacob

Jones; across the Pacific under Master Commandant William Bolton Finch aboard the sloop of war *Vincennes* to the Marquesas, Macao, and the China coast, and thence around the world back to New York. It was the first circumnavigation by an American warship.

That was June 1830. Following a leave, he was detailed to school at the New York Navy Yard to prepare for the examination required of all midshipmen at the close of five years' service. He found the place indifferently staffed and organized, and he was already familiar with the textbooks—Bourdon's *Algebra*, McClure's *Spherics*, Playfair's *Euclid*, and Bowditch's *Navigation*. After a little over two months, and feeling increasingly suffocated and frustrated, Maury got permission for self-study away from New York until the examination scheduled in March. He went down to Washington and lodged with a cousin in Georgetown. There his program of study ranged much wider than the relatively narrow fields of his Navy textbooks, especially navigation as covered by Nathaniel Bowditch. With this last book, standard issue on all Navy ships, Maury felt that officers were being sent blind out onto the briny deep, being required to merely memorize a few navigation formulas without understanding any of the mathematical principles behind them. The rote lessons both bored and alarmed him, something he tried to convey to a number of fellow midshipmen likewise preparing for the examinations, whom he tutored.[7]

On March 3, 1831, in Washington, Maury should have been able to predict the outcome. One by one his friends filed in before the board of old-school officers and a "professor of mathematics," and under the latter's stern eye they recited the Bowditch formulas as if they were poetry. Maury's turn came, and when posed the same question went to the blackboard and computed his answer using spherical trigonometry. The professor soon got lost within the formula, and when Maury finished, his answer was declared to be wrong. The midshipman insisted. The professor was adamant. The navigational mathematics were even more incomprehensible to the examining officers, who of course sided with the professor. Maury could have actually

flunked—instead of earning his rightful place at the head of his class—
but finally the board decided to pass him, ranking him 27th in a class
of 40; his pupils may have had the benefit of Maury's coaching ses-
sions, but their recitations in the key of Bowditch earned them high
placement and earlier promotion. Maury was paying a price for insis-
tence on principle.[8]

Though reward would not come easily, his next orders gave him
a heavy responsibility that would send him in the right direction. He
was appointed acting sailing master of the sloop of war *Falmouth* on
the long journey from New York around Cape Horn, where it joined
the Pacific Squadron in patrolling the west coast of South America,
Maury was in charge of navigation as well as the amount of sail to be
carried at any given time, and answered only to the captain, Master
Commandant Francis H. Gregory. They, and a number of the other
officers, had served together on the nearly identical *Brandywine*; familiarity would help the voyage go smoother for all. During each day of
his duty, Maury would keep running inventories of supplies and reports on the condition of every inch of rigging, lines, and sails as well
as delicate compasses, chronometers, and hourglasses used in navigation. Into the log book all during each day would go the *Falmouth*'s
course and distance; the velocity and direction of currents and winds
it encountered; the weather, barometrical, and temperature readings;
and, in the process of determining location, the results of astronomical
observations. Whenever in sight of land, he would record descriptions
of landforms to aid future mariners; comparing his observations and
measurements with available charts, he would note any variation. At
one point he would begin to wonder what would become of his logs,
with their vast amounts of data.[9]

He busied himself to prepare for the voyage: certainly, he
thought, with all of the naval and commercial traffic around South
America, with all the logs and experience, there should be ample
printed information about the winds and currents encountered. He
found nothing of the sort after several weeks of searching, although he

amassed a clutter of raw data from diverse sources. When the *Falmouth* sailed out of New York Harbor in early July 1831, navigator Maury was, like the others before him, on his own.

By October, as the *Falmouth* approached Cape Horn and Maury readied for this serious test of his navigational abilities, he noticed that while the west winds were rising toward a gale, the barometer's mercury level shot up and down with little connection to the atmospheric pressure. Faced with three methods of doubling the Cape, he chose the longer and safer route, standing out southward to sea until *Falmouth* found favorable winds that took it safely around and then northward up the Chilean coast; the two other routes, through either the Strait of Le Maire or the Strait of Magellan, would have required bucking headwinds and the danger of being cast against the rocky shores.

Maury's choice of route had required 24 days to round the Horn, and at Valparaiso he found a convenient comparison when a British ship, H.M.S. *Volage*, arrived from the Horn after 38 days' rounding. The *Volage* had encountered the same westerly gale as *Falmouth* when nearing Cape Horn; the English sailing master favored the "inshore" passage, but it took three attempts before it conquered the strait's stormy winds. Afterward the ship needed to put into Talcahuano to repair damages from the gales, which cost it another 20 days.[10]

Analyzing and ordering the two ships' notes with other navigators' experiences in his tiny cabin on the *Falmouth*, Maury began to write the very kind of sailing directions he had been unable to find. It would ultimately be his first scientific paper to be published. From the raw data he detected order in what had been haphazard, tumultuous, and extremely dangerous, finding that mariners should follow certain courses based on their compass heading—west or east— around the Cape as contrasted to the wind direction. *Don't struggle*, he warned. "The fact," he wrote, "that winds with *westing* are more prevalent than those with *easting*, in them, is established from the circumstance that the return is less dreaded and shorter than the outward bound passage. The ratio of winds with *westing* in them to those with easting is as *three* to *one*." When winds were favorable, he advised, pursue the "inshore passage" close to the mainland and the Diego Rivera Island group just southwest of the Horn. But when the winds were contrary, longer, wider berth far out to sea was safer. "Common practice teaches," he said, "that good passages are more frequently made by those vessels, which finding contrary gales off the Cape, stand boldly to the south, than by those that lie to in them, keeping near the parallel of the Cape." Each leg of the journey, and its variations, received precise sailing directions in the article, and he scrupulously warned against relying on a barometer in the tempestuous pressure zones of the southern seas.[11]

When "On the Navigation of Cape Horn" by Passed Midshipman Matthew F. Maury arrived in the office of the *American Journal of Science and the Arts*, it made a quick believer out of the editor, the eminent scientist Benjamin Silliman of Yale, despite its young author's lack of academic credentials and his lowly status in the nautical hierarchy. His only claim to competence was in his argument and his data, but these alone made the paper shine. Almost as a postscript, Maury had also enclosed another item for consideration, "Plan of an Instrument for Finding the True Lunar Distance." Exhilarated at his discovery of a wunderkind, Dr. Silliman bought both items for inclusion in the July 1834 issue.

That was a good month for Passed Midshipman Maury, as it also marked his marriage to Ann Hull Herndon, a distant cousin, after an engagement of several years. They had postponed the marriage as long as possible because he could still hardly afford to keep himself, let alone a wife and family. Finally, though, they decided they could wait no longer. The groom gave the last $20 in his wallet to the minister who married them. After several weeks of honeymoon visiting various Virginia relatives, still in straitened circumstances, they rented a room from a cousin in Fredericksburg. For some time, since August 1833 in the Pacific Squadron at Callao when Maury had transferred

from the *Falmouth* to the schooner *Dolphin* with the duties of first lieutenant, he had been receiving that higher grade of pay—continued a
few months later after he transferred again to the homeward-bound
frigate *Potomac*. It had been evident once the *Potomac* anchored at
Boston in early summer 1834 that the higher pay would be insufficient
for domestic life, not that that deterred the couple once they were
reunited.[12]

Keeping house and making do on the half pay of extended shore
leave—a paltry $40 per month—the Maurys set about producing their
first child, Elizabeth Herndon Maury. She was born in June 1835,
while the midshipman was finishing labor on what he would always
tell his family was his true "first born," a textbook entitled *Treatise on
Navigation*, since it had been engendered back on the *Falmouth* after
his confidence-building work on Cape Horn. He pinned much hope
on the book, that it would encourage theoretical as well as practical
navigation, ending the dumb tyranny of rote learning in naval ranks
and empowering a new generation of mariners. It went without saying—he was altogether desperate—that it would be nice if the book
earned some money and helped him in his career.

Maury would not pretend that he was setting forth new theories.
He rested on giants of mathematics and science, but he wanted to
present their work systematically and understandably to a student as
well as a mossback. He drew on algebra, geometry, logarithms, plane
and spherical trigonometry, nautical astronomy, and navigation. Following his lead, a mariner could forthrightly find the time, latitude,
and longitude using chronometers, lunar observations, and single and
double altitudes, and could determine different latitudes as well as the
ship's course and relative distance.

After some 10 months of work, Maury finished his manuscript in
April 1835 and submitted it to Key & Biddle, general interest publishers in Philadelphia, where it was accepted. Eager to hasten its publication, which might help end his financial woes, Maury went to
Philadelphia to read proofs, for 10 days living on cheese and crackers

in a cheap rented garret chamber. He enterprisingly obtained supportive statements on the book from Alexander Dallas Bache of the University of Pennsylvania, later superintendent of the Coast Survey, as well as from Nathaniel Bowditch. The book, *A New Theoretical and Practical Treatise on Navigation*, was published in April 1836.[13]

It received high acclaim, most notably from the editor of the *Southern Literary Messenger*, Edgar Allan Poe, who besides being a poet and story writer was highly versed in politics, current events, and the sciences. He celebrated an auspicious debut, perhaps even the dawn of a new era. "The spirit of literary improvement has been awakened among the officers of our gallant Navy," Poe wrote.

> We are pleased to see that science is also gaining votaries from its rank. Hitherto, how little have they improved the golden opportunities of knowledge which their distant voyages held forth and how little have they enjoyed the rich banquet which nature spreads for them in every clime they visit! But this time is coming when, imbued with a taste for science and a spirit of research, they will become ardent explorers of the regions in which they sojourn. Freighted with the knowledge which observation only can impart, and enriched with collections of objects precious to the student of nature, their return after the perils of a distant voyage will then be doubly joyful. The enthusiast in science will anxiously await their coming, and add his cordial welcome to the warm greetings of relatives and friends.[14]

Equally warm was the reaction of a number of senior naval officers and Navy instructors in mathematics who personally as well as publicly made their praise known, beginning the process that would result in the adoption of Maury's *Navigation* as the required textbook for midshipmen. As Maury's editor at the *American Journal of Science* would note approvingly in his review, copies of *Navigation* were ordered "placed on board all our national vessels." Five weeks after the book's publication, by which time it was already selling well, Matthew Maury finally received word from the Navy Department that he had been promoted to lieutenant.[15]

Sea orders, however, did not immediately follow. By then Maury had been on land, at half pay, for three years. This was not an inordinate spell in that time where there was a shortage of Navy ships and officers' berths, and the service was accustomed to mothballing its personnel, but it was especially hard on a young officer with a growing family to limp along for three or four years.

At least, living at home in Fredericksburg, Maury kept himself as busy or busier as if on a full-time job; after he finished with his book project he had embarked on ambitious self-study of mineralogy, geology, and astronomy, the inspiration of future scientific papers and books. Meanwhile, in Washington, D.C., thoughts were turning in the direction of the South Pacific.[16]

As Maury put together his roster for the great exploring expedition, Commodore Jones personally interviewed him back in the summer of 1836 and subsequently Maury was named executive officer under Captain Thomas A. Dornin on the expedition store ship, the *Relief*, a plum of an assignment for him. Maury was well aware of how the struggle of politics, personality, and ambition was haunting the expedition. He even knew that family friends and politicians back home had been pressuring the Navy secretary to acknowledge his scientific gifts and award him command of one of the ships—a prize he knew he did not deserve, since the thought of a mere lieutenant commanding a ship was absurd. Maury feared the expedition would end up a "bungling concern" and knew that he had already attracted the dislike of Secretary Dickerson and a number of old-line officers. But he respected Jones and trusted Dornin—the two had worked closely together before and all seemed promising: Dornin asked Maury to rate a group of passed midshipmen for the *Relief* duty. But Maury was crushed some weeks later in September 1836 when he learned that the naval secretary had decided the *Relief* needed three lieutenants, not one, and the greater seniority of the others meant he would be the lowest ranking officer with duties that were more of a demotion than a promotion.[17]

Swallowing his disappointment, Maury waited through the expedition's serial delays of fall and winter into 1837, arranging several times to break up his household and board wife and daughter with relatives only to have that reversed, mindful of more disquieting rumors of disarray and incompetence and even that the whole project was doomed to be abandoned. When, in March 1837, he inexplicably received orders from Dickerson posting him not to *Relief* but to the frigate *Macedonian*, Maury lost his patience with the whole enterprise. Though he badly needed the increase in pay of sea duty—his wife was expecting another child in June—he declined the appointment and requested a furlough.

That might have been that—but soon after the baby, a second daughter, Diana, was born, on June 25, Maury received a letter from Dornin. Apparently, behind the scenes people were still fighting on his behalf; Dornin begged him to reconsider, saying that Commodore Jones would wait until they were at sea and beyond Dickerson's baleful reach, and then he would name Lieutenant Maury the official astronomer of the expedition.

This he could not refuse.

Meanwhile, the other scientists of the mission, as well as Jeremiah Reynolds, were butting their heads against the redoubtable Secretary Dickerson's determination to wreck the whole enterprise in the early months of Van Buren's new administration. He delayed their appointments, stalled their pay, shorted them of compensation for six months of preparation, and withheld cash advances. Try as he might, though, Dickerson failed to shake any of them off, with the notable exception of Citizen Reynolds. The latter rose to the bait of the naval secretary's calling for the number of ships and personnel to be reduced —as it would threaten the Navy's ability to protect commerce—and Dickerson demoted Reynolds to merely Jones's assistant. Reynolds published a series of letters (under the pseudonym "Citizen") in the newspapers ridiculing Dickerson for his obstructionism and urging the expedition to set sail. The naval secretary replied in similar heat. Congress finally became impatient. The result, in August, was that Reynolds, whose years of eloquent advocacy and popularity had spurred the whole enterprise, was edged firmly out of the loop, although he would be kept dangling without an outright dismissal for another year.[18]

That same month, the baffled and demoralized scientists finally grouped to meet Commodore Jones. They were impressed and reassured by their leader's faith and determination.

Maury, too, drew comfort. In September after being named astronomer, he went to Philadelphia, where the Franklin Institute's Walter R. Johnson had established an office to manage the expedition's physical sciences. Maury lodged in a boardinghouse and began boning up in astronomy in what he described as "a planked observatory in Rittenhouse Square where our telescopes, transit instruments, chronometers, theodolites, . . . clocks, sextants etc. and all sorts of magnetic apparatus had been gathered." After six weeks in Philadelphia, he returned home to Fredericksburg via Washington, where he saw Dickerson, who had acquiesced to the Maury appointment and promised a signed letter imminently. The official letter arrived in Fredericksburg on October 21. Retroactive to September 5, it more than doubled Maury's lieutenant's annual salary to $2,500, ending his worries about providing for his family.

His eagerness unleashed, Maury wrote to Secretary Dickerson hoping to establish his anticipated official duties as astronomer, while also expanding them in ways consistent with Maury's established expertise in winds, tides, and currents—an area not yet covered by any other scientist in the enterprise. He thought it important to collect "observations on ebb, flow, and other tidal phenomena," he told Dickerson, and "on the set, rate, breadth, depth, and the like of currents at sea; on the prevailing winds of whatever sea; on the variation of the needle; on the latitude and longitude of places already known, or which may be discovered; and on any other subjects of general interest to the navigator, and which may serve to guide mariners in the navigation of whatever seas the expedition shall visit."[19]

Such rosy hopes, though, soon began to dim as Maury found himself injected into a tug-of-war between Jones and Dickerson just as he collided with a new antagonist, an up-and-coming, scientifically minded lieutenant named Charles Wilkes.

Wilkes was the son of well-to-do parents and was born in New York City on April 18, 1798, making him eight years older than Maury. Educated in boarding schools and by tutors, then preparing to enter Columbia College, Wilkes instead made known his desire to go to sea, against his father's wishes. At 16 he was denied a midshipman's warrant and so shipped out in the merchant marine to gain enough sea experience to get him into the Navy. He made midshipman three years later, at 19. In three voyages he saw service on the Atlantic, the Mediterranean, and the Pacific, where he cruised the western coast of South America. He made lieutenant in 1826. With the exception of a brief voyage to the Mediterranean, Wilkes's time would thereafter be spent in scientific study—in part, with his brother-in-law, James Renwick of Columbia College, and with the Swiss geographer Ferdinand Hassler, who had worked on the U.S. Coast Survey. In 1828, when Jeremiah Reynolds first tried to launch his South Pacific Exploring Expedition from the unenthusiastic port of the U. S. Congress, young Lieutenant Wilkes fastened upon the concept with an almost unseemly tenacity. To then-Naval Secretary Samuel Southard, the 28-year-old lieutenant had offered to tap his family wealth to underwrite an additional vessel for the mission—but only if he were awarded its command, as well as being given the post of astronomer.

The bemused Southard passed him along to Reynolds for more scrutiny, and Reynolds was underwhelmed by the confident young man, whom he found "exceedingly vain and conceited" though undoubtedly "enterprising and ambitious." Wilkes had been puffed up by his recommenders, Reynolds decided, and had "a spirit of dictation that I don't like."[20]

In 1833, following his participation in a Navy survey of Rhode Island's Narragansett Bay, Wilkes was given a post superintending the recently founded Depot of Charts and Instruments in Washington. The Depot was a small but important office on Capitol Hill, where charts and old logs were stored and marine chronometers were calibrated. These delicate, precision timepieces were set to Greenwich mean time and used by a ship's navigator to calculate the distance east or west of Greenwich—the longitude; the officer would establish local time by taking an altitude observation of the sun or a star and then compare that to Greenwich. Despite the care (and expense) that went into manufacturing a chronometer, each individual timepiece had to be measured against solar observations to establish its "rate," its slowness or fastness at keeping time, which was crucial to take into account on a long sea voyage where an error of several seconds a day could result in being miles from where one expected. The Depot's superintendent not only maintained these instruments, numbering at least 54 when Lieutenant Wilkes became the second to head the bureau, but he was given the duty of purchasing new ones, which were manufactured in England.[21]

As the U.S. Exploring Expedition plans slowly got underway in summer 1836, Wilkes, who had earlier been asked by Secretary Dickerson to compile a list of scientific instruments for the party, was sent to Europe to purchase them. In his four years working in Washington, Wilkes had assiduously nourished his political and social ties in government. He and the secretary had cultivated each other to mutual benefit, and this continued over the issue of the expedition: neither wanted it to succeed, for their respective reasons.

For Wilkes's part, his hope was to lead one of the ships—perhaps the entire enterprise—despite the fact that he had not commanded a vessel in 13 years.

He returned home after five months, having built an unrivalled collection of navigational and astronomical instruments and books, obtained during travels in England, France, and Germany. He had paid some $20,000 total for the haul, which included 47 new chronometers. The civilian scientists nevertheless complained that Wilkes had forgotten to obtain the important devices and texts used in fields outside his own expertise, even instruments as obvious as microscopes.

That and numerous other gaps had to be plugged in the enterprise during the summer of 1837. Another problem surfaced when Commodore Jones asked for the chronometers and other devices, charts, and books to be handed over to his men in the midst of their preparations. Several written requests went unanswered; Jones dispatched Lieutenant Maury to Washington but his investigations were fruitless. In July he finally got permission to have the supplies examined where Wilkes had stored them in the New York Navy Yard. There it was discovered that the storehouse had been visited: Wilkes seemed to have borrowed most of the chronometers, books, and instruments—with Dickerson's blessing—for use in a survey of his own proposal, the North Atlantic's treacherous shoals and immense fishing waters of Georges Bank. Other books and items had apparently been lent to others. What little was left got packed up and sent to the expedition's own Professor Renwick in Philadelphia for his training observatory in Rittenhouse Square. But Wilkes was finally in command of a ship, the brig *Porpoise*, leading the Georges Bank survey north, so Commodore Jones had to wait until Wilkes returned to Boston in September before he could get to the bottom of the problem.

Another month passed. Jones did not have much patience left, as he indicated to Secretary Dickerson in a letter on November 4.

I again send Lieutenant Matthew F. Maury to Washington, for the purpose of receiving the chronometers and other instruments said to be in depot at that place for the South Sea Surveying and Exploring Expedition. By the enclosed letter I am informed that it is your intention that Lieutenant Wilkes shall select the instruments for the expedition. I hope it is not intended thereby to permit Lieutenant Wilkes or any other person to *withhold* or *make any other appropriation* of any instrument or instruments which have been imported for this expedition; especially do I request that the very *identical books, instruments and charts, etc.,* and everything thereunto pertaining be all sent to the expedition, for which they were purchased. . . . There is no occasion for detaining the chronometers twenty days longer at Washington to obtain Lieutenant Wilkes' rates of those delicate instruments, for they must all be tested to new ratings after they are returned to this place and put on board the respective vessels, and as this indispensable preliminary may require several weeks, at this season, before we can arrive at conclusions sufficiently satisfactory to justify our departure on so important a voyage, the fear of hard winter setting in before we can get away may be justly apprehended.[22]

In another letter sent to Maury on November 12, the commodore minced even fewer words. Lieutenant Wilkes's "conduct in reference to the expedition, since his return to the United States," he wrote, "has been such that I should not be willing to trust him to make any *selections* or calculations whatsoever for the expedition."[23]

Seventeen days later, Maury's report to Jones began to shed light on the situation. He had unearthed a House document with an inventory of Wilkes's European purchases and was able to compare that with what he had found. The results were alarming. Wilkes had apparently scattered the delicate instruments, the books and charts, all up and down the East Coast. Some were in general storage in Navy yard warehouses; some were held by various officers in Boston and

Philadelphia; and some were stowed at Wilkes's own house on Capitol Hill, to which he had relocated the Depot. Even a list of what had been supposedly sent to the Philadelphia observatory revealed absences. Much was just plain missing.[24]

Meanwhile, someone made calculations and announced that when the scientific supplies could finally be found and assembled, they would have several hundred barrels more than they had room for. The *Macedonian* would have to be altered again. It might even be necessary to cut down on the number of scientists, since the books and instruments would squeeze out several berths reserved for them.

After simmering for months the situation had turned volatile—and, to say the least, extremely personal. In Washington, Lieutenant Wilkes decided that these inquiries impugned his honor and demanded copies of all relative correspondence, delaying any inquiry as a document had to be hand-copied by a clerk in Dickerson's small office. And the Navy secretary issued some bizarrely provocative general orders and sailing instructions to Commodore Jones: henceforth, as expedition commander, he could not be trusted with "all journals, reports, records and collections" made by those under his command; he must summon at least two subordinates to certify and then seal up all materials held against the completion of the voyage.[25]

For Commodore Jones, this was more than enough. Writing Dickerson, he announced that the imputations in his orders made it impossible to remain. Citing this as well as his declining health (he was suffering from a chest cold), on November 30 he resigned his command. The secretary agreed that the officer should be relieved of the burden if he were in delicate health. A few weeks later, writing in his diary, Dickerson sniffed that "I do not believe that for a year past he has intended to go out on this expedition. His failure however will make infinite confusion, as no one will take the command in such vessels as he has had constructed, or such arrangements as he has made."[26]

* * *

Immediately after Commodore Jones's departure was announced, Congress and then President Van Buren stepped in to find out what was the problem and ordered a full report from Dickerson, who in the meantime looked for a replacement. Every senior officer offered the post turned it down. The Exploring Expedition was becoming a national, even an international joke. Some feared that leading it, or even taking command of one of its ships, would be a career killer. After the end of January 1838, when Van Buren had digested Dickerson's report and decided the naval secretary was incompetent, the president transferred responsibility for the Exploring Expedition from Secretary Dickerson to Secretary of War Joel Poinsett. A former senator and representative from South Carolina, Poinsett had a keen interest in science, especially botany; while ambassador to Mexico he had imported a decorative winter-blooming plant once prized by the Aztecs, later named the poinsettia.

But he, too, was unsuccessful at finding a commander. Some younger officers, such as Lieutenant Francis H. Gregory, hesitated at the idea of breaking up their families for up to three years of the Pacific cruise. After sending contradictory signals, Gregory even passed up a fast-track promotion to captain offered by the Senate. A more senior officer such as Captain Joseph Smith was tempted, but Smith had little scientific experience and was wary of going without the support of some lieutenants who were competent surveyors. In particular, Captain Smith wanted Lieutenant Charles Wilkes of the Naval Depot, who had once served under him. But Wilkes was anything but accommodating—he told Poinsett he didn't want anything to do with the expedition, and when Captain Smith visited Wilkes, asking him to at least show him how to use a scientific instrument like the pendulum, Wilkes refused so flatly that his old commander was embarrassed and offended. Smith, then, bowed out, feeling he had nowhere else to turn.

At some point, inevitably, Lieutenant Maury received a summons from the secretary. Poinsett bluntly asked him to name the best candidate—without, he stressed, regard to rank. Hearing these words, it headily occurred to Maury that he was going to be offered leadership of the expedition, in the most satisfying nod to his scientific attainments that one could imagine in the Navy. But in answering the question Maury seemed to lose his nerve at the crucial moment. He decorously scrawled out the names of the officers already attached to the expedition—and as the junior member, he put his own name at the bottom. Poinsett "froze in disgust" at what he must have regarded as coyness: indirection did not become a commander. The interview was over.

Maury later consoled himself by thinking that he had "preserved [his] integrity" by refraining from any unseemly politicking for the post. But he had lost perhaps the greatest single opportunity he would ever be offered.[27]

Manipulating, it would seem, was not something Lieutenant Wilkes was above—or at least that is how it appeared to many. The last two years, as his detractors would complain, he may have conspired with Secretary Dickerson; he may have worked to undermine Commodore Jones. He may have claimed disinterest to Secretary Poinsett; he may have boxed in Captain Smith, his old commander who had tried to promote him. Now the esteemed Professor James Renwick of Columbia College in New York spoke to the secretary on his brother-in-law's behalf. It was a compelling suit, and, given the situation, there seemed no alternative.

Poinsett forwarded his secret recommendation that Lieutenant Charles Wilkes be given the command of the whole expedition, not just of one ship. The Navy Department and the president hastily and with no small amount of relief concurred.

The announcement of such a junior officer to such an important command—there were 40 lieutenants on the Navy List, and 38 had more sea service than Wilkes—ignited a furor in Washington and the upper reaches of the Navy. Suddenly a number of senior officers volunteered to take the post, but the irritated Poinsett announced that his decision was final—the command was, he said, more scientific than military and therefore heeded a higher calling than Navy seniority. Twenty-four officers already chosen for duty on the expedition requested other assignments, although four subsequently rejoined. Others signed a mass protest letter evincing no confidence in a mission led by an officer with so little practical experience and so limited a record of commands.

For his part, the party's astronomer was also disconcerted. Matthew Maury's experience with the new commander was mainly in the dismaying, protracted quest and struggle with Wilkes over the missing $20,000 of instruments, charts, and books. He approached Poinsett and told him he could support any officer in the Navy with the exception of Charles Wilkes. The secretary approved Maury's detachment from service with the expedition, which went into effect in June 1838, as Wilkes moved forward to take control of the mission. By then, most observers were so weary of melodrama that they agreed with old John Quincy Adams, who called on Poinsett at the War Department and told him that "all I wanted to hear about the exploring expedition was, that it had sailed."[28]

Maury watched quietly from the sidelines, requesting sea duty and returning home to Fredericksburg to wait for orders. A few weeks later, the official who had presided over the whole embarrassing mess, Naval Secretary Dickerson, submitted his long-awaited resignation, before a congressional inquiry could be organized. His successor was a New Yorker named James Kirke Paulding, an editor and writer on nautical subjects who had served in several civilian Navy posts. An archconservative with many ties to the elder figures in the service, such as the Board of Navy Commissioners, Paulding would favor a few innovations—a Navy academy, for instance—but he was vociferously against steam power—he called steamships "fire-breathing monsters"—and believed that if the Navy possessed only one steamship in 1838, that was one too many. He opposed most other modernizations already taking hold in the world's great navies.[29]

As Maury saw it, the unappealing transition between naval secretaries, the tragicomic opera over the exploring expedition, and his
own part in the events of the past several years gave rise to an exasper-
ation that finally could only be tamed with the pen. Accordingly, he
wrote a series of nine articles under the nom de plume of "Harry
Bluff." He excoriated former Secretary Dickerson for his sundry
errors and limitations, which had wasted so much money, material,
manpower, and morale; though he held few illusions of improvement
under Secretary Paulding, he urged him to get the Navy back on a
firm footing, moving forward, not backward. The articles were published in the *Richmond Whig and Public Advertiser*, an influential newspaper of the day, mostly as front-page articles in August and early
September 1838.[30]

"Harry Bluff" created a great excitement in the service as well as
in Washington—the articles were copied, reprinted, and passed along
by hand—infuriating mossbacks and inspiring reformers, and igniting
much curiosity as to the true author of the pieces; rumor had it that a
captain of high rank had been the author, and Secretary Paulding
vowed to unmask and chastise him. A few months later, Maury picked
up his pen again, writing three new articles, supposedly letters to
"Harry Bluff" from his old messmate "Will Watch." These calls for
reform were published in the *Richmond Advertiser*, in December, causing even more of a stir. The irate Paulding and the Navy Board got
no closer to discovering the writer's identity.

Maury was at home in Fredericksburg, impatiently "hanging
by the eyelids," as he usually put it, on August 18, 1838, when, off
Norfolk, Lieutenant Charles Wilkes gave the order to his little
squadron to weigh anchor after ambitiously having, in some five
months, reshaped the exploring expedition largely in his own image.
Given the snail's pace of the foregoing preparations, it was truly an
extraordinary job.[31]

Wilkes had dismissed most of the assembled civilian scientists, as
well as Jeremiah Reynolds, in favor of picked naval officers. Wilkes

gave himself responsibility for the departments of Physics, Surveying, Astronomy, and Nautical Science, and would also assume the position of mission historian. True expertise, though, was impossible to draw from many of those in the naval ranks willing to serve with him. This measure left the civilians bitterly in arrears for time served and supplies purchased, with their careers having been interrupted for more than a year. They were stuck. "I have referred them to Congress," Secretary Paulding smirked to Dickerson, "the Residuary Legatee of all old good for nothing claims."[32]

Gone, too, would be most of the vessels chosen and elaborately refitted. Understandably, Wilkes rejected the large and unwieldy frigate *Macedonian* in favor of the more nimble sloops of war *Vincennes* (to be Wilkes's flagship) and *Peacock* (Lieutenant William L. Hudson commanding). *Porpoise*, the brig commanded by Wilkes during his Georges Banks survey, was detailed, now to be led by Lieutenant Cadwaladar Ringgold; two pilot boats, the *Seagull* (under Passed Midshipman James Reid) and *Flying Fish* (Passed Midshipman Samuel Knox), were added to replace the schooner *Active* and two brigs, *Consort* and *Pioneer*. The storeship *Relief* (Lieutenant A. K. Long) was retained from the earlier exploring squadron duty for use.

Wilkes asked that the passed midshipmen aboard be promoted to acting lieutenants, just as he expected that Secretary Paulding would elevate him as squadron commander and also William L. Hudson, second in command, to the higher rank of captain. The apprentice officers received their boost, but Wilkes and Hudson were chagrined that, by launch day, they were left holding their old lieutenant ranks. The two had already purchased captains' uniforms. Lieutenant Wilkes decided that because of their squadron commands they should just assume the loftier ranks, the uniforms, and fly the appropriate colors. Wilkes said he would take responsibility for that.

Wilkes's orders were a daunting command for the 40-year-old lieutenant. He was keenly aware that a number of his just-promoted midshipmen had more sea experience. He had the responsibility for six vessels and 346 men expected to be gone at least three years. As outlined by the department—measuring, surveying, observing, charting, sounding, collecting, drawing, preserving, and classifying, on open water and along coasts both known and unknown—they would sail to Rio de Janeiro by way of the island of Madeira off the African coast, a roundabout route dictated by prevailing winds; while in the South Atlantic they would search for an area of shoals in need of delineation. At South America, following the southward coast and pausing to survey the mouth of Rio Negro, they were to proceed down to the cold and largely unknown waters between Cape Horn and Antarctica; they were then to return northward up the western coast of South America, touching at Valparaiso and Callao. They were to strike due westward across the South Pacific toward the Tuamotu Islands, Tahiti, Samoa, northward toward the Marshall Islands and eastward to the Sandwich (Hawaiian) Islands, looping northeastward back to the American northwest coast and touching at Astoria, the mouth of the Columbia River, and San Francisco Bay. Sailing westward again to Hawaii and thence across the great gulf toward Fiji, and then Australia at Sydney, they were to strike boldly southward toward the Antarctic coast and then parallel it for a significant distance. The return home would be both long and elaborate, stringing the landmasses of Sydney, Australia; Hawaii; Northern Luzon in the Philippine Islands; Singapore on the Malay Peninsula; the Java strait; and then the long run west toward Africa's Cape of Good Hope. Once back in Atlantic waters, they would zigzag to St. Helena and westward to Rio de Janeiro and then, finally, wearily, homeward toward New York. Most of the time in the years ahead they would be far from even the slow communication afforded by sea mail from a port halfway around the world from home. Unknown seas, winds, storms, shoals, snags, reefs, diseases, hostile locals, and all of the other perils an imagination could manufacture awaited to endanger them.

Lieutenant Wilkes recognized what a prize he had been granted by this command and how important it might be in his career and his life, but the dangers were hard to minimize—as well as the separation from his wife and their four children, aged 10 years to one month. Most on board the six vessels faced similar situations.

As the exploring squadron vanished over America's horizon and the civilian scientists and officers who were left out contended with regret, bitterness, and relief, Lieutenant Maury tended his wife and two small daughters in Fredericksburg. His "Will Watch" columns on naval reform appeared, making waves in all places but Fredericksburg. Then, also in December, he was ordered to Washington, where the secretary sent him on a survey. Instead of Fiji, Tahiti, and Antarctica, he would be charting certain harbors along the Carolina and Georgia coast, looking for a suitable site for a new Navy yard; he would be serving under Lieutenant James Glynn, six years his senior, on the steamer *Engineer*. Glynn had previously commanded the storeship *Relief*, now bringing up the rear of the Wilkes Exploring Expedition squadron; more poignantly, he had earlier been named—for as long a span as Maury—to the expedition as the hydrographer. Like Maury, he had resigned rather than be commanded by Lieutenant Wilkes. The private conversations between these two officers, outcasts marooned off the exotic shores of Wilmington, Beaufort, and Brunswick, are unknown but can be surmised.

After several months of work were completed, Maury was free to return home until he heard a summons from Glynn for their next survey mission. They eagerly hoped it would be on the Pacific Northwest coast, a challenging and noteworthy goal. But delays, and then more delays—their steamer *Engineer* was withdrawn in favor of the *Consort*, which required refittings—refocused Maury's mind on his family, particularly his aging, infirm parents in Tennessee. He decided to visit them. A soft shoulder on an Ohio backcountry road, and a stagecoach accident that would cripple him, bobbed just ahead, and the course of his life required him to steer straight for it.

* * *

He remembered being flung through the darkness. From his perch next to the stagecoach driver, suddenly the horizon tipped; he flew head over heels and landed hard in an explosion of pain. When the driver and some passengers scrambled to help him, he begged not to be moved until a doctor could be summoned, so a man unhitched one of the horses and rode off through the darkness toward the nearest town. While he waited, his right leg in agony, Lieutenant Matthew Fontaine Maury considered his naval career, which had seemed so promising, and dreaded that it was over.[33]

He would remember this date for the rest of his life: Friday, October 18, 1839. When his overloaded and top-heavy stagecoach stopped at the last coach station, Lieutenant Maury had gallantly given his seat inside to a lady who joined them, though not without misgivings: the passengers' complaints of too many riders and luggage had been rebuffed by the station agent, with this calamity out in the middle of nowhere the result. Obviously Maury's leg had been badly broken—what chance would a cripple have on the deck of a tossing schooner?

After another coach was obtained, and he had been conveyed to an inn of the nearest town and examined, his fear about the injury was confirmed. His thigh bone, or femur, had been split lengthwise in two places like dry kindling; his knee joint was transversely dislocated; his patella ligament was torn; and there was a depression below his kneecap. With no anesthetic, the local doctor correctly readjusted the knee but erred in setting the longitudinal fractures of his thigh bone. Maury had to send to a larger town for a better doctor. The bone was rebroken and then reset, again without anesthetic. He could not be moved to a hospital but had to contemplate three or four months of recuperation in a squalid little country inn with vile food and a hostile staff, fearful of a secondary infection and the certain loss of his leg. Nearly a month after the accident, a young cousin from home arrived to help nurse him, but Maury was unable to escape his prison until after the New Year. Snowfall made it possible for sleigh transport across eastern Ohio and the Alleghenies; from Frederick, Maryland, he took a series of railroads to New York City.[34]

There, he was chagrined to find that his ship, the *Consort*, had sailed for Vera Cruz without him. Never before had he failed to follow orders. Lieutenant Maury journeyed back home to Virginia. He could stump around a little on crutches, but he could not get out of bed unaided nor dress himself. He owed large sums to several relatives. But during his recovery he had taught himself French. And he managed, immediately upon reaching Fredericksburg and his wife, to sire his third child, a son. How he would solve the problem of his career, however, was an open question.[35]

He ought not to have worried. We who have the advantage of hindsight would like to have reassured the man who would be remembered as the "Pathfinder of the Seas" in low moments, for after all, he had fiber: he had bounced back from serious injury before; also, as a midshipman, taking his qualifying board, Maury had known far more than his examiners; moreover, three years before the stagecoach accident, he had published a book that began transforming the science of navigation; additionally, reforms he had championed in the face of personal peril would remake the character of the Navy he loved, just as work in his near future would change the way humanity looked at the earth. Cripple though he may have been, Matthew Fontaine Maury, one of the nineteenth century's most extraordinary scientists, more than any other, would preside over a remarkable age of American exploration.

After the accident, confined in early 1840 for the most part at home in Fredericksburg with a mangled knee, Lieutenant Matthew Maury attempted the kind of active convalescence with regular exercise that he hoped would restore him to vigor and sea duty. If his knee kept collapsing, his spirit, however, seemed even more forceful. He had invested 15 years in the United States Navy, 9 years of it at sea, and the popular attention drawn to his reformist articles on his beloved service encouraged and emboldened him to continue. This time he sought a larger venue than the Richmond *Advertiser* newspaper: the *Southern Literary Messenger*, an influential magazine published by Thomas W. White and formerly edited by Edgar Allan Poe, who had contributed the admiring review of Maury's *Treatise on Navigation*. Maury continued to disguise his identity, writing again under the name of "Harry Bluff." Only the editor, Maury's wife, and a couple of relatives knew the secret author of "Scraps From the Lucky Bag," an allusion to the lost-and-found receptacle one saw aboard ship. Metaphorically, it would be a capacious miscellany for many opinions.[36]

Five articles appeared in the *Messenger* between April 1840 and June 1841. They were widely reprinted in other journals. Both the world and the responsibilities of the Navy had changed since its founding, "Harry Bluff" said, and "necessity *calls loudly* for reorganization." The service was becoming "respectable in force—sending its squadrons to different seas—boasting of the largest ships and the finest specimens of naval architecture in the world." But officers operated at a distinct disadvantage, he complained, being restricted to only a few rank levels compared to other navies. "Their want of rank," he said, "often places American officers in embarrassing situations" when confronted with the kind of disparities that made grizzled and beribboned seniors the inferior in rank to other nationalities' counterparts.

Even more important was the still yawning need for a naval academy whose curriculum would include navigation, the sciences (notably chemistry, natural history, and astronomy), naval architecture, gunnery (especially the new hollow-shot ordnance increasingly employed over the old-fashioned solid-shot cannonballs), tactics and discipline, international and maritime law, and foreign languages. "In a national point of view," he said, "the *building* of officers, or, which is the same thing, the fitting them for the duties of their profession, is quite of as much importance as the building of ships." The course of study should stretch over four years with a two-month cruise each summer;

after completing instruction, each midshipman should serve for two years at sea. Following a rigorous examination, he would receive an officer's commission. Instructors should be picked carefully from within the service ranks, instead of being drawn willy-nilly from civilian teachers, he argued. And although a school ship might have seemed adequate for such a program, he thought, there was really a powerful need to locate the Navy academy on land. "Harry Bluff" advocated Memphis as a good centrally located venue, but it needed to be underway "even if it has to be built on top of the Rocky Mountains."

The *Messenger*'s publisher, Thomas H. White, was excited about all the attention generated by Maury's articles and believed it would catapult the lieutenant to a place where he could actually effect the reforms he called for. "I am hard at work," White wrote Maury on December 13, 1840, "for I intend to be the instrument of placing you at the head of the Navy Department." Maury pooh-poohed the idea, having no interest in getting involved in the muck of politics—look at what Thomas Paine effected with mere pamphlets—wanting to concentrate only on policy.[37]

His next article, published in January 21, 1841, drew blood. It concerned ship construction and the criminal use of public funds. Corruption riddled the shipbuilding process—graft was a given, he charged. Ships cost twice as much to build as they should. Then, repairing those ships cost more than twice as much as required to construct (a $294,000 vessel was repaired at a cost of $600,000, for instance). Similarly, when it came to ships' ordnance and stores, the service had been billed for repairs at a rate twice that of the original costs. Moreover, there was a maddening disparity to the charges for ship fittings and supplies: sometimes one piece of material was four or five times the price of a duplicate item used elsewhere. The fault principally lay with the three-man Board of Navy Commissioners, officers who were lazy and incompetent, "Harry Bluff" charged. They should be tossed out—and replaced by the checks and balances of a bureau system that would keep a lid on costs and extirpate corruption. The

Navy commissioners and their supporters in and out of the service were infuriated, but they were outnumbered by those officers—and the congressmen who noticed the altercation—who picked up the firebrands and encouraged them to spread.[38]

Word soon began to go round as to the identity of "Harry Bluff." Late in the spring of 1841, as the letters column of the *Messenger* were filled with retorts from officials and many more statements of support from others, a brother officer stationed in Norfolk warned Lieutenant Maury that everyone knew and, though they cheered him on from a distance, considered that as far as his future career in the Navy was concerned, he was a marked man. Maury replied that he was putting his faith in the majority who shared his passion for reform.[39] In July, he was unmasked—White published a statement identifying him along with a biographical sketch of Maury written by a "Brother Officer." It bore some stylistic similarities to Lieutenant Lynch's writing. Around the nation, Maury's essays had stimulated "an enthusiasm which has not subsided," the biographer exclaimed, "and will not subside until the whole navy is reorganized."[40] Maury kept it up with a new posting published in the October issue of the *Southern Literary Messenger*, advocating support of a steam-powered merchant marine through federal subsidies and cooperative ventures.

By this time, Maury had received an exhilarating message from Thomas ap Catesby Jones, his former commander, who had been named commodore of the Pacific Squadron and now raised the prospect of sea duty. Jones thought that Maury's "game leg" would not prevent him from serving as Jones's flag lieutenant on the frigate *United States*. Maury enthusiastically turned to Naval Secretary George E. Badger, writing that the light duties in such a post did not require much bodily exercise and that he would be delighted to so serve the Navy. After Maury was visited at Fredericksburg by Commodore Jones in late September, the sea orders came; while the *United States* was being readied at Norfolk, Maury waited at home for the November sailing, certain that his career was regaining momentum.[41]

When a letter arrived in the middle of that month from the new secretary of the Navy, Abel P. Upshur, Maury's hopes were crushed. To his shock, the secretary revealed that, instigated by members of Maury's own family, a group of influential Fredericksburg friends and neighbors—a judge and three physicians—had written Upshur saying that the lieutenant's leg injury was still so bad that his ability to walk and perhaps his life were endangered if he were to take sea duty. Faced with this urgent medical intervention, his situation exposed to the new departmental secretary, Maury had no choice but to ask to be relieved from his sea orders. The exotic Pacific horizon sank from view in his imagination, and he finished 1841 rudderless and in a desultory mood.[42]

Maury was no better in February 1842 when Navy friends in Washington urged his attention toward the Depot of Charts and Instruments, to which a heightened amount of interest and influence was being paid. It was currently being run by Lieutenant James Melville Gilliss, a 30-year-old Washingtonian and astronomer who had taken qualifying courses at the University of Virginia and in Paris, and who had served as Lieutenant Wilkes's assistant when the latter had headed the Depot. Still occupying the rented and worn frame house contracted by Wilkes, the Depot suffered from the site's inadequacies as well as a stifling budget. Gilliss, however, had been campaigning for the establishment of a Navy Observatory. Secretary Upshur, a Virginian educated at Yale and Princeton and until recently a prominent jurist until chosen to head the Navy Department by President John Tyler, was at heart a reformist, and he persuaded the Navy Board to support Gilliss's proposal for a depot building, observatory, and expanded budget; Upshur also encouraged the resulting House and Senate legislation, to which Lieutenant Gilliss devoted several months of promotion. At the same time, Upshur obtained sponsors and enough support to put through a bill reorganizing the Navy. It aimed to abolish the Board of Navy Commissioners and institute a system of five new bureaus attending to material matters and procurement, finally injecting professional management and technical control into the service: one bureau would superintend naval yards and docks; a second, construction, equipment, and repairs; another, provisions and clothing; a fourth, medicine and surgery; the last, ordnance and the science of hydrography.[43]

Of course, Maury was excited by news of this ferment on Capitol Hill, having so strenuously advocated service reform along exactly these lines. However, to his friends arguing that he should now strategically use influence to be ordered to the Depot of Charts and Instruments, he hesitated, allowing that he found it repugnant "going *secretly* to work about it." (Indeed, mores of the times frowned on campaigning for a job and like forms of ambition.) But he was encouraged to hear that the naval reorganization bill might advocate a separate bureau of hydrography. Washington was as much of a rumor mill as it ever has been, and there were whispers that a civilian such as a local publisher of maps and charts might be named to head the new bureau. This sent Maury into a rage—underemployment was already rife in the officer class, and there were now enough young officers with scientific attainments to qualify. He wrote Upshur to consider him a candidate to head it.[44] In any case, a separate hydrographical bureau was not created that year. Leadership at the Depot, though, was about to change, thanks in part to the return of Lieutenant Charles Wilkes, whom neither Maury nor Gilliss was particularly eager to see.

On June 11, 1842, the flagship of the great United States Exploring Expedition—the sloop of war *Vincennes*—arrived in New York harbor. The other ships of the squadron (with the exception of the schooner *Sea Gull*, lost in a Cape Horn gale, and the sloop *Peacock*, lost on a bar off the mouth of the Columbia River) would begin trickling in at the end of the month. Lieutenant Wilkes arranged to be taken quietly ashore at Manhattan's Battery, before the *Vincennes* was towed to its mooring off the Brooklyn Navy Yard. There were no enthusiastic public displays at Wilkes's return, in contrast to his leave-taking. His men grumbled that the lieutenant disembarked early to avoid notice (and reprobation) for having adopted a captain's uniform and displaying the broad blue pennant of that rank on the *Vincennes* for the four years of the circumnavigating expedition.

Worse derelictions would be alleged in the coming days and months, similar to that having leaked out two years earlier when the expedition's storeship, the *Relief*, had returned early from South America full of angry officers and seamen who had clashed with the tempestuous Wilkes and been dismissed. Soon after Wilkes's return, the *New York Morning Herald* disclosed the bitter atmosphere that had permeated the expedition. "We understand that there is to be a nice mess dished up in a short time," it said on June 13, "in the shape of court martials, courts of inquiry . . . etc., in the eating of which nearly all of the officers of the Exploring Expedition are to participate with finger glasses and napkins. It is said that there are at least a bushel and a half of charges already preferred against Lieut. Wilkes, the commander-in-chief, and that several officers of the squadron have come home under arrest."[45]

Admittedly, it was an extraordinary achievement. Under Wilkes's command, the four-year expedition—the last naval circumnavigation of the world to be done under canvas—had sailed some 87,000 miles across three oceans and along the shores of six continents, discovering and charting many new islands and reefs, retrieving many tons of specimens, and adding immeasurably to scientific knowledge. Wilkes would publish a 5-volume narrative (and 1 volume just of maps), and edit some 20 volumes of scientific reports and 11 atlases, writing the volumes on meteorology and hydrography himself.[46]

However, the achievement was soured in the minds of all the adventurers as well as the public, thanks largely to the unpredictable, stormy temper and paranoid suspicions of Lieutenant Wilkes. Return of Wilkes's "castaways" on the *Relief* in 1840 was just the beginning.

Of the 524 who shipped with the expedition during its four years, 126 had deserted. Wilkes had been so besieged by requests for transfer from his flagship that he finally issued a blanket edict forbidding it. The number of courts-martial held by its commander, and the degree of punishment meted out, particularly the floggings, would widen the eyes of even the severest Old Salt. Upon their return, four officers filed charges against Wilkes and he against them. Altogether, 19 cases consumed the time and attention of the Navy's court of inquiry over 105 days. Wilkes's accusations against his men ran the gamut from disrespect and disobedience to misuse of government property; their countercharges in the court included oppression, cruelty, illegal punishments, scandalous conduct unbecoming an officer, and contributing to "destruction of good morals" (and, one must not forget, morale). Newspapers highlighted the excessive number of floggings he ordered, which, it was noted, frequently exceeded even the regulation limit of 12 lashes (Wilkes had ordered at least 25 men flogged between 18 and 41 lashes, his chief physician charged).[47]

But perhaps the most startling charge against Wilkes for that voyage of discovery and scientific knowledge was that in public statements as well as his official report to the secretary of the Navy, he had falsely asserted to have "discovered" land at Antarctica on the morning of a certain day in January 1840, to beat a competing claim uttered by a French exploring expedition. Corroboration by his own men was spotty at best. Consequently, in the public mind a great deal of scientific accomplishment by many brave and enterprising men came under a cloud.

Many of the charges and countercharges were to be ruled out for defects in places or dates. The 15 weeks of naval hearings resulted only in guilty verdicts (17 of them) for Wilkes of illegal punishment, earning him a reprimand, and for his officers in a few acquittals and several reduced sentences or admonishments.

All this, though, was months in the future when, shortly after disembarking at New York, Wilkes hurried down to Washington.

Indifference in Congress would be remarkable, given the amount of energy expended to launch the expedition in the first place, but it might be partly explained by the fact that the lieutenant was strongly identified with the eclipsed Democrats, then out of power at the Capitol. A friend in the Senate proposed inviting Wilkes and his officers to appear and was roundly voted down, thanks to the prevailing Whigs; in the House, advocates put forth a resolution commending Wilkes and his gallant men but so few stood in its favor that it was dropped.[48]

When Wilkes made his official call to Navy Secretary Upshur, his reception was sufficiently muted that the lieutenant lost his famous temper, his complaints and charges of disrespect and conspiracy rising to threats and maledictions; Wilkes stormed out of the secretary's office "prepared for war to the knife," while the bemused Upshur could only shake his head, take off his spectacles, and try to polish off what he had just witnessed.

Wilkes next called on President Tyler at the White House. He complained later that the president did not seem to know who he was although Tyler made a place for Wilkes before the fire amid a circle of friends, who Wilkes thought looked like ruffians, "all squirting their tobacco juice into the fire, and over the white marble hearth." The lieutenant soon fled, "glad to get beyond the vulgarity and boorishness of this squad of politicians, who had not the least idea of the respect due our chief magistrate, and I must add neither had the President any idea of the position he occupied as the head of the country."[49]

Wilkes's return to his old quarters at the Naval Depot was of a similar cast. By then he must have been in a truly ferocious mood. He immediately served notice of eviction to the Navy, giving Gilliss two weeks, to the end of June, to find new arrangements for the Depot. Furthermore, Wilkes insulted the younger officer and complained to the department that Gilliss had not taken care of the property. In light of all that Gilliss was doing for the Depot and the cause of science in the service, this was perplexing.

Soon, though, Lieutenant Gilliss would be following another lead, and fortune would change for Lieutenant Matthew Maury, who had now been waiting for orders for three years. On June 29, 1842, Secretary Upshur named him to succeed Gilliss as superintendent of the Depot of Charts and Instruments. Gilliss, who had found new temporary quarters for the Depot at a privately owned frame house on Pennsylvania Avenue before tendering his resignation from the post on July 2, received thanks and a commendation from the Navy Board. As he watched the progress of that summer's congressional legislation reorganizing the Navy, and enlarging the Depot and creating a naval observatory—it would be passed and signed into law that August—Gilliss prepared for his next duty as naval emissary and agent. His job would be to equip the observatory with instruments and books drawn from diverse American and European sources, the research, travel, and procurement of which would happily occupy him for the next two years. Naturally, Gilliss assumed he would eventually be named its director; that it would require nearly two decades would surprise him.[50]

Meanwhile, Maury settled into his new Depot office, performing the many required astronomical sightings, tending his stores of chronometers and other instruments, and supervising the traffic of charts loaned to outgoing naval vessels or thereafter returned. He wrote his cousin Ann Maury that he was sometimes on his feet from 8 or 9 in the morning until 11 at night, but the exercise steadily strengthened his game leg. His wife and children remained 30 miles away in Fredericksburg for the duration of his wife's latest pregnancy (she would bear their second son, John Herndon Maury, in October). Maury planned for them to move in with him afterward and live upstairs over his office, as had been the fashion with his predecessors.

His solitary life changed, though, with the addition of his brother-in-law, just returned from coastal duty in Florida and now attached, at Maury's request, to the Depot. William Lewis Herndon was born in Fredericksburg and had spent half of his life of 28 years in the Navy, cruising the waters of the Mediterranean and the coasts of South and North America; he had received his lieutenant's commission the previous year. He and his wife had their meals with Maury—it "takes away the bachelor character of the establishment," Maury wrote. Herndon aided his brother-in-law in a new and seemingly Sisyphean task at the Depot. Dirty and exhausting it might have been, inhaling quantities of dust and straining the eyes, but it would begin to effect a worldwide transformation of maritime cartography and navigation—perhaps Maury's greatest project.[51]

Soon after the Depot's founding in 1830 by Lieutenant Louis M. Goldsborough, the Navy had expanded its consolidation efforts from gathering all unused chronometers and other navigational instruments from various Navy yards for care and cataloging at the Depot. From 1831 it added all charts and books to its purview, and soon grew to all the ships' handwritten log books kept by skippers. Until then traditionally submitted to yard commandants and stored locally, where they were forgotten, they thereafter swelled the storerooms kept by Goldsborough's successors, Wilkes and Gilliss, but slept on, neglected. These hundreds of dusty, water-stained log books represented virtually every voyage completed by a Navy vessel since 1775. They were still in their wooden crates as Maury unpacked and arranged his new offices. He did not have to flip through many of those entries before he recognized the immense amount of valuable information stored inside. Maury realized that if he culled all of these old mariners' recorded references to natural phenomena that they had experienced— daily, even hourly—in their voyages—direction and force of wind and ocean currents, calms, storms, rain, and fog, for instance, along with depth soundings, duration of sailing times, and so on—he could deduce the average conditions a mariner would encounter, during each season, for any given route.

It was a numbing, overwhelming prospect. But it could be organized and kept under control. One can imagine the stunned expressions of the young officers and midshipmen in his small staff when he began explaining the task ahead of them.

The first job was relatively easy: all the log books were to be divided into groups, each stack representing one nautical route: Boston to Halifax, or Capetown to the Canaries, or Valparaiso to Honolulu, or Gibraltar to Beirut, and so on. In picking his inaugural project for them, Maury probably remembered back to his time as sailing master to the *Falmouth*, 11 years before in 1831, when he had searched in vain for any collected data on conditions along the sailing route between New York, Cape Horn, and Valparaiso, but found only old, unannotated sea charts mostly of foreign manufacture. The crew at the Depot thereupon turned to log books concerning the much-traveled route between New York and Rio de Janeiro.

Maury would later succinctly explain the project. "By putting down on a chart the tracks of many vessels on the same voyage, but at different times, in different years, and during all seasons," he would write, "and by projecting along each track the winds and currents daily encountered, it was plain that navigators hereafter, by consulting this chart, would have for their guide the results of the combined experience of all whose tracks were thus pointed out." A navigator could thus venture into waters entirely unknown to him, he reasoned, and the wind and current chart

would spread out before him the tracks of a thousand vessels that had preceded him on the same voyage, wherever it might be, and that, too, at the same season of the year. Such a chart, it was held, would show him not only the tracks of the vessels, but the experience also of each master as to the winds and currents by the way, the temperature of the ocean, and the variation of the needle. All this could be taken in at a glance, and thus the young mariner, instead of groping his way along until the lights of experience should come to him by the slow teachings of the dearest of all schools, would here find, at once, that he had already the experience of a thousand navigators to guide him on his voyage. He might, therefore, set out upon his first voyage with as much confidence in his knowledge as to the winds and currents he might expect to meet with, as though he himself had already been that way a thousand times before.[52]

Instead of mariners fighting an eternal struggle against nature, they would use nature and human experience to find the natural pathways across the seas. Not only would voyages be shortened for vast savings—many lives would also be saved.

A couple of months of arrangement and research gave him enough to take his plan to his new superior, the head of the Bureau of Ordnance and Hydrography. Commander William Montgomery Crane was formerly of the Naval Board of Commissioners and a much decorated officer; although emphatically a leader of the service's old guard, Commander Crane was excited at this new approach to navigation. He urged Maury to double his efforts and approved an ambitious program to use the full force of the U.S. Navy to gather even more data. Maury prepared a four-page circular to be distributed to all vessel skippers, who were ordered to provide the Depot with a prodigious amount of navigational, hydrographic, and meteorological observations during each voyage. There would be much grumbling about the incredible amount of paperwork necessary—but the complaints would turn to stunned approval after the Depot produced Maury's first wind and current charts, and the savings in time, money, and human life began to be realized.

With the new year of 1843, living above his office with his wife, their two daughters and two sons, and busier than he had ever been, the 37-year-old Lieutenant Maury entered into a bounteous phase of his life, though the work took its toll on the creator. "We are all in our usual state of health, except perhaps myself," he wrote his cousin Ann

Maury in February 1843. "The doctor said I was destroying myself with overmuch head-work, and, in consequence, I have had to hold up somewhat. But it is a hard case that one's brains will not stand the work of one's will. Certainly it was that, after working all the time from nine or ten in the morning till one or two at night, I began to look and feel badly, and that since I have knocked that off, I am looking much better."[53]

This lessening of his load could only have been temporary, given the momentum taking place in Maury's career as well as a growing public recognition of his achievements. And characteristically, the more he learned, the more ambitiously he stretched to learn more. In March, the first small fruit of his data-collection project appeared, sailing directions for mariners heading across the Indian Ocean for the western coast of Sumatra, a once treacherous run; it attracted favorable comment in the *Army and Navy Journal* and among seasoned navigators. In the summer, lecturing at Washington's National Institute for the Advancement of Science to an audience that included cabinet members and legislators, he outlined the benefits if all Navy skippers took part compiling meteorological and hydrological observations; the institute's endorsement went straight to the secretary of the Navy, producing even more support for Lieutenant Maury's inquiry. An article Maury published in the August issue of the *Southern Literary Messenger* widened interest on the subject to the public at large. By September he had collected enough observations on the Atlantic Ocean to begin a general chart.

The forward strides in his career continued. In September 1843, his publisher issued the second edition of his *Treatise on Navigation*; within a year, *Navigation* would be the Navy's primary textbook for midshipmen. His observations and explanations of how the Gulf Stream influenced not only navigation but also the world's weather were unfolded in an April 1844 keynote talk during a conference hosted by the National Institute and including the membership of the

American Philosophical Society and the Association of American Geologists and Naturalists, and dignitaries including President Tyler. Maury's talk was reprinted in the July *Southern Literary Messenger* and later as a pamphlet. In all three venues Maury urged active study of how the sea's currents affected meteorology, a subject he returned to in May before the annual meeting of the Association of American Geologists and Naturalists. This spurred yet another committee of scientists to extol Maury's program to the new secretary of the Navy, who had recently been appointed by the president in the aftermath of a grave naval tragedy.

The accident had occurred in February, and concerned the U.S.S. *Princeton*, the first screw-propelled steam warship in the Navy. Built in the Philadelphia Navy Yard, commissioned and passed in its sea trials in 1843, the *Princeton* had been outfitted in New York. It was equipped with two huge guns. One was called "Oregon" in honor of the growing American enclave, to which a thousand wagon pioneers had left the "jumping off point" of Independence, Missouri, that spring of 1843. The other gun was ironically dubbed "Peacemaker." Weighing some 27,000 pounds, it was considered the epitome of deadly force as well as safety for its crew. In February 1844, the warship proudly steamed up and down the Potomac River, displaying its firepower and carrying many groups of dignitaries. On Thursday, February 29, Naval Secretary Thomas Gilmer, a Virginian who had succeeded Abel Upshur and taken office only nine days before, entertained a party that included President Tyler, his entire cabinet, and some 200 guests. Wanting to please the partygoers, Secretary Gilmer ordered "Peacemaker" to be fired, overriding the warnings of the *Princeton*'s captain, who was worried that the big gun was still overheated from shots earlier in the day. "Peacemaker" fired—and it exploded, killing Secretary of State Upshur, two congressmen, the Navy's chief of construction, the president's servant, and Naval Secretary Thomas Gilmer.[54]

Gilmer's successor was a former congressman, Judge John

John Young Mason,
Secretary of the Navy.
(Library of Congress)

Young Mason of the United States District Court for Virginia. He would prove to be as devoted to naval reform as his recent predecessors, especially Upshur. For the year that he served—he would become attorney general under President Tyler's successor, James K. Polk of Tennessee—Mason defended the Navy against congressional cutback attempts, presided over the founding of a new naval yard on the Mississippi River at Memphis, and supported research into new technology.[55]

One other pressing issue facing Secretary Mason in that spring and summer of 1844 was the naming of the superintendent for the Naval Observatory. After nearly two years of work, the facility that would not only house the observatory but also be the new permanent home for the Naval Depot was approaching completion at Camp Hill, or University Square, a mile west of the White House on property at

23rd Street between D and E streets—the neighborhood to be called "Foggy Bottom" thanks to the swampy land reaching down to the Potomac River. There were a number of candidates to lead the Naval Observatory, but three finalists: the civilian scientist William Cranch Bond, director of the Harvard Observatory; and the former and current superintendents of the Depot, Lieutenants James Melville Gilliss and Matthew Fontaine Maury.[56]

Whoever would be awarded the post of superintendent would be doing so at the dawn of an exciting new era of scientific knowledge, of which the three best candidates were well aware. "Who is to have it," Maury had written a friend late the previous year, "I do not know—I suppose the competitors will be multitudinous and I shall not swell the list. I am trying to leave my mark before they wipe me out."[57] He did not like to admit to ambition, though when he heard it rumored that Secretary Mason was being pressured toward awarding the post to the civilian scientist "under the plea that no one in the Navy was fit for it," he complained to Mason of the "practical libel" on the service and pressed his own case. Maury realized his own strength was hydrography—his astronomical experience was mostly limited to the intensive instruction he had received in Philadelphia around the time he had been named to the South Pacific exploring expedition, and a number of the new instruments installed at the new observatory were still mysteries to him. But he was confident he would master the new field, somewhat pridefully aiming to do so without asking for help from the "savants."

If Secretary Mason accepted the logic of Maury's argument for supporting a naval officer, then he would still be free to name Lieutenant Gilliss, whose practical experience in astronomical observations was added to the short formal studies he had undertaken earlier; on his side, too, were the two years he had spent researching and equipping the Observatory. But Maury was published widely and well, and he enjoyed a higher profile. The secretary clearly believed that his fellow Virginian would continue his ascent and become notable in the field of astronomy. On October 1, 1844, Lieutenant Maury was named superintendent.

No ribbon-cutting over at Foggy Bottom seemed necessary, although the new Naval Observatory gleamed like an elegant gift in the autumn sunlight. A dignified-looking, two-story brick building in the Georgian style, painted in a light cream color, with pilasters rising to visually support an ornate roofline and balustrade, it was capped by a large copper-clad dome; small one-story ells ran east, west, and south. A tunnel led from the basement to the underground magnetic observatory. However enticing the space may have been, there was much to do before Maury and his staff could begin work.

Though he remained circumspect about assigning blame or even mentioning names, Maury reported that all of the delicate and expensive scientific instruments purchased in London, Berlin, and Munich, and installed by his predecessor, Lieutenant Gilliss, had been improperly mounted and would have to be removed, thoroughly cleaned, and reinstalled: some had been placed using caustic sulfur adhesives that had reacted with the humid air of the Potomac basin and begun to eat away at the metal; others had been set up while the new building was still settling, and had to be removed and readjusted.[58]

Some months later, though, all was ready: the entire year of 1845 would prove to be a strong beginning for the Observatory. In the south and west wings, telescopic transit instruments would observe the transit of stars from the east-to-west points of the horizon; the east wing held the instruments called the meridian circle and the graduated mural circle, used respectively to determine right ascension and declination and measure the arc of the meridian. Upstairs in the revolving hemispheric dome was the large and powerful equatorial refracting telescope and the comet-seeker.[59]

With a staff enlarged to include several professors of mathematics augmented by his trained naval officers and midshipmen, Maury embarked upon an astronomical program that at first focused on navigational stars. To this was added an effort to catalog every star found from the zenith to 20 degrees north with a brightness of 6th magnitude or greater. Then, Maury added the even more ambitious aim to begin, as he described it, a "systematic review and exploration of the whole heavens, in ascertaining Right Ascension, Declination, and assigning position to every star, cluster and nebula" viewable from the Observatory, which went all the way to the dim glow of 10th magnitude. Significant descriptions of comets commenced in the summer of 1845, but after the year turned, Maury's personal observations of Biela's Comet as it split in two attracted worldwide notice.[60]

Official support gladly came from new naval secretary George Bancroft, appointed to fill Judge Mason's place when the latter moved to occupy the attorney general's chair in the administration of President James K. Polk. Bancroft, a nationally prominent Democrat from Boston, was a brilliant educator and historian, author of what would grow to become the 10-volume *History of the United States of America*. He would make many important contributions to the department in the 18 months of his tenure as secretary, but his greatest was to found the U.S. Naval Academy.

It took a particular inventiveness and determination; Bancroft succeeded where so many had failed by making an end run around Congress, which had historically resisted the notion of a national naval academy for budgetary and political reasons. At the Capitol there was even less interest in naval matters than usual, with the great focus on the recent annexation of Texas, done with a joint congressional resolution of the 28th Congress just two days before its term expired. Crowding the Capitol after Polk was inaugurated on March 4 and they themselves were sworn in, members of the new 29th Congress seemed in a similar non-nautical mood, what with the breakdown of relations with Mexico over Texas and the subsequent saber rattling on the freshly independent soil south of the Nueces River, to which

General Zachary Taylor had been ordered with up to half of the U.S. Army.

In Washington, though, perhaps encouraged that Congress was pointedly looking the other way, Naval Secretary Bancroft pressed the issue of his academy. He found a location for the school—the Army's underused Fort Severn, at Annapolis, Maryland—and persuaded Secretary of War William L. Marcy to transfer the nine-acre fort to the Navy at no cost. To open and fund operations, Bancroft squeezed the needed $28,200 out of the department's existing instructional salaries, though that earned him the resentment of several laid-off professors. The academy opened on October 10, 1845, superintended by Commander Franklin Buchanan and with a faculty of seven, some drawn from a small precursor in Philadelphia. The first class of 50 consisted not only of midshipmen returned from their five years of sea duty but also young men with appointment letters who had yet to go to sea. Curriculum consisted of mathematics, navigation, chemistry, natural philosophy, English, French, gunnery, and steam mechanics; the five-year course began and ended with a year of classroom instruction separated by three years of sea duty. Secretary Bancroft thus had the naval academy up and running before he approached Congress with his fait accompli, asking for an operating budget; he impressed leaders of Congress, and Annapolis, as it would come to be popularly known after 1850, was thereafter supported.[61]

Of course, the self-taught Maury was delighted, having advocated the concept since his midshipman days; his encouragement and advice about the academy project to Bancroft that year went full circle with the naval secretary's enthusiasm for Maury's stargazing, a reciprocity similarly in evidence between Maury and a number of other leaders in Washington. This was especially so with Congressman John Quincy Adams, who, as president 20 years before, had so eloquently called for an American Enlightenment with new colleges and universities and research laboratories and astronomical observatories— "light-houses of the skies." The 78-year-old Adams would have preferred something like the Naval Observatory to be in direct civilian control, but as he entered the Observatory with its sky-blue interior walls and beheld the gleaming brass instruments, it took his breath away. He did not miss the unfinished details of the building, the "unhealthy," damp air and even pools of water seeped onto the basement floor, but still it was a dream realized. As he left that first day, with an invitation to return the first clear evening, he allowed that the Observatory would not be complete without an attached house for its superintendent.[62]

Sure enough, as Adams would exult in his memoirs, he went to "look through the large refractor at the nebula in the sword of Orion." Maury also guided him to see "a cluster of spangles in Auriga, the blazing light of Sirius and the double stars, orange and blue, in Andromeda." And Maury thereafter had a faithful advocate in Congress, and not the only one, either. South Carolina's legendary Senator John C. Calhoun brightened when a visiting English journalist brought up Maury's "admirable regulations at the Observatory, his eminent professional knowledge and industry, his good judgment in political affairs, and his exceeding moral worth," as she would write. "Pray ask him to come see me often," replied Calhoun, "he is a man of most excellent thought."[63] Maury opened his observatory to Washington, as well as to academe: through Harvard's Professor Benjamin Peirce, he pledged "the civilities of the Observatory" to anyone at the university who happened to be in the neighborhood. "I shall be glad," wrote Maury to Peirce, "to open a broadside with you upon the stars."[64]

Scientifically, politically, and socially, his amiable personality served him well, and Lieutenant Maury had more friends than enemies. However, the latter would prove to have extensive reach, in important ways affecting his reputation long after his death as an old man heaped with honors. For instance, the competitive friction between Maury and Lieutenant Charles Wilkes seemed enough to set the rigging ablaze, with both having to grit teeth in order to pry a courtesy out of the other in the instances when they needed to com-

municate about Observatory business or Wilkes's consuming duty to
publish a record of his South Seas expedition. Similarly, though their
correspondence was outwardly cordial, Maury's immediate predecessor at the Depot, Lieutenant Gilliss, was bitter that he had been
passed over, for all the years of Maury's tenure at the Observatory;
perhaps resentment contributed to Gilliss's relatively few attainments
in those years.

A similar climate seemed to exist in the Naval Observatory during the 12 months that the civilian scientist Sears Cook Walker, Mas-
sachusetts-born and Harvard-educated, worked there. Walker, who
could not adapt to a government job's formality, much less to a military atmosphere and hierarchy, let it be known that he was more
deserving of the superintendent's post and had words with Maury over
what he considered work beneath him; ironically, he had been told by
Maury to concentrate his astronomical observations to the planet
Neptune, recently discovered by astronomers at Paris and Cambridge
University. The task included the Maury-like (and mind-numbing)
retracing of Neptune's path through the heavens and thus through
much earlier astronomical findings. Maury suspected that the planet
had been observed before and deemed a fixed star. Months of work
later, Walker found that his superintendent's suspicion was verified
and that Neptune had been identified as a fixed star during two sightings in May 1795 by a French astronomer, who had published his
findings in 1802. This created the opportunity of discovering the orbit
of the newly named planet, using the sightings of 1795 and 1847.[65]

Having a part in such a notable success—or, at least, being entitled to share in it—was insufficient to keep the civilian scientist happy.
After an argument with Maury, he quit. "Mr. Walker was unwilling to
comply with the rules of the office," Maury wrote to a friend, "as the
officers do, and it was better therefore that he should quit. He wanted
to be excused from attending the office entirely and occupy himself
upon such subjects only as he should fancy. Mr. W., moreover, was a
much better computer than observer; he could compute day in and

day out but our night observations would knock him up."[66] Unbeknownst to the superintendent, Walker took his papers with him.

Some months later, Maury was flabbergasted to read an abstract of the Neptune work in an important German scientific journal. Walker had apparently left the Observatory and gone directly over to the Smithsonian Institution, dazzling the recently appointed director Joseph Henry with his discovery and asking his aid in getting it published in a European publication. Henry, a New York mathematician and magnetism expert, happily agreed and then scheduled the full report for the Smithsonian's annual *Transactions*. Maury's subsequent complaints—that as the discovery had occurred at the Naval Observatory by an employee, credit and publication rights belonged to the Observatory—were approved by his chief at the Bureau of Ordnance and Hydrography and by the secretary of the Navy. Henry, though, refused to acknowledge that any wrong had been done and stopped responding to the complaints, and Maury had an influential enemy.[67]

Another was the superintendent of the Coast Survey (later to be called the Coast and Geodetic Survey), Alexander Dallas Bache. The West Point-trained Philadelphian and former professor at the University of Pennsylvania pridefully traced his lineage back to his great grandfather, Benjamin Franklin, and thus considered himself an inheritor of an august scientific mantle with all the rights and responsibilities pertaining thereto. Bache had been a cordial supporter of Maury, lending him an endorsement for Maury's *Treatise on Navigation* ("I consider the work fully to sustain the high character for scientific attainment which I have always heard attributed to its author," he had said).[68] The luster on their relationship apparently wore off when Maury, and not Bache's friend Gilliss, became superintendent of the Naval Observatory. It cannot have been improved when Bache's close friend Joseph Henry poached the Neptune sightings history, nor when Professor Bache hired Sears Walker fresh out of the Observatory for the Coast Survey office. This last must have seemed like several fingers, not one, in the eye: the Coast Survey was for obscure reasons under the purview of the Treasury Department, although it used naval officers for the actual surveying; everyone in the Navy believed it should be in the Navy Department.

Academic and scientific territorial skirmishes can be corrosive affairs, but this was possibly more annoying because these men looked down on Maury for his ordinary pedigree and nonuniversity background, though in most respects this was equal to that of Lieutenant Gilliss and the eminent Joseph Henry, and certainly to Bache's revered great-grandfather. Maury's detractors disliked his embrace of the military and his identity as a Virginian, which would put his reputation and scientific gifts under a near-permanent cloud after the Civil War.

In the day-to-day scheme of things for Maury, however, these were but high passing clouds in an otherwise clear and promising sky. There was too much work to be done. And he had the support of a loving family, with whom he spent all of his free moments—he and his wife Ann were up to four daughters and two sons—and a good number of friends, among whom were many distinguished persons of the day. Also he had a group of close cousins, his brother-in-law and Observatory associate Lieutenant William Herndon, and longtime friends such as the Lynchburg newspaper editor William Blackford, and a faithful comrade from midshipman days, Lieutenant William Francis Lynch.

In his work, rewards continued. A record of the Observatory's astronomical observations for the year 1845 was published in April the following year. A bulky 538 pages, it was, Maury wrote proudly, "the first volume of Astronomical Observations that has ever been issued from an institution properly entitled to the name of Observatory on this side of the Atlantic," and as such it was widely noted.[69] Indeed, Maury was putting the Observatory on the map. "The colleges . . . are warm in their commendation of the volume," he would write to his friend William Blackford. "They all think more of it than I do; but what amuses me, that almost every one expressed surprise that *Navy* officers should be able to do such things. We have beat Greenwich all hollow, there is no doubt; yet we shall do better next time. . . . I have solved a problem that has often blistered my heart and proved that Navy officers are fit for something else besides scrubbing decks at sea and tacking ship."[70]

In the face of this demonstrated scientific value of astronomy, and the immense promise of the wind and current charts project, the Atlantic phase of which in early 1846 was in sight of completion, Lieutenant Maury and all his officers and midshipmen at the Observatory nevertheless tendered reassignment requests to Naval Secretary George Bancroft on May 11, seeking duty on the waters off Mexico. Fighting between the Mexican and American armies had broken out in Texas north of the Rio Grande, and General Taylor had quickly won several battles and repulsed the Mexicans back across the river. Official declaration of war came two days later despite mounting Whig opposition in Congress; generally, though, there was much popular support for war with Mexico and the notion of expanding the western boundary of the United States to the shores of the Pacific Ocean—the "Manifest Destiny" as coined in a phrase a few months later by John Louis O'Sullivan in his *United States Magazine and Democratic Review*. "Our manifest destiny," wrote O'Sullivan, "is to overspread the continent allotted by Providence for the free development of our yearly multiplying millions."

Like most, Maury "cordially approved" of the Mexican War, as the English author of a profile reported, adding breezily in her own words that he "was zealous that the Navy should share the glory of the strife. He, himself, forgetful of the . . . suffering limb, and of a constitution injured by its effects, would instantly seize the boarding pike and cutlass and leap to the oar."[71] But Secretary Bancroft refused to consider detaching him from his "valuable work" in Washington. The pressure increased on the Observatory staff, though, as a number of junior officers were sent off to war duty in the closing months of 1846 and early 1847.[72]

Dispatches then began pouring in from the Mexican seacoast, where the U.S. Navy's Home Squadron, under the cautious Commander David Conner, blockaded the eastern ports. By February 23, the Army's General Zachary Taylor had defeated Mexico's General Santa Ana at the battle of Buena Vista; two weeks later, on March 8 off the bristling fortress of Vera Cruz, commenced the first large-scale amphibious operation in American annals: 10,000 troops under the command of General Winfield Scott were shifted from transport ships to newly constructed landing craft, and then stormed the beaches under covering fire from naval gunboats. In the resulting siege, U.S. naval shore batteries and a procession of artillery craft—using diagrams of the Vera Cruz defenses drawn by Maury's assistant at the Observatory, Lieutenant William B. Whiting—pounded the formidable walls. The fortress surrendered on March 27.

Aside from blockade work and transport, the Navy's job was over. General Scott would move his soldiers toward Mexico City, defeating large forces at Cerro Gordo on April 18, Churubusco on August 20, Molino del Rey on September 8, and later in that second week of September, swarm over the fortified hill of Chapultepec outside Mexico City, and enter the capital on September 14.

Too late for the war effort was Maury's first sheet of eight charts of the Atlantic Ocean—depicting the Gulf of Mexico, drawn by Lieutenant Whiting, and published immediately after the victory—but the Observatory's strategic role in the landing at Vera Cruz, launching the final push, was commended. The accolades would increase as the remaining Atlantic charts were issued in the next several months, found their audience, and won their adherents. It was a great satisfaction to Maury as he contemplated the inauspicious birth of that five-year project in the neglected crates of old ships' logs, and he looked forward to continuing the cartography across the rest of the world's oceans, illuminating the waters as well as Quincy Adams's lighthouses in the sky.

CHAPTER THREE

Ambition Within the Ashes

THE RESPECTIVE ELEMENTS IN THE LIFE OF WILLIAM FRANCIS LYNCH —grief over his daughter's untimely death, marital failure, nagging infirmities, career sluggishness, finances, middle age—were swirling like motes in the air; if one could not see a pattern, one could at least understand that they were accumulating a greater urgency. He scrutinized the ebb and flow of naval administration—what captains were nearing retirement (or incapacitation, or mortality) to open up a senior officer's berth; what naval ships were going to require a new captain.

Back at the family home in Frederick, as was the case throughout the United States in the autumn of 1846, most conversations faced West: about the new state of Texas and territory of Oregon; about the 6,000 infantry and cavalry under General Zachary Taylor, sweeping down into Mexico, winning gloriously at Monterrey; Stephen Watts Kearny's conquest, New Mexico, annexed; an increasing number of ox-driven covered wagons rumbling toward Oregon and California; a louder call for a national railroad to link the Atlantic and Pacific, stirred by a speechifying New York merchant named Asa Whitney. The whole pulse was quickening.

If anything, Lieutenant Lynch stepped up his campaign with the naval secretary to get himself moving again. He had the fortune, at least, to have a sympathetic ear in his fellow Virginian, Naval Secretary John Young Mason. When, in December 1846, Lieutenant Lynch learned that a side-wheeled steamer named for the president had finished construction in Richmond and was destined for service in the Gulf of Mexico, he wrote to Mason asking for command of the *Polk*, getting his hopes up. Mason replied in a polite letter that the post would go to another officer. Lynch, disappointed and hurt, uncharacteristically pushed back a little and asked why: since he was eminently eligible for the promotion, the secretary must have personal reservations about him. Mason's reply came in a kindly tone—it was nothing personal, he said, but was based on other considerations.

Lynch had counter-suggested that he be given command of one of the new, so-called bomb vessels—in effect a floating siege engine with one huge mortar on board, used for shelling land fortifications and towns—and reminded Mason of his experience with artillery gleaned aboard the *Fulton* and other craft, including having "served at gun practice under Commodore Perry, and he will satisfy you that I can plant a shell with accuracy." Secretary Mason promised that his petition would be "respectfully considered."

Across ensuing weeks the anxious Lieutenant Lynch, worrying that he would miss out on the action, pored over dispatches from Mexico. In late March, the defeat of Mexican forces at the town and castle of Vera Cruz was also, in Lieutenant Lynch's disappointed eyes, a defeat of his own aspirations. "There was," he would conclude glumly, as General Scott's army marched off to fight its way toward Mexico City, "nothing left for the Navy to perform." One might envision that landbound naval officer reading the adulatory dispatches and populating the quarterdecks of those important naval ships—those transports bearing the infantry, those landing craft riding the Gulf's surf in toward the beaches beneath the protective whistle of artillery shells, those attacking steamers *Vixen* and *Spitfire* and their gunboat flotilla, lobbing ordinance against Vera Cruz's defensive walls—with all of the lucky or well-connected naval officers who had scored while Lynch had lost. The ambitious images of himself commanding the side-wheeler *Polk*, or a bomb vessel blasting out breaches in castle walls, faded.

His ambition, however, did not fade.

Instead, his visions of command began to arch out over peace-time again, vividly enhanced by memories of his many voyages tracing ancient mariners' routes across the length and breadth of the Mediterranean.

How many times had he gazed out at the old ports, yearning for the kind of exploration a tourist on shore leave could never manage? How many times had his ships paused off the coasts of the Barbary States, of ancient Rome, Greece, Phoenicia, Israel, and Egypt, and he felt the adventurer's pull? How many times had he steered by the stars that had shown down on Homer and Caesar and Alexander and Pliny and—most reverently, he would add—Christ himself? And again he would have felt the adventurer's pull.

The Holy Land exerted the most powerful gravity. And from Lynch's long-felt urges, intensified by his readings of two popular travel memoirs of the region, came the express nautical purpose through which he might obtain departmental—and probably congressional—approval of a scientific mission, on the heels of war, and in a climate indifferent to the naval heart.

The lieutenant's soul may have always yearned to be a novelist, but as a frequently land-bound naval officer Lynch satisfied at least some of his restlessness in reading travel memoirs. Particularly strong was the bestselling *Incidents of Travel in Egypt, Arabia Petraea, and the Holy Land* by an American, John Lloyd Stephens, published 10 years before in 1837. Stephens, a young New York lawyer of literary bent, had adventurously journeyed up the Nile from Alexandria and Cairo to Thebes, visiting temples, ruins, tombs, climbing pyramids and ducking into "mummy pits." By camel caravan and in Arab disguise he had traveled westward to the Red Sea and across the Sinai desert and beyond to the ancient lost city of Petra, carved into the precipitous red walls of a twisting gorge, and visited by only a handful of Westerners, after resting for a thousand years and being known only to Bedouins: Stephens was the first American to see Petra. Next he followed an old Roman road across the desolate terrain of Edom to the Holy Land, where he visited the tombs of the Patriarchs, Bethlehem, Jerusalem, Jericho, the Dead Sea, the Jordan River, and finally the old Crusader port of St. Jean d'Acre where he departed for home.

Filled with adventure, exotica, erudite history and cultural commentary, and written with wit and literary flair, Stephens's *Incidents of Travel* was a runaway bestseller, selling some 21,000 copies in its first two years, running through multiple editions and translations and staying in print with its original publisher, Harper and Brothers, for four and a half decades; its appearance in the fall of 1837 was heralded by the young critic Edgar Allan Poe, who in his 12-page critique in the *New-York Review*—it was his first piece for the *Review*—said it was "written with a freshness of manner, and evincing a manliness of feeling, both worthy of high consideration." Poe concluded by hoping "it is not the last time we shall hear from him. . . . Mr. Stephens writes like a man of good sense and sound feeling."[2]

William Francis Lynch had been stationed on the U.S.S. *Fulton* along the Atlantic coast in October 1837, when Stephens's *Incidents of Travel* was published; it was, he would say, "one of the most interesting books of travel which our language can produce."[3] From 1840 to 1842, while aboard the *Fairfield* in the Mediterranean, Lynch was free to ponder the lure of Stephens's adventures—to whom he might add those of Edward Robinson, professor of biblical literature at Union Theological Seminary in New York, whose own remarkable travel memoir had appeared in the fall of 1841. *Biblical Researches in Palestine,*

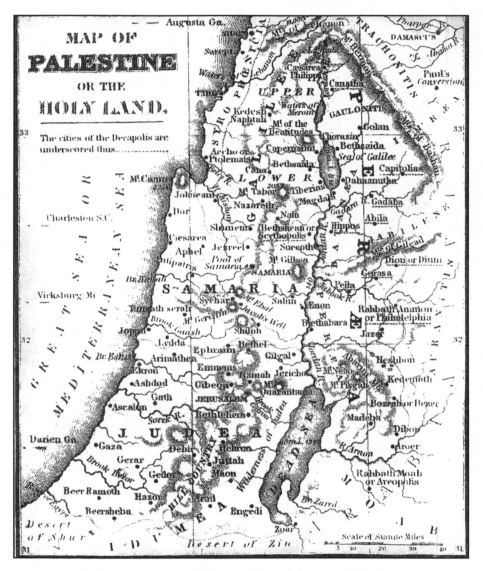

Palestine at the time of the Lynch Expedition, as published in
the competing journal by Edward P. Montague, 1852.

(Author collection)

Mount Sinai, and Arabia Petraea was a journal of travels taken in the year 1838 by Dr. Robinson and his former pupil, the Reverend Eli Smith, American missionary in Beirut. The pair traveled from Cairo and the Nile to Suez, Sinai, Aqaba, Jerusalem, traversing the length and breadth of ancient Israel. In some 900 pages of exquisitely detailed and exhaustively researched material, Dr. Robinson closely examined purported physical remnants from the biblical era as well as the topography of the Holy Land's terrain, authoritatively establishing the physical locations of biblical stories as well as triangulating with science and with established histories such as that of the first century's Flavius Josephus much of what had previously been collected only in scripture and commentary. His footnote-crammed but compellingly written book became the foundation of biblical geography, inciting generations into the field, as well as one of the most important works on Palestine in the nineteenth as well as the twentieth century. After publication in two volumes in 1841, *Biblical Researches* sold out its first edition in America as well as Britain; among a number of awards was the gold medal from the Royal Geographic Society.

The effect of these two books upon Lieutenant Lynch was profound, and the geographical place description in both that pulled him most was that of the Dead Sea, with its fabled history as well as its host of unanswered questions. In his narrative, John Lloyd Stephens had confessed that "nothing, not even the thought of visiting Petra and the land of Idumea, affected me so strangely as the idea of making the tour of [the Dead] Sea." Poe had quite agreed in his review, finding it "the most interesting if not the most important portion of his book." For his part, Edward Robinson had also lingered on the Dead Sea shore as he strove to steer through faith and superstition toward amassing solid history and science about that remote and mysterious body of water.

Terrible associations were attached to the Dead Sea from its earliest Old Testament stories of the five cities of the Vale of Siddim—Admah, Zeboiim, Zoar and the notorious Sodom and Gomorrah, wrathfully destroyed by Jehovah for the sins of their citizens: *"And Jehovah rained upon Sodom and upon Gomorrah sulphur and fire—from Jehovah, from the heavens—and He overturned those cities, and all the Circle, and all the inhabitants of the cities, and that which grew upon the ground. And Lot's wife looked back as they fled to Zoar and became a pillar of salt. And Abraham looked down upon Sodom and Gomorrah, upon all the land of the Circle, and saw, and, behold, the smoke of the land went up like the smoke of a furnace."* Popular belief placed the ruins of the blasted cities at the bottom of the Dead Sea. Adding to the region's grim reputation, there had been the New Testament account of the beheading of John the Baptist by the murderous King Herod, said by the first-century historian Flavius Josephus to have taken place in the deep dungeons of Herod's cliff-top fortress of Machaerus overlooking the Dead Sea. Also, there was the still obscure but awe-inspiring story of the terrible resistance against Roman legions of a besieged Jewish garrison, high above the sea at Masada, ending in the suicide or massacre of 960 soldiers and civilians, including women and children, rather than surrender; Edward Robinson reported in his book that after he had spied mountaintop ruins overlooking the sea's southwest coast, he was willing to vouch that they were of ancient Masada.[4]

Known to be vastly saltier than the Mediterranean, the Dead Sea had no outlet and was supposedly filled with deadly chemicals from the bowels of the earth, giving off fumes that not only prevented life beneath its waves but killed any bird that flew over it. The water was said to be so heavy that winds could not ruffle it. Ancient writers from Aristotle to Pliny had remarked about the water's buoyancy. "It is," wrote Josephus around AD 75, "so light or thick that it bears up the heaviest things that are thrown into it; nor is it easy for anyone to make things sink therein to the bottom." Great clods of oily, black bitumen were released from its bottom; this had given it the name known during the Roman occupation as Lake Asphaltites.

Its major tributary, the Jordan River, which spilled into the Dead Sea from the Sea of Galilee (or Lake Tiberias, the old Roman name) from the north, was said from ancient Christian times to flow into the Dead Sea without blending with the noxious waters—such were the sacred associations of the river said to have been blessed with Jesus's presence. But the sea, ringed with bare, blasted mountains, connoted death and ancient destruction to all who visited it, including Josephus. "It is related how," he wrote, "for the impiety of its inhabitants it was burnt by lightning; in consequence of which there are still the remainders of that divine fire; and the traces [or shadows] of the five cities are still to be seen, as well as the ashes growing in their fruits, which fruits have a color as if they were fit to be eaten; but if you pluck them with your hands, they will dissolve into smoke and ashes."[5] Over succeeding centuries, other travelers and commentators, particularly during the Crusades, had repeated and imaginatively embellished the accounts, all the way to the present century.

But what was the modern day's reply from science and reason?

All previous attempts to map and sound it had failed, though thanks to recent travelers including Robinson it was known that the Dead Sea was between 38 and 40 miles long, depending on seasonal water fluctuations, with a breadth some 9 miles at midpoint; it lay beneath shoreline cliffs as high as 1,500 feet westward and 2,500 feet to the east.

Beyond that, however, in the annals of science the Dead Sea and the Jordan River were stuck in mystery and controversy. Two members of Britain's Royal Geographical Society, G. H. Moore and W. G. Beke, had visited the sea in March 1837, intending but not succeeding to map it; they were surprised, though, while trying to discover its relative altitude level by measuring the boiling temperature of water, that the Dead Sea seemed to be some 500 feet below sea level of the Mediterranean. Verification by the more accurate aneroid barometer, a cumbersome and extremely delicate instrument prone to breakage, was attempted by successive travelers, to confusing results. In 1838 a Frenchman measured the depression as 1,332 feet, and a German came up with 1,400 feet. Subsequent inquiries by these men and other travelers found the below-sea level of the Sea of Galilee to be variously, 535 feet or 756 feet, but they compounded the confusion by also finding places along the lower Jordan to be either *above* sea level—did they mean to represent that the river water actually ran uphill?—or to be sufficiently below to require huge cataracts as high as Niagara Falls, seen by no traveler since antiquity, to account for the drop in altitude between the Sea of Galilee and the Dead Sea.

Within recent memory, scientists from across Europe had pondered these mysteries. In England alone, the Royal Geographic Society had published a slew of articles on various aspects of the subject, with its counterparts in France and Germany not far behind. In his influential tome on biblical geography in 1841, the frustrated Edward Robinson had said that the question could never be decided until "the intervening country shall have been surveyed and the relative level of the two seas trigonometrically ascertained."

As it happened, that very year a Lieutenant J. F. A. Symonds of the British Royal Engineers attempted that kind of survey within a larger colonial project involving the entire Judean area. The Sea of Galilee, he reported, was 84 feet below the Mediterranean, and the Dead Sea was 1,337 feet below sea level; his methods and figures were later challenged, but the fact remained that there seemed to be a drop of more than a thousand feet along the length of the lower Jordan, taking it to the lowest, deepest place on all the earth.

As Lynch pondered the mysteries of the Dead Sea and the Jordan River, he read of the man who had apparently taken the sole exploration in modern times across the noxious lake, only to have it end in tragedy. John Lloyd Stephens had uncovered the story and publicized it in his bestselling book: it concerned a 25-year-old Irish adventurer named Christopher Costigan who upon arrival in the Holy Land in 1835 had felt compelled to explore and map the Jordan and the Dead Sea. Unfortunately for Costigan it was the height of summer. He had hired a Maltese sailor as his servant, purchased a small boat, and had it transported by camelback from Beirut to the Sea of Galilee. Costigan and the Maltese had begun a descent of the Jordan but within days crawled back out, nearly drowned in its tumultuous rapids. They finished their descent along the riverbank and re-embarked upon the Dead Sea, measuring, sounding, and charting as they zigzagged its full length and breadth.

Days later they staggered ashore suffering from heat stroke, dehydration, severe illness from drinking sea water, and malaria. The Maltese servant recovered—but poor Costigan had lingered for some time after being carried to the nearby village of Jericho and died soon after being evacuated to Jerusalem. No notes of his historic voyage were ever found. "Nothing . . . affected me so strangely," wrote Stephens, "as the idea of making the tour of this sea." Having found poor Costigan's boat intact in Jericho, where it had been pressed into service to hold up the roof of a lean-to hovel, Stephens had procured oars and sails to duplicate the voyage, but his own illness and lack of an adventurous companion compelled him to abandon the idea. "If I had succeeded in this," he mourned, "I should have considered my tour the most perfect and complete ever made by any oriental traveler."[6]

Modern science and reason had more to do in that ancient region, Lieutenant Lynch believed. Even then in that year of 1847 Edward Robinson would be preparing a paper to be read at the New-York Historical Society and in London at the Royal Geographic Society, calling the Jordan's fall in altitude a "remarkable phenomenon" and the question of relative levels of river and sea still a "burning issue" for scientists everywhere. He would call upon the nations of England, France, and Prussia to "not let the matter rest until it shall be fully accomplished." It was, he continued, "a remarkable configuration of the earth's surface, respecting which we have as yet no accurate knowledge." That this was square in the center of the biblical Holy Land gave it even greater intrigue.[7]

To Lynch's mind, the U.S. Navy was as fit to make those measurements as any European service.

* * *

At his office in Washington, Secretary of the Navy John Young Mason received a letter from his fellow Virginian, Lieutenant Lynch. It was Monday, May 10, 1847. In the eight months since returning to head the Navy —at President Polk's request—most of Young's daily concerns referred to the Mexican War, most recently matters such as how many of his marines were casualties during the bloody infantry assault on Cerro Gordo just three weeks before; how Commodore Matthew C. Perry fared in pounding the Caribbean coastal towns of Alvarado, Tuxpan, and Tabasco, while on the Pacific the effectiveness of the naval blockade of Mexico's western ports; and whether (perhaps most worrisome of all) the approaching spring and summertime plagues of fever would again ravage his men. As usual for any cabinet officer, his correspondence load leaned heavily toward deflecting office-seekers; the closer General Taylor got to Mexico City and victory, the more frantic they seemed to become.[8]

Therefore, it must have been with some surprise that Mason began to absorb the proposal of the ambitious Lieutenant Lynch, who only a few months before had been so eager for war service. A small stack of books aflutter with place markers came with the letter.

Washington City
May 8, 1847
Sir,

In the hope that it may receive your sanction, I respectfully submit a proposition to circumnavigate and explore the lake Asphaltites or Dead Sea, and its entire coast.

The expense will be trifling, and the object easy of attainment.

Our ships of war frequently touch at Acre in Syria. That place is forty miles distant from the foot of lake Tiberias or Sea of Galilee. Through and from the last, the river Jordan, a bold and navigable stream runs about sixty miles in a southerly direction, and debouches into the first named sea.

The frame of a boat, with its crew and their provisions, can be transported on camels from Acre to Tiberias. At the latter place the frame can be put together, and the crew embark and accomplish the desired work in fifteen days. Arms and a tent, a few mathematical instruments, provisions and water, are all that will be required. The tent can be made on board ship—temporarily used, and the canvas afterwards applied to other purposes. The arms from the ship, and the ordinary ration will suffice—and the boat itself can be safely returned.

The Dead Sea has been circumnavigated but by one traveler, Mr. Costigan. He very nearly accomplished it in eight days. Unfortunately, he embarked at a most insalubrious season of the year, and died at the termination of his voyage, without leaving a journal or notes behind.

For the information now possessed and to convey an idea of the desire felt to require more, I respectfully refer you to Voltaire and Chateaubriand; to "Rees' Cyclopedia" (article Asphaltites); to "Travels of La Martine" page 234, and to "Incidents of Travel" by Stephens, page 204-216, vol. 2.

The three last works, with the places marked, I have left with the Register of your Department subject to your call.

This proposition pertains to a subject maritime in its nature and therefore peculiarly appropriate to your office, and it is involved in mystery, the solution of which will advance the cause of science and gratify the whole Christian World.
I have the honor to be
Your obt. Servt.
W. F. Lynch
Lt. U. S. Navy[9]

Lynch's proposition may have been unconventional but it was hardly a lunatic idea. Secretary Mason firmly supported the notion of science in the service, and the lieutenant's enterprise was admirable, even taking advantage of existing situations to keep costs down, recognizing that the Navy was, as always, strapped for cash. It also happened to be strapped for a Mediterranean fleet, its ships having been absorbed by the Home Squadron for Caribbean duty at the onset of hostilities with Mexico—but Mason had been pressuring the president to restore their presence since he took office, knowing it was just a question of time before U.S. merchant shipping there got into trouble.

Mason tabled the letter in order to consult the State Department and, as he always preferred, a few close authorities. As it turned out, the superintendent of the U.S. Naval Observatory, whose province was the collection and coordination of scientific data on the world's oceans, was more than happy to support such a mission as Lynch's. Over the years, Lynch and Maury had stayed in touch, encouraging each other with the energy of youth and ambition in agitating for a larger, more modern, and more professional Navy—one in which they hoped to play substantial roles. Lynch had cheered Maury's daring but pseudonymous newspaper essays on reform; Maury had egged Lynch, as the more senior officer, to take some of their proposals to a predecessor of Navy Secretary Mason's. "The Secretary directed Lynch to leave Washington," Maury would recall, "for . . . he—the Secretary—wished to bring up the bill and have the credit for originating it."[10]

From his place at the Naval Observatory, Maury would be a steadfast champion of the Lynch expedition, both to Secretary Mason as well as to political Washington and the rest of the world. "The spot to be explored," he would write, "was a mysterious one; those who had visited it before, had died, and by their fate invested it with deeper interest and shrouded it in darker mystery. From infancy up, associations of terror and awful vengeance, were, in the minds of millions, associated with the name of that spot, and throughout the entire length and breadth of Christendom, there was an eager, not an idle, curiosity with regard to it; to explore it would redound to the glory of the navy and the honor of the nation. Expeditions from other countries had been attempted and had failed. The American navy never fails; and one of its most accomplished officers, willing to risk his life and reputation upon success, appeared entreating for leave to go."

Not only was there the scientific challenge of determining the Jordan's path and fall, and the Dead Sea's level compared to that of the ocean, Maury argued. Science also needed to know about the Mediterranean currents, especially the perplexingly violent one pouring through the strait of Gibraltar. Moreover, "what effect might a conjectured difference of level between that sea and the Dead have upon this current, and other phenomena? An expedition there would improve geography, and therefore navigation; for by giving the height of the mountains along the coast, you could afford the navigator the means to determine his distance from them and to fix the place of his ship at sea, when the light of heaven themselves may fail him in his straights."

Besides, he continued, as the legendary natural scientist Alexander von Humboldt had said, "He who elicits a fact from nature, often makes a discovery of more value than he who discovers an island in the sea." The Navy was being given the opportunity of gathering a "bundle of facts," argued Maury, "the importance and value of which, like the bearings of every new fact gathered from nature, it is impossible to foresee."[11]

The weeks pressed on across Lynch's tabled proposal. General Scott halted his forces at Puebla, 80 miles from Mexico City. He would remain there for three months as a significant number of troops went home when their enlistments expired; the remainder struggled against yellow fever, malaria, and typhoid. Meanwhile, the Navy continued to exert force along the southeastern Gulf Coast between Matamoros and Vera Cruz, many of the sailors also falling ill. While Lieutenant Lynch chafed, waiting to hear back from the Navy Department, he decided to visit relatives in Connecticut.

* * *

Secretary Mason was at his office on Thursday, May 27, valiantly —perhaps impatiently—working to tie up loose ends before a much-anticipated pleasure trip would take him out of Washington for several nostalgic days of festivities surrounded by friends and associates at his alma mater. Mason toiled away, anticipating the touching convocations of Tarheels, the sight of the campus's grand Davie poplar and the stately Old East residence hall of his youthful days; the naval secretary could have predictably most looked forward to the socializing, as his fondness for food, drink, and companionable laughter were well known. But, before he could join his friends and they could fill their coach with cigar smoke and kick their boots off for awhile, there was the matter of one particular correspondent.

Secretary Mason's letter would reach William Francis Lynch in New Haven a few days later.

Navy Department
May 27, 1847
Lt. Wm. F. Lynch
U.S. Navy
New Haven, Conn.

Sir:

The Department has considered the proposition contained in your letter of the 8th inst. with much interest, and will be disposed to act favorably upon it at the most convenient opportunity.
Resfy YrobSevt
J. Y. Mason[12]

* * *

Maury, too, was on the move. He had received word that he was to be awarded an honorary degree at commencement of the Univer-

sity of North Carolina at Chapel Hill. The honor was made greater
by circumstances: the lieutenant of humble beginnings and little formal education journeyed to North Carolina in the august company
of Secretary of the Navy John Young Mason, class of 1816, and President James Knox Polk, class of 1818. A number of other dignitaries,
including a governor, several former governors and cabinet members,
would also be present. Even a special correspondent from the *New
York Herald* was going. Secretary Mason was to give the alumni association address in Gerard Hall the evening before President Polk
would deliver the commencement address in the university chapel.
Polk and Mason were to view the seniors' examinations in Constitutional and International Law, while Maury was to sit in on Astronomy—"he was so struck by the brilliancy of our mathematical
champion," an observer would write, "that he offered him a situation
in the Observatory, which was accepted." Secretary Mason's address
would be fondly recalled for his "well-modulated silvery voice" and
electrifying words; President Polk would be praised for his "total
absence of ostentation, his sincere and unassuming courtesy," while no
one could refrain from comparing his appearance to that of a classmate,
Thomas J. Green of Virginia, who looked 20 years younger as opposed
to the president's "anxious countenance, his silvered hair and careworn
features, denoting incessant toil and perhaps suffering." Aggressive war
and forceful annexation seemed to be taking its toll.[13]

On the minds of several in the presidential party during the 270-
mile journey by rail and special coach from Washington to Chapel
Hill was a certain place far removed from that bucolic campus, and
from the other concerns occupying their minds, be they of war or
other matters of state, of the naval bureaucracy and operations,
or even of most matters hydrographic or astronomic. The faraway
and unexpected place was the hard kernel of an idea that, once one got
over one's surprise, seemed to seize enough of the minds of those
extraordinarily burdened men to compel them to support it. The faraway place was of course the Dead Sea, of great and biblical renown,

and the idea was that of Lieutenant Maury's old friend and fellow Virginian, Lieutenant William Francis Lynch. That weekend's gathering, that talk, did as much to solidify the future of Lynch's daring proposal as did his own initiative and daring.

Our great surprise, or at least bemusement, as we imagine the conversations of two Virginians and one Tennesseean as they sat swaying and no doubt wreathed in cigar smoke in the carriage conveying them to Chapel Hill, is that such a pure-knowledge enterprise would find favor in the midst of war and acquisition, and of a crushing array of weighty and demanding matters concerning those men of 1847—much less that it would succeed.

One more fateful event had to make its contribution. A few days later came startling news from Europe: an American merchant schooner had been captured by a privateer, the *Unico*, flying Mexican colors, and the prize was taken into the port at Barcelona. Washington, as well as vessel owners, shippers, and insurance companies, and corresponding entities in England and elsewhere, was much alarmed. Due to the war with Mexico there had been no protective American fleet in the Mediterranean for well over a year. Nervousness was only partly abated by a subsequent report that Spanish authorities, citing a treaty between Washington and Madrid in 1795, had immediately released the captured schooner and condemned the actions of the privateers.

Nevertheless, events called for action. On Monday, June 7, Secretary of State James Buchanan met with President Polk, who promptly issued orders for a formidable steam warship, the *Princeton*, to be sent to the Mediterranean to run down the *Unico* "and any other vessels that may be insulting our flag there." Secretary Mason (who never forgot that it had been because of the *Princeton*'s exploding gun in 1843 that he had been propelled into the president's cabinet) promised that ship would be provisioned and ready to weigh anchor within the week.

Soon there was a compounding alarm: an American barque arrived in the port of Boston from Gibraltar with reports that "four feluccas, under Mexican commissions, were known to be cruising in the Mediterranean, and one, formerly belonging to Gibraltar, was said to have been stopped by the French authorities while fitting out at or near Oran, on the coast of Barbary." These privateers were said to be carrying their prizes to a river on the Barbary coast, with one seen cruising outside the strait of Gibraltar.[14]

With the specter of insults to the flag as well as the menace to Mediterranean shipping, the *Princeton* hastened from Mexico's Caribbean coast toward Gibraltar, soon to be joined by the sloop of war *Marion* and the revenue cutter *Taney*. Later in the year the esteemed old seahorse Commodore George C. Read would be shifted from the African squadron to take over the restored Mediterranean squadron at Port Mahon, the all but deserted American naval base at Minorca in the Balearic Islands. However, the restoration posed the immediate logistical problem of provisioning ships and crews. Because of long-standing squabbles with France over the islands, Spain had requested the year before that the Americans' warehouses at Port Mahon be emptied and U.S. naval employees transferred.

It would take time to smooth out the diplomatic details—the Navy would begin the search for another sea base—but with ships and their crews rushing eastward across the Atlantic, Secretary Mason needed to keep up with their support. He ordered a recently commissioned storage ship, serving for the last several months off the Tampico coast, to sail to New York where it would be outfitted for Mediterranean duty. A 547-ton ship-rigged sailing vessel with four 24-pound guns, it was called the *Supply*, an apt if unimaginative name for a storage ship. Its original name had been the *Crusader*.[15]

It would be a perfect answer to satisfy the enthusiasm of his friend Maury and the ambitions of Lieutenant Lynch in his quest for the Holy Land. The Navy could profit in the public eye from the publicity such a feat might bring. Lynch would be given command of the *Supply* for its important mission to support the Mediterranean Squadron, and the *Supply* could then be justifiably dispatched to the coast of Syria as a part of "showing the flag." It was time to unleash Lieutenant Lynch; he could begin by commissioning a metal boat for his expedition down the River Jordan to the Dead Sea.

> Navy Department
> July 31, 1847
> Lieut. Wm. F. Lynch
> U.S. Navy, Washington, D.C.
> Sir:
> You will proceed to New York, and procure a copper boat of the dimensions proposed by you, & superintend its construction. You are also authorized to ship, or select from those already shipped, one petty officer and twelve seamen for the service on which you are to be detailed.
> I am respectfully,
> Your ob. Serv't,
> J. Y. Mason[16]

The puzzle-pieces seemed to be falling into place by themselves, perhaps for the first time in Lynch's life. And the Lynch Expedition to the Holy Land would turn out to be the beginning of a new era of discovery, one that would try to avoid the devilish shoals that had threatened to scuttle the great Pacific Exploring Expedition of the haughty Charles Wilkes, and one that would capture a great public attention.

CHAPTER FOUR

New York to Palestine

FOR THE NEXT TWO MONTHS OF PREPARATION IN NEW YORK, Lynch seldom rested. He immediately wrote to his friend Matthew Maury for advice about appointing members for his expedition. Obviously, he said, he needed men who knew surveying and had good eyes and hands for mapping and drawing. "Please sit down," he asked, "with the Navy Register of officers before you and give me the result."[1]

The junior officers presented to Lynch were both from Virginia and came highly recommended. Lieutenant John B. Dale was the son of an eminent officer; his father was Commander Richard Dale of Norfolk, who had served with distinction in the Revolutionary War under John Paul Jones on the *Bonhomme Richard* in its famous battle with the *Serapis*, later on the *Alliance* and *Ariel*, being wounded three times, and who had commanded the Mediterranean Squadron against the Tripolitan pirates in 1801–02. The younger Dale had served on the *Vincennes* as well as the *Constitution* in the latter's recently returned around-the-world cruise. A superb draftsman, Dale's drawings had been included in the published reports of the United States Exploring Expedition under the command of Lieutenant Charles Wilkes between 1838 and 1842. However, Dale, serving on the *Porpoise* and like many junior officers sailing under the tyrannical and paranoid Wilkes, had been detached from the expedition by the commander after a blameless minor incident off Tierra del Fuego; Dale returned to the United States aboard the storeship *Relief* in its long, episodic journey from Callao on the Peruvian coast by way of Hawaii and Sydney, Australia. Courts of inquiry cleared Dale of charges, leaving him a spotless record of accomplishment and gentlemanly deportment under all his other commanders; his relationship with his new superior, Lieutenant Lynch, would be one of mutual respect and deep friendship.

Second to Dale would be Passed Midshipman Richmond Aulick, who had the distinction of being the first graduate of the new naval academy (in other words, first in his class, in the academy's first graduating class) when he received his commission a year before. Auburn-haired, gray-eyed, he was the son of Captain John H. Aulick of Winchester, former head of the Washington Navy Yard and now commanding the *Vincennes*, just back from East India. Young Aulick, like Dale considered a good draftsman, was 21.[2]

Lynch was to apply a rigorous standard to the selection of his expedition members—"young, muscular, native-born Americans," he would specify, "of sober habits, from each of whom I exacted a pledge to abstain from all intoxicating drinks."[3] Sailing experience in all climates and conditions had convinced him that alcohol sapped a man's power and perseverance. He set about his interviews of the 10 men who would accompany him and his officers on the expedition—an 11th he already knew well, having chosen his 16-year-old son, Francis, known as "Frank," to manage herbarium duties. Interestingly enough, another son would be detailed to serve on the *Supply* (but not on the expedition): John Y. Mason, Jr., appointed by his father as ship's purser.

In New York, consulting with the boat designer and builder Joseph Francis for the vessel he would launch on the Sea of Galilee,

Lynch originally wanted a small sailboat fabricated of copper, some 28 feet long by 6 feet wide. However, material shortages forced him to switch the order to two 18-foot lifeboats of corrugated sheet metal along the lines of the famous patent won by the designer. One would be of copper and the other of galvanized iron. Their design allowed them to be taken apart and reassembled if necessary for transport inland from the Mediterranean shore, but because Lynch worried about the "experimental" process of dismantlement, he ordered carpenters to construct two low wheel-trucks so the boats could be towed across land by horses or camels. The boats would be lightened by dispensing with the metallic flotation chambers of the original design; instead, Lynch purchased a number of vessels of gum elastic, which after their use for storage of supplies, could be filled with either air or water for use in flotation or ballast, when needed. Lynch sentimentally named the lifeboats after the young daughters of supportive commanders—the copper boat would be "Fanny Mason," after Secretary Mason's daughter, and the galvanized boat would be "Fanny Skinner" after the daughter of Commodore Charles Skinner, formerly of the African Squadron and now superintendent of the Gosport Naval Yard at Norfolk. For the ocean passage the boats would be stowed upside down in special cradles on the quarterdeck of the *Supply*.[4]

The two men in the world who probably knew the most about his destination—who in their books had written of standing on the shore of the Dead Sea yearning to explore it—happened to live in New York, and Lynch lost no time in contacting them. John Lloyd Stephens had followed his bestselling account of travels in the Holy Land with popular books on journeys through Eastern Europe and then Central America and the Yucatan, the latter filled with many adventures struggling through jungles and discovering ancient, overgrown Mayan ruins. He had just returned from a quick summer trip to Europe—having become a director of the Ocean Steam Navigation Company, he had gone on the maiden voyage of the 1,640-ton wooden side-wheeler *Washington* on its new mail run to

Southampton and Bremerhaven—and was full of impressions of his interview with every explorer's and naturalist's hero, Alexander von Humboldt, then 90 and a guest at the imperial palace at Potsdam. Stephens was happy to hear about Lynch's expedition and wrote a long list of recommendations.

Dr. Edward Robinson received Lynch and Dale at his office at Union Theological Seminary, and the biblical geographer opened his extensive files of field notes and maps as well as contributed letters of introduction to associates in Beirut. Further, Robinson proposed to send his endorsement and suggestions about the Dead Sea expedition directly to Secretary Mason.[5] In his journal, *Bibliotheca Sacra*, he would thank Lynch and Dale for doing him the honor of consultation. "How far they will be able to carry out their plan," he said, "remains to be seen; but so far as they shall be permitted to proceed, the public have reason to expect a great accession of accurate and valuable information."[6]

From his office in Washington, Secretary Mason sent a letter to Secretary of State James Buchanan on October 13, informing him of the Lynch expedition and asking him to smooth the way in diplomatic circles. Accordingly, Buchanan wrote Dabney Smith Carr, minister at the U.S. consulate at Constantinople, instructing him to aid Lynch in obtaining permission for the party from the sultan. "As this project is purely in the interest of science, and for the gratification of an enlightened curiosity," Buchanan wrote, "it is not conceived that the slightest objection will be raised by the Turkish Government in opposition to it, or that the request will not be promptly granted." A stack of handsomely printed American art portfolios were to be carried to Constantinople by Lieutenant Lynch, to be presented to sultan Abdul Mejid.[7]

Then, on October 15, while visiting Philadelphia, Lynch received some news from his friend Commodore Skinner that briefly threatened to put the entire enterprise in jeopardy: it was rumored that an English government party had just carried out a survey of the Dead Sea. "I beg you to be assured," Lynch immediately wrote to Secretary Mason, "that both previous and subsequent to my first application respecting the survey, I thoroughly examined every book and review I could find, at all bearing upon the subject, to ascertain whether it had been made. If it has been, I shall ever deeply regret the unnecessary trouble I have given you and the expense that has been incurred with no promise of an equivalent." He promised to get to the bottom of the rumor. If it was well founded, he presumed that Mason would call everything off. Then, Lynch said, he could not in conscience go forward to the Near East merely as commander of the storeship *Supply*. "If prevented from advancing the interests of Science and the cause of Christianity," he went on miserably, "I cannot desire, while war exists, to be employed peaceably cruising on a distant and otherwise attractive sea, and will ask you to permit me to proceed as a volunteer to our army in Mexico."[8]

In his reply, Mason said he would be "pained" if the rumor were true and would of course give consideration to letting Lynch go off and pick up an Army carbine. Soon enough, though, Lynch found enough information in Philadelphia and New York to cast doubt on any English success already accomplished. They were all, to be sure, cognizant that they might be taking part in an international race. Preparations in New York continued.[9]

Almost every day, more material for the Mediterranean Squadron as well as for the expedition was hoisted aboard the *Supply*. A small library of geographic and scientific works, requisitioned to uplift and prepare the men during their long voyage, was approved. To keep them safe, Lynch's arms included a blunderbuss, 14 carbines with long bayonets, 14 pistols (4 revolvers and 10 with bowie-knife blades attached), and ammunition belts; all officers additionally carried swords. They also would take sails, oars, flags, tents, gum elastic beds and covers for tents, gum elastic overcoats, preserved meats, and cooking utensils. For trade and presents to the Arabs they might meet along the trail, there was 80 pounds of tobacco and 50 pounds of coffee.

USS *Supply*, commissioned in 1846 and in service during the
Mexican War, transported the Lynch Expedition to the
Holy Land.

The scientific instruments, though, presented a problem: as
Lynch wrote Maury, the mountain barometers were uncrated only to
be found broken and their mercury leaked out. "If so easily damaged
when transported by railroad," he fretted, "they cannot stand being
carried on the backs of animals." He proposed substituting two
French instruments that were "capable of more accurate adjustment
and transportation," and instead of the supplied transit instrument,
which was "so large and heavy that it will be impossible to take it in
the boats," Lynch begged Maury's aid in securing a small universal
instrument that would serve the same purpose. This would turn out
to be in Lieutenant Charles Wilkes's possession; although Maury
would instinctively wonder if Wilkes would purposefully annoy them
by balking, he cooperated. Also, Lynch needed reconnoitering telescopes instead of common spyglasses, and a set of leveling instruments; Professor Robinson had urged him to ascertain the depression

of the Dead Sea below the Mediterranean by running a level line from seacoast to lakeshore in two places.

Maury helped his friend with all the acquisitions, which would arrive in time, and sent a long, finely detailed letter of instructions to Lynch's second-in-command, Lieutenant Dale, urging the simple fallback process of boiling water at various heights and depths of terrain and using an ordinary thermometer. "There is an empirical rule," Maury wrote, "which is near the truth: it gives 604 feet to a degree." He also went over using moon and star observations for determining longitude, using the universal instrument and sextant for latitude, and recording movements of various heavenly bodies.[10] Chronometers could not be promised to arrive before their departure, so Lynch asked that a London firm send them for pickup at Gibraltar.[11]

News of the expedition had crept through New York, rousing curiosity in the columns of the *New York Herald*, and Lynch took it upon himself to write the editor to elucidate. "For upwards of four thousand years, the Dead Sea has laid in its deep and wondrous chasm, a withering record of God's wrath upon his sinful creatures," Lynch colorfully said. "Itself once a fertile vale, teeming with population, and redundant with the products of a favored clime, it now lies inert and sluggish, a mass of dark and bitter waters, with no living thing upon its shore, or above or beneath its surface." It was said to have no bottom, indicated in one place "by incessant bubbles and agitated surface. Whether or not this be the crater of a submerged volcano, forming a subterraneous aqueduct with the ocean, who can tell?" He proposed to ascertain "whether the sea and its shores are of volcanic or nonvolcanic origin, and to refute the opinions of infidel philosophers with regard to its formation." Not only Science but "the whole Christian world" would be gratified. "Strabo, Diodorus, Pliny and Josephus, among the ancients, and Maundsell, Pocoke, Abbe Martine, Chateaubriand, La Martine, Stephens, and Robinson, among the moderns, all differ as to the extent, and many of the peculiarities of this sea." All, he said, "is vague, uncertain and mysterious." The U.S. Navy would get to the bottom of it.[12]

By the second week in November, the readiness date was almost upon them. Secretary Mason wanted to see Lynch in Washington before issuing his final instructions, and Lynch needed a last consultation with Maury, so once more he journeyed to the capital. Mason's formal orders, marked "Confidential," then followed him back to New York, arriving on November 15. As soon as the *Supply* was cleared for sailing, Mason said, Lynch was to take the ship directly to the Mediterranean, reporting to the squadron's Commodore George C. Read and calling at the Navy facility at Port Mahon. Then, seeking official permission—an Islamic royal decree was called a "firman,"—for the Dead Sea expedition, he was to sail to Smyrna (now Izmir) on the Turkish coast and then head overland to Constantinople. If he was refused permission, Mason wrote, he should just return to the ship and carry out its regular duties. But if the Turkish government agreed, Lynch was to proceed with his well-laid plans, surveying the Dead Sea and the river and terraces of the Jordan as well as the Sea of Galilee, if time permitted. "The object," Mason stated for the record, "is to promote the cause of Science, and advance the character of the Naval Service, to accomplish which a more favorable opportunity will probably not occur." Lynch was warned in his relations with inhabitants to be "circumspect, conciliatory and forbearing; paying fairly for all provisions obtained or services rendered, and prohibiting those under your command from committing the slightest act of aggression." [13]

Such was his zeal to see the object of his aspirations, Lynch anxiously felt it necessary to pry one more concession from the naval secretary. "The Turkish Government," he wrote Mason on November 17, "supposed to be incapable of appreciating the value of a scientific research, and prone to suspect other motives than the avowed ones, may refuse to grant a firman. In such an event, I beg permission to leave this ship in the Levant and to return in her, or some other ship of the squadron, or direct to the U. States within the year." Obviously, if an official American naval party could not go inland, Lynch was determined to do it as a "tourist." Mason would acquiesce to the year's detachment, hoping as did Lynch that it would not be necessary.[14]

On Friday, the 20th of November, the *Supply* dropped down from the Brooklyn Navy Yard to an anchorage abreast of the Battery where it waited for the weather to open. For a week it kept raining and blowing, but finally, November 26 dawned clear with a fresh breeze from the northwest, the ship weighed anchor, and, notwithstanding that it was a Friday, the day thought to be unlucky by superstitious seamen, the ship formerly known as the *Crusader* got underway for the Mediterranean. "We are all well and in buoyant spirits," Lynch wrote Mason in early afternoon with his final mail packet and muster roll as the harbor pilot was released off Sandy Hook, and "are pressing forward with great velocity."[15]

Boisterous winds propelled them across the Atlantic in 23 days. During the passage, Lynch's aspirations expanded, wanting to wheedle one more concession from Mason, as he had begun to address in dispatches forwarded just before the ship left American waters: after he and his men had finished their Dead Sea and Jordan reconnaissance, he hoped to continue eastward, and survey the Euphrates. With the passage of weeks and the growing distance between them, the issue would take a long time to resolve.[16] Meanwhile, he noted down his sightings of rainbows, stars, planets, and, short of the Azores, a pod of sperm whales "sporting in the wild chaos of waters, and exhibiting their glossy backs as they rose occasionally to the surface, and blew high in air volumes of water from their capacious nostrils." He was ever mindful of his old and older predecessors, sighting Cape St. Vincent, "the southwestern extremity of vine-clad Portugal, as it is of Europe also," and calling it as the Romans did, *Sacrum Promontorium*. Making Cape Trafalgar and the site of the "great conflict between the fleet of England and the combined fleets of France and Spain," he meditated on Admirals Collingwood and Nelson. Mid-channel in the Strait of Gibraltar, sighting the southern point of Europe at Tarifa and, enshrouded in mist, the "lofty and majestic" mountains of Africa, his imagination summoned the flotillas of Saracen invaders bearing down on the Spanish coast. Passing between Calpe and Abyla, the pillars of Hercules, the *Supply* closed in on the bay of Gibraltar and found anchorage below the magnificent rock, which to the lieutenant resembled a couchant lion—"his forepaws gathered beneath him, his massive, shaggy head towards Spain, his fretted mane bristling against the sky, and his long and sweeping tail resting upon the sea."[17]

The safe ocean passage, favorable winds, and, as he reported to Secretary Mason, the "utmost harmony" among officers and crew, portended success, he hoped. Not even a slight case of varioloid, the mildest form of smallpox, which befell a crew member several days out of New York, had seemed to threaten Lynch's mission—the ship surgeon was not alarmed and said no isolation was necessary. At Gibraltar, though, after the ship was given a clean bill of health by the port medical officer and the *Supply* waited for the arrival of the two ship's chronometers ordered from London by Matthew Maury, Lynch developed a blinding headache and high fever, which the surgeon was unable to diagnose or treat.

A few days later the lieutenant developed the characteristic rash and open sores in his mouth and tongue, then spreading all over his body, that meant smallpox. From his cabin sickbed, Lynch immediately ordered all communication with the shore halted, had the yellow pennant of pestilence hoisted, and directed that the *Supply* sail for Port Mahon at Minorca in the Balearic Islands, off Spain's eastern coast. There a good *lazaretto*, or hospital, could take him; there, too, the flagship of the Mediterranean fleet was berthed. The badly needed chronometers would have to be forwarded.

"Prostrate with a disease as malignant as it is loathsome," Lynch would write, "with a body inflamed and swollen" with running pustules, his mind "so racked with fever that reason, from time to time, fairly tottered on her throne," he suffered his illness confined in his stifling cabin for the eight-day passage until, at Mahon, he was hoisted out of the ship and carried to the hospital. The crew was quarantined aboard the *Supply* for eight days, anchored at a safe distance from other vessels while port medical officials began the tedious process of fumigating the ship. Only one additional case appeared, a steward named Edward Montague who was also sent to the *lazaretto*.[18]

With quarantine finally lifted, the crew set to unloading stores for the Mediterranean fleet. On January 20, 1848, word came that after much suffering, Captain Lynch was entirely recovered. It had been generally known since Gibraltar that, illness notwithstanding, this delay at Port Mahon was a boon, for newspapers were full of dispatches reporting a bad cholera epidemic in Smyrna and Constantinople, at which Lynch intended to request the Ottoman firman permitting his expedition to the Jordan and Dead Sea. Better to delay there at Mahon in the Balearic Islands off Spain, with the comfort of the American fleet and shore leave, than be stuck in a long quarantine off the Syrian coast.

But then, regaining his strength, William Frederick Lynch contemplated news in a brief item from an English paper picked up at Gibraltar, which waited his return to the ship: a lieutenant in the Royal Navy, commanding a party surveying the Dead Sea, was killed during an encounter with Bedouin Arabs. As he wrote to Naval Secretary Mason back in Washington, "This intelligence rendered me the more anxious to reach the ground of our operations." On the evening of Friday, February 4, having to leave their remaining seaman behind at the *lazaretto* because he was still too ill to move, the *Supply* weighed anchor and steered toward the east under a light but favorable wind.[19]

Every nautical mile eastward across that ancient sea summoned forth associations, which Lynch commended to his diary, notes to contribute to the book he planned to write. Sailing abreast of Sardinia and then the "blue outlines" of Sicily, they touched at the island of Malta and anchored briefly in the port at Valletta, and as he stared up at the abrupt promontories dotted with Saracenic edifices and beetling fortifications, "fretted with artillery," he was moved to exclaim, "Here, too, has Napoleon been! From Moscow to Cairo, where has he not?"

But more insistent were reminders from deeper histories, as, on February 12, they entered the blue Aegean sea and made the island of Cerigo; he recalled Cerigo as ancient Cythera, "reputed to have been the birthplace of Helen, the frail heroine of the Trojan War." Further to the northwest was the Gulf of Athens and Cape Colonna, "ancient promontory of Sunium, where Plato taught, and where are the ruins of a temple of Minerva." Bypassing the coast of "poetic" Greece, wishing that he could stop to fulfill a long-held dream to plumb its mysteries, gape at its ruins, and climb Mount Olympus, he would be somewhat consoled once the *Supply* passed into the Gulf of Smyrna and closed in on the harbor of Smyrna, or Izmir, and he had a view of the snowy ramparts of Homer's Mysian Olympus, another resort of the ancient gods. As the sun set, casting the many sails of feluccas on the harbor, the olive groves of the coast, and the mountain range beyond in various shades of purple, the Americans standing there on deck heard the distant tinkling of bells: "a caravan of camels rounding a distant hill. In a long line, one after the other, slowly, sedately, with measured strides," Lynch would record, "they passed along the road towards the west."[20]

After a day sightseeing around the unprepossessing city of mostly one-story houses overshadowed by many mosques, Lynch left on the overnight, Constantinople-bound *Prince Metternich*, a steamer under the Austrian flag. His goal was an audience with the sultan and permission to visit the Ottoman province around the Dead Sea. The ship steamed north and northeast up the Gulf of Smyrna, passing the ancient island of Lesbos, birthplace of Sappho, and past dawn, the ruins of Alexandria Troas where, as at the former place, St. Paul had visited. Lynch was as much captivated by the picturesque humanity on deck, "Turks, Greeks, Armenians, Jews, and Syrians," each of course in his native dress and attended by piles of baggage. As they were turning east toward the mouth of the Hellespont strait, his eyes took in the barren plain of Troy and, far beyond, white-capped Mount Olympus. Past the fortified castles of the Dardanelles, after sunset and the arrival of pelting showers swept in from the hills of Thrace, the officers went below to bed, leaving their umbrellas to benefit a small number of the throng of deck passengers, who huddled miserably in the rain.[21]

By the sunlit morning, they emerged on deck to see that the ship was anchored in the Golden Horn—the harbor of Constantinople, "filled with ships and vessels of every class, and rig, and nation; and hundreds of light and buoyant caiques flitted to and fro among them," and, "flanking the harbor in an oblique line, were the heavy ships of war of the Turkish fleet." And there was the city and its suburbs, an expanse of brown, tile-roofed houses, interspersing mosques with domes and minarets, occasional cypress groves, and a rising mass of palaces, gardens, and kiosks, overseen by the largest mosque of all, "its roof a rounded surface of domes, the central and largest covered with bronze, and glittering in the sun, with a light and graceful minaret springing from each angle of its court."[22]

There would be a six-day wait until Lynch's audience with the sultan; he met with the U.S. minister, Dabney Smith Carr, a grandnephew of Thomas Jefferson who had in Baltimore been both a naval officer at the Port of Baltimore and a newspaper publisher; he conducted Lynch on a sightseeing tour of Constantinople's mosques, castles, and tombs, on a boat trip up the Bosphorus, and on a walk through the slave market. Every place summoned forth musings on ancient history, but the slave market brought up deep sentiments about the curse of slavery and the general degradation of women, free or not, in that predominantly Muslim empire.

Through Minister Carr, Lynch met Henry Bedlow, a 27-year-old American from New York, of a literary bent but with a little medical training, who eagerly volunteered to join the expedition. This was

Henry Bedlow, from a portrait taken late in life, decades after serving as a medic and poet in residence with the Lynch Expedition. *(Author collection)*

an offer Lynch was delighted to accept. Bedlow had until recently served as attaché in the Naples office of the American minister, his friend William Knox Polk, brother of the president. Bedlow had attended both Yale and Harvard Law School before studying medicine in New York. He was a highly intelligent dabbler whose name would be found on the Social Register in New York as well as Newport (his great-grandfather had owned a good proportion of Manhattan real estate as well as the island in New York harbor that had been named after the family and would, in 1886, become the site of a 305-foot-tall statue, "Liberty Enlightening the World"). For Lynch, Bedlow would serve as a backup scribe and assistant medical officer, contributing a detailed journal and saving the life of at least one member of the party following a serious accident.[23]

On February 26, Lynch was admitted to the Cherighan palace

fronting on the Bosphorus, and after a ceremonial interview with several palace officials, was escorted to the throne room of Grand Sultan Abdul Mejid, 31st sultan of the empire. There was a delay outside the chamber when the chamberlain instructed Lieutenant Lynch to leave his sword outside and the American refused, saying it was part of his uniform, and as an officer of the United States on an official call, it would be impossible to relinquish it. But after a half hour of whispered consultations the chamberlain finally acquiesced, and Lynch was ushered inside.

The sultan was only 25, and although he showed great kindness and friendliness, Lynch was struck by his wan, melancholic demeanor, his paleness presumably a result of the tuberculosis that would kill him at 39. Abdul Mejid had received a European education and was fluent in French, and he would be remembered as a reformer who brought in various modernizations while contending with the imperialist threat of Russia and with several rebellious provinces in the sprawling empire. As a gift from the president of the United States, Lynch offered some biographies and a portfolio of prints depicting the character and habits of North American Indians as done by American artists.

"He looked at some of them," recalled Lynch, "which were placed before him by an attendant, and said that he considered them as evidences of the advancement of the United States in civilization, and would treasure them as a souvenir of the good feeling of its government towards him. At the word civilization, pronounced in French, I started; for it seemed singular, coming from the lips of a Turk, and applied to our country." Much later, the lieutenant decided that his 72-year-old nation had not been slighted in that palace of ancient Turkey, and that what had occurred was either an error in translation or, perhaps, the sultan's grasp of French—Lynch presumed "that, by the word 'civilization,' he meant the arts and sciences."[24]

The day after that cordial audience, the sultan sent word to Lynch that he wanted to give a present to the lieutenant, who should name it. "More than any present," replied Lynch, "I would prize the granting of the firman" for permission to "pass through the Turkish dominions, in Syria, to the Dead Sea."

There would be a nervous wait of 10 days in Constantinople for the sultan's answer, while Dabney Carr did his diplomatic utmost to advance their case. Meanwhile, Lynch and his accompanying officers visited the city's historic sites, which testified to how the tides of power and belief had washed successively over the imperturbable capital. There was the ancient chariot racetrack of the Hippodrome, constructed by the Emperor Severus in the year 203 when the city was known as Byzantium; and the white marble Fethiye, or Victory Mosque, erected overlooking the Golden Horn in the eleventh century as the Greek Orthodox monastery of St. Mary Pammarkaristos. There was the breathtaking white-domed Mosque of St. Sophia, built, with elements of ancient pagan Greek and Roman temples, in the fourth century by Emperor Constantine and rebuilt by Emperor Justinian in the sixth century, and then taken from the Christians for Islam in the fifteenth century after the Ottoman conquest. There was the Sultan Ahmed, or "Blue" Mosque, with its six attending minarets, built in the sixteenth century; and the fifteenth century Seraglio, or Topkapi Palace, the sprawling administrative center of the Ottoman Empire built by the sultan Mehmed the Conqueror. And there was the Sufi Convent of the Whirling Dervishes, at which, at its small mosque on the Islamic holy day of Friday, Lynch caught a glimpse of Sultan Abdul Mejid in a royal procession, on foot. Once again the naval lieutenant was struck by the sultan's "almost tottering" melancholy, which to Lynch was symbolic that "the Ottoman rule upon the European side of Turkey is drawing to a close."[25]

He had begun to muse on historical parallels between the fall of Rome and the present Turkish state of affairs when, finally, on Tuesday, March 6, Lynch was given the long awaited firman from the sultan's Grand Vizier, addressed to the pashas of Sidon and Jerusalem and instructing them to give Lynch "all due aid and cooperation in

his explorations." He lost no time: in a half hour he was aboard the
French steamer *Hellespont* to return to Smyrna, musing during that
passage on matters less political than very personal. "As to protection
against the Arabs," he would write of the royal document he tucked
carefully away, "it could afford none whatever; for Eastern travelers
well know that, ten miles east from a line drawn from Jerusalem to
Nablus, the tribes roam uncontrolled, and rob and murder with
impunity."[26] Rumors persisted about the English party attacked
recently in the Jordan Valley; its commander had reportedly been
mortally wounded during the assault. In Lynch's luggage, therefore,
were fresh purchases from Constantinople—three military swords,
two of which had pistols attached to the blade at the hilt—to augment
his regular arsenal.[27]

Back in Washington, Secretary Mason wrote Lynch to address
his question as stated in several December letters on whether he
could get permission to lengthen his explorations to the Euphrates
River. It could not be approved, he said—Mason had worded his
instructions to avoid "a special direction by law" and keep the exploration within the department's purview. To go any farther would in-
volve a fractious U.S. Congress, the State Department, and naturally,
President Polk. Lynch would have to be satisfied with sticking to his
original plan.[228]

It seemed clear, however, that Lynch's exploration of the Holy
Land was exciting comment in all levels of American culture, ever
since the first notices published the past November in the *New York
Herald* and reprinted in many newspapers around the country. "We
may justly anticipate from the expedition," opined the *Baltimore Sun*,
"accurate information on points heretofore wholly conjectural, yet
invested with deep interest." The influential, much-quoted *Journal
of Commerce* thought the project "not only convenient, but oppor-

tune," and the modest Massachusetts sheet, the *Berkshire County Whig*, thought it "would be most gratifying to the whole Christian world." Not all papers hewing to the Whig party and opposing the general policies of the Democratic president Polk—who claimed to be a strict constitutional constructionist—were as supportive, especially after Massachusetts senator Joseph Grinnell spoke out in faux outrage during a December debate on internal improvements. "Our Democratic administration that denies the power of Congress to improve our lake harbors, or remove snags from our rivers," grumbled the *Keene* (New Hampshire) *Sentinel*, "is about sending an expedition to explore the Dead Sea in ancient Palestine, and so settle a question touching upon the density of the water!" Many Whig papers not only agreed but reprinted the complaint, or other jibes, like the much-reprinted editorial of the laconic little *Maine Farmer*: "The design of our government in sending an expedition to the Dead Sea, may be to fish up Sodom and Gomorrah and annex them to the United States."[29]

What could not escape Secretary Mason's attention, however—indeed, all members of Polk's administration, and grudgingly admitted by their political enemies—was that across the country, citizens were transfixed by the idea of Americans applying a scientific approach to ancient mysteries in as deeply venerated a place as Palestine. It would seem as if every newspaper in the country ran at least one item each week on the progress of the Lynch Expedition. Each sighting, direct dispatch, or even a competing press mention of the adventures, appeared and reappeared in journals everywhere, from the *Boston Emancipator* to the *Charleston Southern Patriot*, from the *Macon Georgia Telegraph* to the *New London* (Connecticut) *Morning News*, from the *Missouri Republican* to the *Amherst* (New Hampshire) *Farmer's Cabinet*, the *Houston* (Texas) *Telegraph* to the *Norfolk* (Virginia) *Beacon*. Any eyewitness account conveyed by ship's mail would, when it arrived weeks or months after its composition, score a jackpot in reprinting. There even seemed to be an increase in feature articles about biblical history and the Middle East in general; "Dead Sea" became an active metaphor in daily discourse.

The *Supply* rejoined on the morning of March 9, they sailed the next day from the Turkish coast southward through the Aegean isles. When forced in by a gale to the Asia Minor mainland, they paused for a few days at Scala Nuova (modern Kusadasi), which gave them the agreeable excuse to explore the nearby ruins of the ancient trading capital of Ephesus, once home to the apostles Paul and John. There they scrambled over rubble of an ancient Roman amphitheater, and beside a ruined aqueduct—"amid the tall grass, shafts of porphyry columns, one fragment bright and beautifully polished"—and amid the once great temple of Diana—"a surface of marble fragments, glittering in the sunlight"—and the crumbling gateway of the first of the seven churches of Asia, the Church of St. John—"subverted and unknown among the habitations of the poor and ignorant herdsmen."

Southward the *Supply* resumed on the evening of Saturday, March 18, under a light wind past the small, rocky, treeless isle of Patmos, "where St. John wrote the Apocalypse." In a freshening gale, they sailed under the lee of the isle of Cos where Lynch noted, once "the god Phoebus was worshipped." Later it was visited by St. Paul on the way to Rhodes. Continuing, they came to the isles of Crete, then Rhodes, then Cyprus, raising ancient images of the labyrinth of Daedalus, and the vanished Colossus, and old redoubts of the Crusades, the Knights of St. John, and Richard the Lionhearted. Then, on Saturday, March 25: "This morning the mountains of Lebanon are before us," Lynch recorded, "their shadows resting upon the sea, while their summits are wreathed in a mist, made refulgent by the rays of the yet invisible sun. Brilliant as the bow of promise, the many-colored mist rests like a gemmed tiara upon the brow of the lofty mountain.

Like the glorious sunset on the eve of our departure, I hail this as an auspicious omen."[30]

They anchored off Beirut, but there now was no time for exploration of that old trading port, rich in the influences of Phoenician, Greek, Roman, Arab, and Ottoman civilizations. Now Lynch worried that the flood season in the Jordan River valley was soon to subside. "It seemed better to descend the river with a rush," he thought, "than slowly drag the boats over mudflats, sandbanks, and ridges of rock." With the American vice-consul Jasper Chasseaud, he presented his royal firman to the pasha of Beirut, who affirmed that he would obey it; a message was sent off to the pasha of Damascus, whose jurisdiction over the eastern banks of the Jordan was established. "He evinced during the interview much thirst for information," Lynch noted, "and like his master, the Sultan, expressed a wish to know the results of our labors."

Next, Lynch called on the Reverend Eli Smith, the Yale and Andover graduate who had worked for the American Presbyterian Mission in Beirut for 20 years. He was fluent in Arabic and had combed the Holy Land with Edward Robinson 10 years before for their seminal book on biblical geography, a work Lynch had virtually memorized by then. Smith and his fellow missionaries found him an interpreter, Antonius Ameuny, a Syrian by birth who worked as a translator at the consulate; and an Arab cook, Mustafa.[31]

Lynch picked up more intelligence about the competing party of English sailors that had already descended the Jordan to the Dead Sea. The next day, he would learn much later, in fact, a report on that expedition was read before the Royal Geographic Society in London; it would contribute some to the genre of travel literature but nothing at all to scientific knowledge.[32] It had been commanded by a Royal Navy lieutenant, Thomas Molyneux, and during the river voyage they had suffered an unprovoked attack by Bedouins. Then, while upon the Dead Sea, Lynch learned, Lieutenant Molyneux had been stricken with fever, from which he died—as had his only predecessor, the Irish adventurer Christopher Costigan.

Henry James Anderson, long-time Columbia University professor and trustee, was 49 when he served as physician and scientist on the Lynch Expedition.
(Author collection)

Worried now about diseases both known and unknown as well as gunshot wounds, Lynch came to an arrangement with an American doctor he fortuitously met in Beirut; he was the 49-year-old New York native Dr. Henry James Anderson, a graduate of both Columbia and the College of Physicians and Surgeons, who for nearly 25 years had taught mathematics and astronomy at Columbia and nurtured a keen interest in geology. Dr. Anderson had resigned his professorship in order to take his wife to Europe for health reasons, but she had died and he was consoling himself with travel and scientific inquiry. He leaped at the opportunity to join the lieutenant's adventure and agreed to travel overland from Beirut. He would make a geological reconnaissance and meet them on the road that ran from the seashore at Acre to the Sea of Galilee at Tiberias.[33]

Returning to the *Supply* with the precious pocket chronometers ordered from London, which had miraculously survived the long and rough pursuit of the Americans via Gibraltar and Port Mahon, Lynch ordered the ship southward. Failing winds and heavy seas compelled them to ride at anchor until mid-afternoon of the next day, Tuesday March 28, when a fine breeze from the northwest freed them. The words of a Syrian merchant he had met in Beirut—"*It is madness!*" and "*Oh, how I envy you!*"—were in his ears as, around midnight, they passed Sidon and Tyre, heaved to off the White Cape, glided past the battlements of St. Jean d'Acre, and anchored below Mount Carmel, near the walled village of Haifa.

Lynch eagerly headed in toward shore, but the heavy surf overturned his boat, sending him and two companions into the tumbling waves. There they would have ignominiously drowned—if not for the sudden appearance of several Arab fishermen, "bold and dexterous swimmers," the lieutenant gratefully called them, who rescued and dragged them ashore. With the surf rising dangerously, they were cut off from the ship. All there was to do, upon this inauspicious landing on the edge of their exploit to come, was to trudge wet and miserable toward the village of Haifa, or to the monastery perched on a promontory above. Near there, it was said, the Prophet Elijah had built his altar: *And the fire of the Lord fell and consumed the burnt sacrifice, and the wood and the stones and the dust, and licked up the water that was in the trench.*[34]

PART TWO

Mediterranean to Galilee

Acre—the Syrians' Akka, the Crusaders' St. Jean d'Acre, the Greeks' Ptolemais, the Israelites' and Canaanites' Akko—had long been judged a prime target. "On that little town," Napoleon had exclaimed, "hangs the destiny of the East," by which he recognized the best access to Palestine from the sea. The Plain of Esdraelon (present-day Jezreel) lay beyond, watered with the blood of untold generations of combatants, and the gates, battlements, and citadels of Acre bore the scars of all those assaults to get inland. In living memory there were the unmistakable siege signs from Napoleon's navy and infantry in 1799, repulsed by the Turks with help from British allies after a two-month campaign. The invading Egyptian Ibrahim Pasha had left his marks in 1831, and most recently in 1840, the combined squadrons of Britain, Austria, and France had forcibly restored Acre to Ottoman rule. In his short ride into the city a mere eight years later, Lieutenant Lynch noted ample evidence—breached walls, cannon balls still lodged in buildings, rubble, and wreckage—and even in the courtyard of the American consul, he stumbled over broken bombshells and fragments of masonry.

Near Acre at the mouth of the Belus River on the Mediterranean,
the Americans erected two tents and hoisted the flag.

Before long, Lynch was feeling similarly battered, as were his
companions. They had landed all their effects and the two lifeboats
meant for their inland voyage, and they pitched two canvas tents outside the village walls of Haifa beside a cemetery and a towering carob
tree. Immediately they attracted a large crowd of Arabs "of all ages
and conditions, their costumes picturesque and dirty," not hostile but
intensely curious. Small items began to disappear, including even the
little copper chains which attached their oarlocks to the boats' gunwales—"they thought," said Lynch, "that they were gold." The crowd
pressed so close and grew so clamorous with questions and offers that
the lieutenant ordered the camp and stores moved to the far bank of
the little Belus River; even posted sentries had only mild effect on the
crowd of Arabs following them until the sailors were ordered to fix
their bayonets.

Offshore, their last connection to home was drawing away.
"With conflicting emotions," Lynch would write, "we saw the *Supply*,

under all sail, stand out to sea. Shall any of us live to tread again her clean, familiar deck? What matters it! We are in the hands of God, and, fall early or fall late, we fall only with his consent."

In Acre, Lynch and his Syrian interpreter, Antonius Ameuny, called on Governor Sa'id Bey, meeting him first at an outdoor café and later at the governor's palace. Although the official was cordial, and clearly understood the imperial order implicit in the sultan's firman, he gave forth a litany of reasons why he could not be more supportive of Lynch's expedition needs. "I suspected," noted Lynch, "that he was coveting a bribe, and determined to disappoint him." The horses loaned them from the governor were old, tottery, underfed, and unwilling to pull the two boats tied on their caissons. No more horses could be procured. Loftily, the lieutenant told him "that we were there not as common travelers, but sent by a great country, and with the sanction of his own government; that I called upon him to provide us with the means of transportation, for which we would pay liberally, but not extravagantly; that his own sovereign had expressed an interest in our labors, and if we were not assisted, I would take good care that the odium of failure should rest upon the shoulders of Sa'id Bey, governor of Acre."

Ah, countered the governor, but also his visitors would be in danger. "The tribes were up in arms, at war among themselves, and pillaging and maltreating all who fell into their hands." The Americans could not safely proceed, he said, "with less than a hundred soldiers" guarding them. This could be had for "a modest" 20,000 piastres (a princely $800, Lynch noted). "He could not look me in the face when he made this proposition," recalled the lieutenant. He scorned the idea of buying protection but offered to pay fairly for draft horses or oxen "and a few soldiers to act as scouts," adding that "we were well armed and able to protect ourselves."

The two parties withdrew to think things over for the night. Outside the palace, Lynch and the interpreter caught up and conferred with a Bedouin dignitary—"a great border sheikh"—he had

'Akil Aga el Hasseé,
"a great border sheikh
of the Arabs."

met in the throne room, whose name was 'Akil Aga el Hasseé, and
who had just returned from the Ghor, or Jordan Valley. 'Akil verified
most of the reports about warring tribes but he was impressed with
Lynch's account of the party's weapons, the 14 carbines with bayonets,
the 12 bowie-knife pistols, the blunderbuss, and, finally, Lynch's own
sword with its pistol barrels attached to the hilt. "He examined them
closely," said Lynch, and remarked that they were the "devil's invention." As to whether he thought with such an arsenal they could pre-
vail, he replied, "You will, if anybody can."

However, that evening, Lynch's reassurance eroded when he met
with several fellow Americans who had heard of the naval explorers
and sought them out at the consul's. They were based at Nazareth,
and they confirmed the reports of trouble in the interior—"they had
themselves been attacked two nights previous, at the foot of Mount
Tabor." Lynch was thoroughly alarmed. "To turn back was out of the

question," he thought, "and my soul revolted at the thought of bribing Sa'id Bey, even if I had been authorized to spend money for such a purpose. I felt sure that he had exaggerated in this statement, and yet the attack on our countrymen, so far this side of the Jordan, staggered me. Had my own life been the only one at stake, I should have been comparatively reckless; but those only can realize what I suffered, who have themselves felt responsibility for the lives of others."[1] He did not relish the idea of having to fight his way to Tiberias on the Galilee shore and then southward the length of the lower Jordan.

Twenty-four hours later, though, he began to regain his confidence when, at the consul's residence, he was introduced to "a fine old man, an Arab nobleman," whose name was Sherif Hazza of Mecca, "the thirty-third lineal descendant of the Prophet." Sherif was "about fifty years of age, of a dark Egyptian complexion, small stature, and intelligent features," with dress and demeanor very prepossessing. "We were told," said Lynch, "that from his descent he was held in great veneration by the Arabs; and I observed that every Muhammedan

Sherif Hazza of Mecca, thirty-third lineal descendant of the Prophet.

who came in, first approached him and kissed his hand with an air of profound respect." Finding that Sherif also currently had time on his hands, Lynch impulsively invited him to come on his adventure. To his surprise and joy, the Arab nobleman agreed. Sherif was "considered a saint," the consul would report home. "His presence in this expedition is worth more than one or two hundred soldiers."[2]

That night, Lynch's sleep in the consul's guest quarters was much postponed, partly by a plague of fleas, and partly by the nagging worry about their miserable draft horses. How to transport the two boats and all the gear inland? "There seemed to be no alternative," Lynch thought, "but to take the boats apart and transport them across in sections, unless camels could be made to draw in harness." He concluded to try the experiment, but the fitful sleep that overtook him was hardly restful, an ill way to conclude the 47th anniversary of his birth. "During the night, I suffered dreadfully from the nightmare, and the incubus was a camel."

After Sunday services the next morning, the Americans located a merchant in Haifa who supplied them with camels. Naturally, most of the village followed them back to their campsite, watching with much amusement as the sailors improvised with harnesses. This was met with great hilarity; the Arabs knew that camels were only employed as beasts of burden, so to maneuver them back against the wheeled trucks with their gleaming metal boats and piles of luggage while the sailors fussed over the imperturbable animals, occasionally receiving a spurt of camel saliva for their troubles, gave them an entertaining few hours. The Americans were pleased as much as the local citizenry was amazed when, after being fitted, the camels easily and with no complaint pulled the two loaded caissons.

By Monday, April 3, the boats had been sent ahead on the road to Tiberias, the odd caravan stopping most activity it passed, and Lynch and party prepared to follow their path. That night, having received the last-sought firman for travel from the pasha of Damascus, Lynch again entertained the Bedouin sheikh 'Akil. He "was dressed in the same scarlet cloak, flowing white trousers, and red *tarbouch* [hat] and boots as in the council two days previous," said Lynch. "He was mounted on a spirited mare, and long after our parting I could see his scarlet cloak streaming in the wind as he scoured across the plain."[3] The next day such romantic imagery was displaced by foreboding and then alarm, when, after the caravan had gotten underway eastward across the level plain, Lynch rode ahead and alone toward the Bedouin mountain fortress of 'Akil, responding to his invitation from the night before. As a precaution, he had passed a note to his second in command, Lieutenant John Dale, that if Lynch did not return, Dale should push on and complete the mission. The village of rude, mud-roofed stone huts wreathed in a pall of smoke from camel dung fires, commanded a sweeping view of the coastline. Inside a dark and smoky council room, surrounded by 12 or 15 Arabs "armed to the teeth," and with no interpreter, Lynch began to wonder in a tense silence whether he had been lured into a trap: "The whole business looked like a snare." None of the previous cordiality of 'Akil and the nobleman Sherif, also present, seemed to be recalled.

Then, as the Bedouins began talking in low tones, shooting appraising glances at him, Lynch nervously consulted his pocket watch. It immediately changed the room's atmosphere, and with fierce but friendly curiosity the Arabs crowded around the lieutenant to examine it, and Lynch extended the mood by showing off his sword with its pistol handle, with which he would not part. Then, there was a tumult outside; Lynch heard camel bells and familiar voices; and his compatriots rode in. "From that moment," Lynch said, "there was a marked change in their manner toward me." Later, both Sherif and 'Akil would explain that one of the conferees was an emissary of the Acre governor, Sa'id Bey, and could not be trusted. They had not wanted to tip their hand that they were going on the Americans' expedition.[4]

The caravan resumed, enlarged by 10 Arab escorts, including 'Akil and Sherif. "They had all assumed the garb of the desert," said Lynch, "and each, with a flowing dark *aba* [cloak] on, and the yellow *kufeyah* [scarf] upon his head, bound round with a cord of camel's hair, dyed black; and bearing a spear eighteen feet in length, some of them tufted with ostrich feathers, looked the wild and savage warrior."[5] Via Malta consul William Winthrop, consul Chasseaud in Beirut would communicate his relief to the State Department that Lynch's small group was to be joined not only by Sherif Hazza but Sheikh 'Akil. He was, wrote Winthrop, "a very powerful man among these savages."[6]

The road inland to Tiberias was that in name only: more like a donkey trail winding across rugged terrain. The lieutenant was kept in a constant state of anxiety over whether the caissons would make it. "Wheel-carriages had never crossed it before," Lynch recorded. "In their invasion of Syria, the French transported their guns and gun-carriages (taken apart) on the backs of camels, over the lofty ridges, and mounted them again upon the plain."[7] Three camels were teamed to pull each boat, with 12 spares ambling along behind, and every half hour progress halted while the relief camels were hitched in place.

They passed through the Valley of the Winds, or Wady en Nafakh in Arabic, with Lynch noting forests of white oak on the flanks of the hills, and they stopped for the evening near a water source though it was only 3 p.m.. It was a handsome spot, and when set up their camp was picturesque—the Americans' two white tents, and the two boat-bearing caissons with the Stars and Stripes snapping from two masts, and the Bedouins' dark blue tent with their wild feathered spears planted outside in the ground, and 30 picketed camels and a similar number of horses tearing at the grass, while officers took their solar and barometrical readings. Dinner for all was highlighted by a sheep presented by the escorts. Night fell with two Arab horsemen taking posts at either end of the valley, a half mile away, and near the compound, two sailors and an officer mounted with their carbines next to the blunderbuss. Under a brilliant array of stars, they sighted and recorded Polaris, and all slept well though interrupted at midnight by a sudden violent wind, which rocked the tents and flags and briefly endangered the scientific instruments.

Caissons drawn by camels bore the *Supply*'s metal lifeboats from
the sea to Tiberias.

After they had gotten underway the next morning, the route narrowed into a gorge so tight that the lifeboats on their caissons could not squeeze through. The Americans were forced to have the camels bypass the defile, ascending a steep slope. At the summit for safety's sake the camels were unhitched and the caissons lowered by rope— much as, two years earlier, wagon train pioneers struggling through Utah's Wasatch and California's Sierra had to tug and winch their wagons down and up through the Weber and Truckee gorges. Beyond, the march took them across a plain in places cultivated with grain but largely verdant with wildflowers "of brilliant hues and fragrant odors," past hillside clumps of trees sheltering songbirds.

Mid-morning found them in sight of the remains of the ancient walled city of Sepphoris, torched in war nearly 1,900 years before but rebuilt by Herod Antipas, son of Herod the Great, into a spacious and elegant city, the "ornament of all Galilee" in the words of the Jewish general and first-century historian Flavius Josephus. They were now half the distance to the Sea of Galilee, and only some five miles north of the hallowed village of Nazareth, home of Jesus. "How we grieved," said the reverent Lieutenant Lynch, "that our duties prevented us from visiting a place which, with Bethlehem and Calvary, the scenes of the birth, the residence, and the death of the Redeemer, are of most intense interest to the Christian!"[8]

Their Bedouin escorts provided more than company and a daily lamb. At night, in camp, they welcomed the officers into their tents, where they served dinner, "a whole sheep, entombed in rice, which they pitched into without knives or forks, in the most amusing manner." Usually one of their party would strum a stringed instrument and sing or chant Arab poetry. On the trail, since the marching pace was slowed by the rate of the caissons, the Arabs delighted in displays of horsemanship, galloping and charging at one another, twirling and brandishing their long spears, their cloaks flying. When Lynch stopped to take readings, they offered help with grace and politeness. "Thus far," wrote Lynch with remarkable cultural self-assurance, "these terrible Arabs had conducted themselves like gentlemen. In courtesy, civilization could not improve them."[9]

At dinnertime on Thursday, April 5, Dr. Anderson, the party's surgeon, finally rode into camp, having taken geologic and geographic notes on the coast road down from Beirut. At one point, he told Lynch, while high above Acre in the coastal mountains, he spied the American party, tiny and far below, with its flags and camels and wheeled boats providing a stirring sight.

It was late the next afternoon, when their path intersected with the high road from Jerusalem to Damascus and they encountered a tired band of Christian pilgrims at a watering fountain, that Lynch grew impatient with the slow pace and rode ahead with the cook, Mustafa. From a height, they came in view of the Sea of Galilee, or Lake Tiberias, the sight of which overwhelmed the reverent Lynch for its associations with the ministry years of Jesus of Nazareth. "Like a mirror it lay embosomed in its rounded and beautiful, but treeless hills," he wrote. "How dear to the Christian are the memories of that lake! The lake of the New Testament!" All he saw—the blue water basking in sunlight, the "everlasting hills," the "ruined cities once crowded with men," the cliffs that once "echoed the glad tidings,"—filled him with exultation. Beyond the tiny lake, mountains marched northward toward the distant snowy slopes of Mount Hermon, source of the Jordan River.

Tiberias was still in ruins after a massive earthquake that had leveled much of it over a decade before, in 1837, killing some 800 people and leaving shattered remnants of the ancient imperial city. Between its periodic earthquakes and the successive wars enveloping it, Tiberias—built by Herod Antipas in the 19th year of the Christian era as an administrative and trade center, becoming one of the four Jewish holy cities, and being destroyed and rebuilt a thousand years later during the Second Crusade—was a miscellany of styles and influences from its Roman walls and arches and baths to its Byzantine churches, its Crusader castle, its synagogues, its mosques. Of nine large and influential cities ringing the shore of the Sea of Galilee, Tiberias in its reduced state was the only survivor, and the city was enervated and underpopulated and showed little of the grandeur of the old Judean capital.

The lake was known by Arabs as Buhairet Tabariyya (Lake Tiberias) and by Hebrews as Yam Kinnereth (Sea of Kinnereth). It would prove to be some 33 miles in circumference and pear-shaped, only 13 miles long and 8 wide—small to Americans used to taking their sights on a large scale and shockingly so with its prominence in the mind's eye of the average Christian. In fact, a later-day Holy Land traveler, in 1848 serving as a 12-year-old printer's apprentice in Hannibal, Missouri, would colorfully comment on the miniature scale of that hallowed place. "One of the most astonishing things that have

Tiberias, on the western shore of the Sea of Galilee.

yet fallen under our observation," Mark Twain would write after his tour of the Holy Land in 1867,

is the exceedingly small portion of the earth from which sprang the now flourishing plant of Christianity. The longest journey our Saviour ever performed was from [the Sea of Galilee] to Jerusalem—about one hundred to one hundred and twenty miles. The next longest was from here to Sidon,—say about sixty or seventy miles. Instead of being wide apart—as American appreciation of distances would naturally suggest—the places made most particularly celebrated by the presence of Christ are nearly all right here in full view, and within cannon-shot of Capernaum. Leaving out two or three short journeys of the Saviour, he spent his life, preached his gospel, and performed his miracles within a compass no larger than an ordinary county in the United States. It is as much as I can do to comprehend this stupefying fact. How it wears a man out to have to read up a hundred pages of history every two or three miles—for verily the celebrated localities of Palestine occur that close together. How wearily, how bewilderingly they swarm about your path![10]

Similar thoughts were occurring to Lieutenant Lynch, looking out at the lake and its surrounding hillsides as he was compelled to dismount and lead his horse from the heights, picking his way down the steep, rough, and winding road to the city's tumbled gate.

He also wondered how in the world they were to get the boat caissons down such a sheer slope. That nagged at the Americans as they took an apartment in the lodging house of a Polish Jew by the name of Chaim Wiseman and set about conferring with local dignitaries and arranging further details for the expedition. They saw the governor, who was a relative of their noble Arab escort Sherif; they paid visits to the leading rabbis of the city's Sephardic and Ashkenazic congregations; they quizzed locals about conditions in the Ghor; they consulted with a Janissary, an elite Ottoman guardsman bearing the firman from the pasha of Jerusalem and accompanied by four guards. The expeditionary services of these guards Lieutenant Lynch gracefully declined by paying them off and sending them home. "Our Bedouin friends served as vedettes [scouts], to apprise us of danger," he would write. "It was only ambuscades we feared."

Their landlord had been with the Irish adventurer Costigan just before he attempted to circumnavigate the Dead Sea and was just as acquainted with the story of the English sailors under Molyneux. "Poor fellows! If God spare us, we will commemorate their gallantry and their devotion to the cause of science," Lynch vowed.[11]

Even more details came in from an Arab boatman who had hired on to Molyneux's crew. "He gave a disheartening account of the great, and, as he thought, the insuperable impediments to boats as large as ours," wrote Lynch. "He dwelt particularly upon the rapids and cascades, false channels and innumerable rocks, and was inclined to think that there was a cataract in the part of the river along which they transported their boat upon a camel." As he made notes of the conversation, Lynch forced himself toward optimism. "That we should encounter great obstacles, perhaps seemingly insurmountable ones, I did not doubt," Lynch wrote, "but I had great faith in American sailors, and believed that what men could do, they would achieve. So there was no thought of turning back."[12]

On Saturday, April 8, all the Americans and their escorts went back up the mountain to lower the boats down to water. The process brought out many of the locals as observers, who all became convinced that the gleaming copper boat was made of gold. Many times as they struggled downhill, wrote Lynch, they thought that, like the Gadarene herd of swine in the New Testament, "they would rush precipitately into the sea." But each of the sailors and officers did his utmost, straining at the ropes while trying to stay from underfoot of the camels, until at last rewarded by success, and thankfully with no injuries to humans, beasts, or equipment. "With their flags flying," Lynch exulted, "we carried them triumphantly beyond the walls uninjured, and, amid a crowd of spectators, launched them upon the blue waters of the Sea of Galilee—the Arabs singing, clapping their hands to the time, and crying for *bakshish*—but we neither shouted nor cheered."

It was not mere tiredness; Lynch and the other Americans were overcome with the sight of their vessels and their flags snapping in the wind, on that deep blue lake they and all other Christians venerated. Furthermore, Lynch believed, no craft had plied the lake since the first-century time of Josephus—this seemed to be borne out by more than a millennium and a half of traveler's tales, such as that of the German explorer Ulrich Seetzen, in 1806. "No vessel of any size has sailed upon this sea," noted Lynch, and for many, many years, but a solitary keel has furrowed its surface."[13]

Over the next several days there was little unoccupied time. Each morning, their apartment thronged with local visitors, among whom their cook Mustafa bustled, bowing and scraping and serving tiny cups of bitter coffee to sheikhs and the governor, and treating with studied indifference all of his own station. Lynch, of course, wrote a long report letter to Secretary Mason, which would be dispatched by messenger to the consul at Acre and by ship's mail the long way back to North America; he also kept rigorously to his journal, in his measures of the local citizenry exhibiting most of the Western ethnic and religious stereotypes of the era, yet beyond his cultural self-regard and hygienic fastidiousness, he showed a degree of empathy and an appreciation of justice and, all around him, injustice. Though they far outnumbered Tiberians of Arab descent, Jews were despised and downtrodden, and among the Arab classes, the *fellahin*, or peasants, endured much, as indeed did all of humble rank. "Filth, poverty, avarice, and tyranny," wrote Lynch, had ground the Syrian Jews into "libels upon humanity," and injustice had many victims even among their tormenters. The Holy Land seemed to teem with cruelties.

Work, though, forced him to make shorter use of his pen. He and his officers frequently made their barometrical and thermometrical observations, along with taking sightings to keep track of the rate of their instruments. The Bedouins were delegated to rent new teams of camels and horses for the next stage of their journey, having reached the end of the term stipulated by the owners of their initial teams back in Haifa. Then, Lynch and Dale heard of the existence of an old wooden frame boat, seemingly the only vessel to be found in that shore town, which the lieutenant bought for 600 piastres, about $25, "in order to relieve the other boats, lessen the expense of transportation down the Jordan, and carry our tents upon the Dead Sea; for it was fast becoming warm, and we might not be able to work in that deep chasm without them." The sailors repaired the boat and named it *Uncle Sam*.

Also on Sunday, the Americans visited the hot baths at the southern end of the town—not the original Roman baths, which were in ruins, but the square vaulted chamber and pool constructed during the administration of the Egyptian conqueror of Syria, Ibrahim Pasha, a decade before. The hot springs feeding the large basin were heavily sulfuric and bitter with salts, and an almost unendurable temperature of 143 degrees to which the sailors could accustom themselves with difficulty. They would encounter many other hot springs during their exploration of the deepest lands on earth, where vents from the nether regions were plentiful.[14]

Later, pickled but refreshed, they took out the two lifeboats and rowed up the green shores of the lake toward a small village of stone and mud huts lying at the foot of steep, cliffy hills penetrated by many caverns; it had been built upon the remnants of ancient Magdala, presumed birthplace of the disciple Mary Magdalene. "We had not time to survey the lake," and its shoreline, Lynch mourned, hoping to return for that later. The site of the vanished trade city of Capernaum on the northern shore, to which Jesus had moved from his boyhood home at Nazareth, and where he began his ministry, was a particular draw.

But time overweighed. "The advancing season, and the lessening flood in the Jordan, [was] warning us to lose no time." On the way they did note, however, with a number of soundings, that the concave basin of the lake seemed to have a greatest depth of 27½ fathoms, or 165 feet. The lake water was clear and cool and sweet, and was the habitat of many fish in five varieties (including tilapia, "St. Peter's Fish"), snared shoreside by locals in big, hand-thrown nets, which distinguished every one of their meals while at Tiberias. When a sudden squall swept down one of the ravines and enveloped them, they were forced to retreat to town, not without a new appreciation of the changeable, tempestuous weather on that normally placid-looking little sea.[15]

On Monday, April 10, all was readied to push off.

Lynch divided the explorers into two parties, one to go by sea and one by land. In the water party, Lieutenant Lynch would be in charge of the copper boat, the *Fanny Mason*, and sail it with his team; with a like number, Passed Midshipman Richmond Aulick would command the dull silver, galvanized iron boat *Fanny Skinner*. Several Arabs took to the oars of the repaired lake skiff, *Uncle Sam*. Scientifically, Aulick, a draftsman, was further assigned to render topographical sketches of the lake and the river and their shores; Lynch set himself to record their course and speed and the nature, depth, and color of the waters, their banks and tributaries, descriptions of the surrounding countryside including its flora and fauna, and keep the regular journal of their travels.

As the head of the land party, with a new team of camels pulling the empty caissons and their gear, Lieutenant Dale would make topographic sketches of the land route along the Jordan Valley; Dr. Anderson would record geological observations and collect specimens; Henry Bedlow, the poet-volunteer who joined the expedition at Constantinople, was assigned the journal-keeping; and the 16-year-old midshipman Francis Lynch, the lieutenant's only begotten son, was to keep the herbarium by gathering samples of plants and flowers. The Arabs in their party—Sherif, 'Akil, Mustafa, and 10 Bedouin scouts—would watchfully ride their horses. The previous night, another local dignitary had asked to come along: the emir, or prince, of the Bedouins of the upper Jordan Valley, Emir Nasser 'Arar el Guzzaway, a dark-complexioned and stout Oriental voluptuary in Lynch's view, who was given to holding rose petals to his nostrils. So the emir and his retinue were admitted. All the Arabs assured Lynch that there would be no danger to the caravan, but nevertheless Lynch was worried that if his boats became entangled among the rocks and shoals of the Jordan, they would be sitting ducks for an attack. He urged Lieutenant Dale to keep the land party as close to the river as practicable, "and should they hear two guns fired in quick succession, then leave the camel-drivers to take care of themselves, and hasten with all speed to our assistance. I felt sure that Lt. Dale would not fail me, and in that respect my mind was at ease."[16]

Finally, the land contingent got moving through the ruined and filth-cluttered streets of Tiberias "after much delay and vexation," with the sound of camel bells and the calls of the animal-drivers echoing back to the water party. And at 2 p.m., Lynch and Aulick and their men climbed into the two *Fannies* and pushed out onto the lake surface and hoisted the sails. The air temperature was 82 degrees and the water 70, and their course southeast, with distant, snowy, cloud-wreathed Mount Hermon at their backs. Tiberias receded. Lynch was mindful of how picturesque his modest flag-waving flotilla must have been from shore, as to him indeed appeared the land party, with its 11 stately camels followed by some 30 Arab horsemen, "their *abas* flying in the wind, and their long gun-barrels glittering in the sun, and Lieutenant Dale and his officers in the Frank costume" bringing up the rear. "Little did we know what difficulties we might have to encounter," said Lynch, "but, placing our trust on high, we hoped and feared not."[17]

Behind and above the shore and the camel caravan with its fluttering Stars and Stripes, one could see the land rise to hills, and then to the Plain of Gennesareth, reputed to be the site of the miracle of the loaves and the fishes performed by Jesus. South and westward, the land rose further to the twin peaks of the saddleback hill known as the Horns of Hattin, upon whose flank the Latin church held was the site of Jesus's Sermon on the Mount: *Blessed are the pure in heart; for they shall see God; and Blessed are the peacemakers, for they shall be called the Children of God.* And just below was the site of the terrible Battle of Hattin on July 4, 1187, during which an army of Crusaders from the arrogant but beleaguered Kingdom of Jerusalem were lured onto that arid plain, surrounded and trapped by the army of the Kurdish Sunni general and sultan of Egypt and Syria, Saladin, or Salah al-din Yusuf. With Crusaders weakened by great thirst and fear, and encircled by smoky fires, they were picked off and then routed and mowed down by the sultan's bowmen and cavalry. Thousands slaughtered and only a few taken prisoner and into slavery, the defeat ended the Second

Crusade in ignominy and returned Jerusalem and most of the Holy Land to Muslim control. From the blue waters one could absorb in one long glance these polar opposites of peace preached by religion and war enacted by religion, with only an optimist's faith sustaining the ancient words: *Blessed are they who hunger and thirst after righteousness: for they shall be filled; and Blessed are the merciful; for they shall obtain mercy.*

And so they went.

The lake narrowed as they pulled southward. A grassy sloping shore lay to the west, with the ruins of the ancient city of Tarrichaea visible on the water's edge, and, eastward, rounded, rain-washed limestone bluffs and intervening chasms caught the eye.

Then, at 3:45 p.m., they saw the lake outlet, appearing like a stream draining from a funnel. The lower Jordan opened with a steady rush between low rounded hills that in turn climbed to barren, rough gray mountains. Further to the south they were dimmed by a faint purple mist. Wild ducks disturbed on the water stirred, flapped, or took flight. A long, low mound up the slope marked Khirbet Kerak, the ancient site of a temple to the moon goddess. Stone, mud-roofed huts of Semakh, an Arab village, clung to a hill. The last thing Lynch saw behind them as they were strongly pulled into the outlet and were swept sharply to the right and into the valley was snowy Mount Hermon, fissures in its cap now visible in the afternoon light. As the birds flew they were 65 miles from the Dead Sea.[18]

CHAPTER SIX

The Descent of the Jordan to the Ford of Sek'a

IT BECAME EVIDENT THAT THE JORDAN VALLEY WAS IN TWO LEVELS, a trough within a trough— the river's narrow and deeply cut flood-plain called the Zor, or thicket, rambling at the bottom of the wider upper valley, the Ghor, or rift. The river was 25 yards wide and water was clear to the pebbly bottom, 8 or 10 feet below the keels. There were fish, and the bright air was tropical. Luxuriant grasses and flow-ers—scarlet anemones and yellow marigolds, and the occasional lily drooping over the water's edge, but no trees or shrubs—covered the rounded riverbanks to their crowns, some 30 feet overhead. Lynch constantly checked his pocket chronometer and a compass as he scrib-bled journal notes. They hardly dipped their oars; the current meas-ured out at two and a half knots, a brisk walking pace on land. The land party came into view, following the shore, the Bedouins' crimson and white robes catching the eye before they were again lost from sight.

Twisting and turning in quarter-, half-, and three-quarter loops,[1]

The explorers' camp at the ruined bridge of Semakh, on the Jordan.

they bore west by north, then northeast by north, then west by south-west, then northwest by west, then south. Then, joining and leaving a wide inlet, or lake called El Muh, they skirted rocks, scattering waterfowl, passed low marshy islands tufted with reeds. Finally, shortly after hearing a signaling gunshot, they came around to the sight of their comrades and camels on the western bank, and, down-stream, the picturesque stone piers, their arches collapsed into the water, of Jisr Semakh, the bridge of Semakh, amid an alarming stretch of white water. " 'Akil stood on the summit of one of the abutments," noted Lynch, "in his green cloak, red tarbouch and boots, and flowing white trousers, pointing out the channel with a spear. Over his head and around him, a number of storks were flying disorderly"—he stood amid their nests.

The lieutenant saw the dangers ahead in an instant and signaled that his copper boat would be first to approach the rapids. On shore, Henry Bedlow scrawled his impressions: *We halted at the ruins of an old bridge, now forming obstructions, over which the foaming river rushed like a mountain torrent,*" he wrote hurriedly. "*The river was about thirty yards wide. Soon after we halted, the boats hove in sight around a bend of the river. See! the* Fanny Mason *attempts to shoot between two old piers! she strikes upon a rock! she broaches to! she is in imminent danger! down comes the* Uncle Sam *upon her! now they are free!*" Minutes later: "*the* Fanny Skinner *follows safely, and all are moored in the cave below!*"[2]

Night fell over their four multicolored tents on a grassy, flower-strewn prominence by the rapids. All the Arabs disappeared before dinnertime, riding away to a nearby Bedouin village to take advantage of the culture of hospitality among the tribes. Lynch and Dale had taken the night's astronomical sightings and all the Americans had turned in, save a pair of sentries, when, very late, their escorts returned, riding and splashing across a ford, talking loudly and laughing "and making such a chatter," noted Lynch, "that we sprang to our arms expecting an attack." After all settled down, further alarms broke their rest as one of the excitable horses, Dr. Anderson's, kept breaking free of his picket, "rushing frantically over the tent-cords, attacking some slumbering Arab steed, his bitter enemy."

They were hardly refreshed when they woke to face dangerous rapids ahead. Lynch had decided to stretch rations by restricting them to two meals each day, and they ate a hearty breakfast knowing there would be no pause at midday. After the camel caravan picked its way southward, the water party shoved their three battered craft into the current.

Only 10 minutes' placid stretch of a walking-pace current gave way to chaos, where the river cascaded for 300 yards down a slope between cultivated fields, all white water with ruins of another stone bridge and rock-rubble fish weirs obstructing passage. Stopping, for half a day they worked in waist- or chest-deep water: they emptied the boats and eased them into the quick current, using rope and a grappling hook to control the pace of each boat, one after the other. Finding five successive waterfalls below that plunged the river some

18 feet lower, and recognizing the boats would never survive such a plunge, they took advantage of an old sluiceway. They painstakingly opened it by manhandling large rocks out of the way, guiding the craft downward until they could advance no farther, opening a new passageway between the big rocks, emptying the boats once again, and squeezing them through and downward another 6 or 7 feet back to the main channel. Then it was merely a fast ride of 80 yards of whitewater until they could rest at the base of a 60-foot cliff overhanging the water before portaging down all their gear, scientific instruments, and arms.

By this point, however, a number of unfamiliar but very curious Arabs had appeared on the shore and clustered around the boats. The lieutenant stood one of his men behind the blunderbuss mounted in one of the boats as an unmistakable caution, until their gear was safely stowed and their rifles and sidearms were close at hand again. During the next stretch the emir rode along in the copper boat in five knots' current, which soon more than doubled over several bends as the Jordan turned into a 30-degree chute followed by a shoal rapid, where Lynch's copper boat got hung up on a rock for a few moments before twisting free.

He called a halt while they waited for the other two boats, unseen around several bends, to negotiate the passage. "Wet and weary," he recorded, "I walked along the difficult shore to look for the other boats, when, seeing a cluster of Bedouin spears on the bank above, I went up to see to whom they belonged. It was a party of nine strange Arabs, who were seated upon the grass, their horses tethered near them. They examined my watch-guard and uniform buttons very closely and eagerly looked over my shoulder, uttering many exclamations, when I wrote in my note-book. They repeatedly asked for something which I could not understand, and as they began to be importunate, I left them. Shortly after, while walking further up, I came upon their low, black, camel's hair tent, almost concealed by a thicket of rank shrubbery."[3]

The two lifeboats rowing down the Jordan. "The character of the whole scene of this dreary waste," wrote Lynch, "was wild and impressive."

Back on the river, after the three boats regrouped and got moving again, they were confronted by a set of three scary rapids tumbling past two abandoned mill buildings and their adaptable sluiceway. As in the morning, the sailors worked themselves around the rapids by manhandling rocks and dragging the unladen boats down and through to safety—although one seaman nearly drowned when he lost his footing and then his hold on the gunwales, being swept into deep water and then nearly over a waterfall before finally managing to struggle ashore. After recovery and resumption, they continued downstream beneath "lofty, perpendicular" banks, then into a small valley with cultivated wheat fields, "the wheat beginning to head," as the river grew increasingly shallow and muddy, more than 50 yards wide, and full of life. They saw a partridge, an owl, a large hawk, herons, storks, and caught a trout. At 5:40 p.m., Lynch noted, they rounded a high, bold

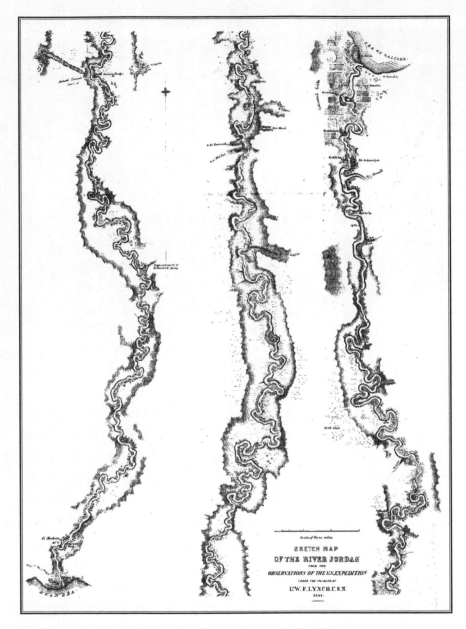

Gatefold map showing the sinuous Jordan River, as
published by Lynch.

bluff, the river clearing and widening considerably. At three knots they were swept past the village of 'Abeidiyeh, "a large collection of mud huts, on a commanding eminence on the right; the people, men, women, and children, with discordant cries, hurrying down the hill towards the river when they saw us. It was too late to stop, for night was approaching, and we had seen nothing of the caravan since we parted with them, at the ruined bridge, this forenoon. If the inhabitants intended to molest us, we swept by with too much rapidity for them to carry their designs into execution."[4]

This long and exhausting day was not over. For two more hours they floated downstream, the current slowing and the river deepening as it flowed between thickets of small vine-tangled willows, tamarisks, wild pistachio, and oleander. Occasional small streams burbled in and there were many fish in evidence, attracting a multitude of storks and other water birds. At 8 p.m., as it rapidly grew dark, they reached the head of the falls and whirlpool of Buk'ah and knew to push no farther. Lynch stumbled ashore and felt his way up a hill until amid the ruins of the Arab village of Delhemiyeh, he blundered into one of their Bedouin escorts, sent from the caravan to find them. The much-fatigued sailors finally made their way under a rising moon to the night camp, where food and blanket rolls in the tents were the only things to hold their interest. The deafening roar of the waterfall ahead enveloped them.

At dawn on Wednesday, April 12, while the officers and men were planning their day's first task, getting past the whirlpool and rapids of Buk'ah, Lynch rode down along the river almost to the confluence of the River Yarmouk with the Jordan. "I saw Sherif coming rapidly towards me, on his spirited mare," he recorded, "and calling out, in an angry tone, to some Arabs, who, I now perceived, were approaching under cover of the bank. They turned back, and when he joined me he said nothing about them, but kept close by me the remainder of the ride." He dismounted often to help Lynch gather handfuls of flowers and quartz and trap for their botanical and mineral

From a sketch made below the ford of Seka: Sherif Masa'ad, Emir Nassir, and the sheikh of the Beni Suk'r.

collections, his watchful presence apparently saving the lieutenant from being waylaid by local thugs.[5]

Back where their boats were moored, they discovered that the *Uncle Sam* had foundered, its wooden planks unable to withstand the previous day's pounding. "Thus ended all our hopes of transporting the tents from place to place along the Dead Sea," rued Lynch, "and thereby protect the party from the dews of night"—but at least, he conceded, Tuesday's worst rocks had proved the superiority of the reinforced metal lifeboats over traditional wood.[6]

Three hours' march from their camp lay the ruins of ancient Gadara, the elaborate Hellenistic-Roman city also known as Antiochia Semiramis, which Lynch's travelers' journals said were in an extraordinary state of preservation. For the day, he detached Dr. Anderson and an Arab detail from the camel caravan, to record notes on the place reputed to be where the New Testament lunatic, Legion, had lived among its old tombs until an encounter with Jesus of Nazareth sent his personal demons into an unfortunate herd of pigs grazing nearby.

By mid-morning their survey of the hazardous stretch ahead had yielded a plan. The two *Fannies* entered the current, shot through the first rapid, and then paused at the second, where a steep, 11-foot fall ended and broke against a great black rock at the edge of a whirlpool, "a caldron of foam." To avoid disaster, they had to simultaneously plunge down the falls and make a mad, sharp turn around the rock. With the help of ropes secured to bushes on the bank, and several naked Arab swimmers clinging to the gunwales and pushing, and with sailors stationed every few yards in the stretch below to rescue anyone thrown helpless into the current, Lynch and another seaman took the *Fanny Mason* first. "I gave a signal to let go the rope," he recalled. "There was a rush, a plunge, an upward leap, and the rock was cleared, the pool was passed, and, half full of water, with breathless velocity, we were swept safely down the rapid. Such screaming and shouting! The Arabs seemed to exult more than ourselves." The *Fanny Skinner* followed, piloted by Midshipman Aulick, "and by his skill and coolness passed down in perfect safety."[17]

The feat merited a break for hot coffee, which was proffered first to the Arab swimmers, two of whom had lost their hold on the boats and had been carried a distance downstream before their rescue; one was slightly injured. They passed the confluence with the Yarmouk River, flowing in from the east and about the same size as the Jordan. Several hours got them all through a new series of ugly rapids.

During a pause Lynch climbed on his hands and knees up a steep, 300-foot-high hill on the shore to survey ahead. The view was "wild and peculiar," he wrote. "The high alluvial terraces on each side were everywhere shaped by the action of the winter rains into a number of conical hills, some of them pyramidal and cuneiform, presenting the appearance of a giant encampment, so perfectly tent-like were their shapes. This singular configuration extends southward as far as the eye can reach. At intervals I caught a glimpse of the river in its graceful meanderings, sometimes glittering like a spear-head through an opening in the foliage of its banks, and again, clasping some little island with its shining arms, or, far away, snapping with the fierceness and white foam of a torrent by some projecting point."[8]

Safely back down on the river, further perils awaited him in yet more white water, "one of the most frightful rapids we had yet encountered," negotiated with the aid of ropes fastened to bankside bushes. It was nearing sunset when the two lifeboats reached the graceful Saracenic arches of Jisr Mejamia, Bridge of the Uniting, named for the Jordan's confluence with the Yarmouk. There, beneath the spans, the river fell steeply and broke for a time into several channels, so before it became entirely dark, the two *Fannies* shot beneath the bridge and down a long and slightly pitched, 200-foot chute. Tents of their land caravan stood nearby.

Not long after the tired crews had collapsed, Dr. Anderson returned from his excursion to the ancient ruins of Gadara, with detailed notes and many samples. He had picked his way over a large, elaborate Roman theater constructed—like the habitation ruins, necropolis, and giant, broken columns scattered and almost buried by weeds and brambles—of the local black Hauran basalt. On the brow of a hill, the professor came in view of distant Mount Hermon and the entire Sea of Galilee to the north, and, opposite, the valley of the Yarmouk. His transit back to the Ghor and the Zor included several encounters with local tribesmen, but nothing of any threat. If the exhausted wayfarers dreamt that night, Lieutenant Lynch's would have been of white water and menacing dark rocks, while Dr. Anderson's would have featured haunting broken black columns rising out of thickets, and the stair-stepping procession of stone arena seating, from which vanished ancient Romans had cheered chariot races and gladiatorial contests.[9]

* * *

Just west of their riverside camp near the Bridge of the Uniting was the village of Beisan, which had known several names. As Bethshean, it was the onetime Canaanite town on the road winding from Egypt to Jerusalem to Damascus. After Saul, the warrior king of the Israelites, was defeated by the Philistines at nearby Gilboa and avoided capture by falling on his sword, his body and those of his sons were hung by the victors on the walls of Bethshean. Later, in the Hellenistic period, the town was called Scythopolis, and after the Roman conquest of Palestine it became the capital of Rome's Decapolis. The 10 cities of Samaria, sketches of those ancient Roman ruins—acres of tumbled basalt building stone, intact walls and odd standing columns, a theater, a hippodrome—would soon be gathered by Lieutenant Dale, who, early on the morning of Thursday, April 13, was dispatched with the interpreter and an Arab escort to pay a call on the Ottoman district military governor, Muhammed Pasha, reputed to be camping outside of Beisan.

Navigating through extensive wheat fields, Dale passed near the famous Crusader hilltop fortress, Belvoir, once controlled by the powerful Hospitallers—Knights of Rhodes and Malta—for two stormy decades of the twelfth century until it was besieged by Saladin's army for a year and a half. It finally fell in 1189. Dale observed that the courtyard of the battered old fortress had been converted to a cow yard by the Arabs, whose rude village stood beyond. In his ship's library, stocked by Lieutenant Lynch, was the authoritative *Travels in Syria and the Holy Land* by Johann Burckhardt, the Swiss explorer for the British Royal Society. Burckhardt had stopped at Beisan in 1812, finding "a village of 70 to 80 houses, whose residents are in a miserable state" from four centuries of feudal existence and burdensome Ottoman taxes. Little seemed to have changed, in Dale's view. A mile distant, on the plain of Jezreel, he beheld a sight that would have been unsettling to any Arabs in the Jordan Valley: a large Turkish encampment of black cavalry tents, their thousand horses grazing nearby.

Dale was ushered into the presence of the Turkish commander,

Muhammed Pasha, "a fat Osmanlie," who received him "frankly and kindly," and said he had been alerted and was expecting the Americans. The general had been poised to raid some troublesome Arab tribes in the lower Ghor Valley, but he had held off to avoid stirring the Arabs who might then seek revenge upon the Western sailors in their boats on the Jordan. The territory ahead of the explorers was very unsettled and dangerous, he warned, and insisted that the Americans must accept a Turkish escort of 12 cavalrymen.

Back on the Jordan, Lynch was anxiously watchful all day. His honorable escort, Sherif, warned him in early morning that henceforth as they descended into the lower Ghor, they would be in danger from the warlike tribes. Lynch had the blunderbuss mounted on the bow of the *Fanny Mason*. "Formidable it must have looked," Lynch said, "with its gaping mouth, pointed down stream, and threatening slugs and bullets to all opponents."[10] Once they got moving, a number of villages periodically appeared on either side of the Jordan, most distant, but as they passed several riverside settlements, their sudden appearance startled throngs of Arabs, who rushed shouting and waving down to the water as the two lifeboats were swept on downriver and out of sight. What they might have done was matter only for conjecture.

Between the heightened alert and the serpentine, quick-flowing river with its intermittent cascades, the day's journey was tiring. Rocks in a perilous rapid had come close to destroying the copper boat in mid-morning, but it righted itself and survived with bad dents; other downriver stretches of white water kept them on guard as they also kept watch for the great number of downed trees in the river. With each successive day, they noticed, the heat grew worse. "We were changing our climate in a twofold manner," Lynch explained, "by descent and by progress southward."[11]

Some hours after the meridian observation, later that afternoon and farther downriver, Lynch's men and boats rendezvoused with their land-party comrades and caravan of horses and camels. The lieutenant was surprised when the shrugging Dale returned from his mission with 12 Turkish soldiers. "I regretted that the Pasha had sent the horsemen," Lynch would write, "for their presence would tend more, perhaps, to endanger than to aid us; but, as it was meant in kindness, it would have seemed rude to send them immediately back, particularly as the march of the Turkish detachment had been delayed on our account. But the presence of the horsemen increased my anxiety: the sight of them might exasperate the Arabs, and I had no faith in their courage or fidelity."[12]

Dale also brought an invitation for Lynch to dine with the general, who would brook no refusal, so the lieutenant dutifully rode off with a token few officers and with Sherif and 'Akil and the other Bedouins. The pasha beamed with delight to see not only the Americans but to have the honor of entertaining Sherif Hazza, lineal descendant of the prophet. But there was a momentary altercation as they arrived—"an Arab woman screamed out and wept bitterly at the sight of 'Akil," said Lynch. "In him she recognized the murderer of her husband, in a foray the previous year. If 'Akil felt remorse, as he certainly must have done, he possessed too much of the stoicism of the savage to let it become apparent." The ensuing feast was rice and huge bowls of stewed mutton, but the Americans were unable to avoid watching the sheep being killed and dressed right outside the pasha's tent as the officials exchanged niceties; that, and the unhygienic appearance of the cook, took their appetites. The most they could do was pick at the food or pretend to eat. When, after the long evening, they finally had ridden back to their own tents on the riverbank, they went to bed hungry, and several of the men were quite sick the next morning.[13]

When the rivermen parted from the camel caravan and descended the Jordan bank to their boats, they were surprised to see the steep, overhanging bluff opposite them was ringed with faces of villagers lying "full-length . . . with their heads projecting over the bank, and looking at the floating wonders beneath; turning, from time to time, to regard the race to whom belonged such rare inventions and famous mechanisms, as boats and six-barrel revolvers."

That day's journey, on Friday, April 14, proved dramatically less difficult than those preceding it: the milky-colored river flowed at a good clip along its never-ending serpentine curves, occasionally joined by tributary streams, with occasional sandbars or thickly vegetated islands, the banks sometimes fringed with low, sandy hills, or cane thickets, or wall-like, overhanging jungles. They saw "the fresh track of a tiger on the low clayey margin, where he had come to drink," and later startled a wild boar, which bounded out of his lair and thrashed into thick vegetation. The Jordan was well populated with cranes, storks, herons, ducks, snipes, swallows, hawks, and bulbuls, the latter a gentle, brown-breasted, scarlet-headed, and crimson-winged creature—one of which was shot and retained as a scientific specimen. Later, when Sherif used his carbine to take a potshot at a standing stork, shattering one leg and causing it to flounder and be swept downstream until it beached and agonizingly tried to drag itself to safety, Lynch could not restrain himself from lecturing the elder dignitary, he later claimed in his book—"it was a pity to shoot a bird unfit to eat, and not required as a specimen, and which, by the Muhammedan law, was regarded as a sacred one." Sherif seemed to stand corrected—the shot had been done in a moment of excitement, but immediately afterward he seemed "sincerely sorry about it." Within moments of the shot they were borne out of sight of the little drama.[14]

All day, Sherif seemed anxious and watchful as they passed through enemy terrain. At the times that they pulled in to shore to investigate the path ahead, and try to spy their friends on a parallel path in the land caravan, his scout never set foot on land without strapping on his pistol belt. That evening the ground around their tents bristled with spears when land and river parties rejoined; they supped and fell into exhausted sleep. The sick among them had been vomiting all day. It was decided that the next morning it would be safer for the parties to keep within sight of one another, with camels and drivers on the eastern shore and the Bedouins on the western, with lookouts taking to vantage points on the hills when the path took them out of sight of the Jordan.[15]

Saturday proved an oppressive day, rising from 78 at half past 6, when they set out, to 86 degrees, with no wind, and a hurtful glare that gave a number in the party headaches. The camel caravan crossed the river at a boisterous ford called Wacabes, and proceeded down along the eastern side of the valley, with the Bedouins continuing on the west. For most of the day, the rivermen caught no glimpse of the land parties, and, given the increasing sense of alertness conveyed by their escorts, Lynch and his comrades remained anxious.

The Jordan varied in width from 40 to 80 yards and depth from 2 to 4 feet, requiring the boats to descend 6 ugly and 10 moderate rapids as it passed high conical hills to the west. Opposite stood high terraces of clay and conglomerate ridden with caves, from which clouds of pigeons emerged. In those caves, and within those thickets in the Ghor, the warriors of the Jewish rebel leader, Jonathan Maccabee, long evaded the search parties of the king of Syria, 150 years before Christ.

With the quick current every hairpin curve sent the boats off on a tangent toward dangerous rocks or surface-scraping tree limbs, which threatened to comb the mariners out of their vessels. Ravines, or wadys, opened up ashore, some dry, some carrying little streams down to the river. Canes, thistles, tamarisk and ghurkud trees bound the waters, and they could tell by deposits of driftwood that the Jordan was falling daily by a rate of two feet. At Wady el Malakh (Ravine of Salt), they examined the brackish stream falling down from the gloomy, desolate mountains rising to the east. There were tiger tracks on shore. They sampled some wild fennel and spit out tastes of ghurra, a purple-stemmed, light green-leafed and exceptionally bitter plant. On a distant hilltop, 'Akil and a few scouts kept watch over them.[16]

The day's journey ended before 3 p.m. at the ford of Sek'a, where

Lynch and his comrades were relieved to see that the caravan and escorts had rejoined and camped. 'Akil told Lynch that there was a friendly village nearby, and several locals soon appeared, greeting the Bedouins with familiarity but bearing a report that their village had been attacked the night before by a force of some 200 warriors—the bad tribe 'Akil and Sherif had been concerned about. Several villagers had been killed, and the raiders rustled off most of their horses, cattle, and sheep.

With hours of daylight remaining, Lynch got busy with his field notes and then his highly colored journal entry began, trying to skirt the Americans' nervousness. "Beneath a sky hollowed above us like a brazen buckler," he wrote,

> and refracting the shafts of smiting sunlight, we journeyed on, heeding neither light nor heat, hunger nor thirst, danger nor fatigue; but each day looked cheerfully forward to the time when we should be gathered on the margin of the river, the tents all spread, the boats fastened to the shore, the watch-fires blazing, and the sound of human voices breaking the tyrannous silence, and giving a home-like aspect to the wilderness.
>
> The character of the whole scene of this dreary waste was singularly wild and impressive. Looking out upon the desert, bright with reverberated light and heat, was like beholding a conflagration from a window at twilight. Each detail of the strange and solemn scene could be examined as through a lens.
>
> The mountains towards the west rose up like islands from the sea, with the billows heaving at their bases. The rough peaks caught the slanting sunlight, while sharp black shadows marked the sides turned from the rays. Deep-rooted in the plain, the bases of the mountains heaved the garment of the earth away, and rose abruptly in naked, pyramidal crags, each scar and fissure as palpably distinct as though within reach, and yet we were

hours away; the laminations of their strata resembling the leaves of some gigantic volume, wherein is written, by the hand of God, the history of the changes he has wrought.[17]

That their little expedition had settled into a routine was comforting. "The scene of camping for the night is ever a busy one," Lynch wrote.

The uprearing of tents, the driving of the tent-pins, the wearied camels standing by, waiting to be disburdened, all remind one forcibly of the graphic descriptions of the Bible. There are other features, too, illustrative of our brotherhood with the children of the desert—Sherif, seated beneath a tree, or under the shadow of a rock, issuing commands to his immediate followers, and 'Akil reconnoitering from the summit of a hill, or scouring about the plain, stationing the outposts. With us, too, everything bore the aspect of a military expedition through a hostile territory. The boats, when practicable, were securely moored in front, and covered by the blunderbuss; the baggage was piled between the tents, and the sentries paced to and fro in front and rear. Among the trees which bordered the river-bank, the horses of our Arab friends were this evening tethered, while our own luxuriously enjoyed a clandestine supper in the wheatfield near at hand.

At this time, our benign and ever-smiling Mustafa, with his bilious turban and marvelous pants, wide and draperied, but not hiding his parenthetical legs, seemed almost ubiquitous. At one time, he was tearing something madly from his laden donkey; and the next, he was filling pipes, and, hand on breast, presenting them with low salaams; or, like a fiend, darting off after the Doctor's horse, which, having evaded the watchful Hassan, was charging upon the others, and frightening "'the souls of his fearful adversaries" with the thunder of his nostrils.[18]

He continued writing until sunset, at which point the Christians and the Muslims bathed in the invigorating waters of the Jordan. That evening, Lynch and Sherif debated the qualities of their respective religions, each coming away politely but privately convinced that the other's faith was backward and barbarous. But the evening ended companionably at the edge of a campfire, while the Arabs took turns singing songs accompanied by a two-stringed *rebabeh*, while the rest sipped coffee and smoked from the communal pipe. Out beyond the firelight, though, the sentries were on heightened alert, mindful that the "bad tribe" raiders vastly outnumbered their valiant little force of warriors.[19]

CHAPTER SEVEN

The Descent of the Jordan Past Jericho

As BEFORE, THE EXPEDITION SPLIT INTO THREE PARTIES EARLY ON Sunday, April 16—Palm Sunday to Christians—but the lieutenant was troubled that his guides "were utterly ignorant of the course of the river, or the nature of its current and its shores." But all they could do was press forward. Downstream, an hour later, he ordered the crafts ashore to examine the place where, he had been told, the Molyneux party had been attacked.

He would not learn the details until much later, but the English sailors, three in number with four Arabs escorting them, had been waylaid as their boat passed into a narrowed valley, on Monday, August 30, the previous year. Lieutenant Molyneux, when it happened, was with the mules and camels and out of touch with the Jordan. As the boat, carrying three sailors and two Arabs, rounded a curve, they saw a crowd of 40 to 50 Arabs on either side of the river, who immediately let fly with rocks, with a few carrying carbines shooting into the water ahead of the vessel. The marauders waded into the river and seized the boat, dragging it and the terrified occupants ashore. One sailor drew a pistol, but he was knocked into the water by a stick-wielding tribesman. All were stripped of their weapons and much of their clothes. The guides were threatened with death but sustained only a stiff beating, and they were separated from the three Englishmen. They rejoined Molyneux later that day, and went with him as he cut short the river journey and fled overland to the fortress at Jericho.

No word of the fate of the missing men would be heard until the expedition's end, nearly two weeks later, when the lieutenant rejoined his ship in the Mediterranean and was reunited with his three sailors, who had retraced their path north to Tiberias and west to the sea-coast.[1] As he examined the place of ambush eight months later, Lynch saw no clues to help him assess the earlier event, but there were numerous wild animal tracks, including that of a tiger. They rejoined the lifeboats, still on guard.

Nerves were tense uphill from the river, too. Lieutenant Dale and Henry Bedlow, traveling as usual with the camel caravan, noted that the Bedouins were in a state of heightened alert. Emir Guzzaway, in particular, seemed out of sorts the further he got from his home territory adjoining Galilee: he had pled that a headache kept him from his accustomed perch in one of the lifeboats, which had struck the Americans as odd.

But in clinging to the land party that morning, the stout "voluptuary" scored a fright. Early that morning, a strange Arab was sighted lurking beyond a deep ravine, and scouts spied a large number of black goat-hair tents hidden there. Sure there would be a skirmish, the Bedouins halted the camels, drew themselves and their mounts in front, loosened their swords in their scabbards, and unslung their carbines, all while pivoting their stamping horses and singing a war song. Dale saw they were working themselves into a frenzy; he was instructed to lay aside his hat and don a *tarbouch* and *kufeya*.

At a signal, they advanced, ready for a fight. But when they neared the strangers, those Arabs "kept aloof," recounted Dale, "proving neither hostile nor friendly." The bristling horsemen and their caravan rode by, and " 'Akil, as he passed, contemptuously blew his nose at them." Not long after, their path intersected with an ancient trade road and its ford at the Jordan, called Damieh. Since breaking their journey there would make the next day easier, they made camp at the ford and waited for Lynch and men to appear. When they did, the lieutenant and his comrades in the copper boat were soaked, with all of Lynch's papers and notebooks wetted, thanks to a stretch of whitewater and an obtruding boulder.[2]

The intersecting road ran from the west bank town of Nablus—ancient Shechem, where the great patriarch of Israel, Abraham, was said to have received his Lord's affirmation of the special covenant with the Israelites, and where many believed the tomb of the patriarch Joseph was located—to the hilltop village of Salt, identified of old with Shoaib, the father-in-law of Moses.

At the Damieh ford of the Jordan, the high-arched stone ruins of a Roman bridge stood as a mute reminder of the days when Emperor Titus Flavius Vespasian founded a city adjacent to old Shechem, naming it Flavia Neapolis, after himself, the illustrious conqueror of Judea. The partially collapsed Roman bridge was examined by Dale and Aulick, who had to fight through dense thickets to get close; it now spanned the old, dried-up main channel of the Jordan. From one of its approaches they could see down the barren eastern hills a line of green tracing its way almost parallel to the Jordan—marking the course of the River Jabbok, the deep torrent valley that meandered west and south from Amman until it joined the Jordan.

Back at camp, the Arabs predicted they would reach that point tomorrow, but what really stirred the Americans was the knowledge that they were nearing the ford of Bethabara—traditionally held to be the baptism place of Jesus by John the Baptist. According to travelers' reports of the valley, the mouth of the Jordan lay perhaps a day further.

Long before dawn brightened over the mountains of Gilead on Monday, April 17, the camp bustled for breakfast and the coming journey, which would be unusually long if they were going to make the next ford. "Although the air was damp and chilly," Lynch wrote, "we knew, from past experience, that before noon the sun would blaze upon us with a power sufficient to carbonize those who should be unprotected from its fierceness." Downriver, beneath a purple haze, sterile rocky heights fell toward unappealing sand hills and river banks that were now strikingly bare of the flowered greenery to which they had grown accustomed. Nowhere was there a sign of tilled land or habitation—"all before us was the bleakness of desolation."

Before he launched, Lynch called his Arab escorts together and told the emir that since they were well out of his territory, his services and those of his retinue were no longer required. Paid what had been previously agreed, but no more, they headed back up the valley after an embrace between 'Akil and the emir.[3]

The river was becoming more choked with uprooted trees from the earlier floods, many still well in foliage. Owing to the declining waters of the approaching dry season, the going was more difficult as the Jordan, 50 yards wide with a pebbly bottom, flowed around islands through high red clay hills. Vegetation, though sparser, was more tropical, and there were a number of thorny thickets, and much bird-song above the river, though few birds were visible. High up in the hills Lynch saw "immense caverns and excavations, whether natural or artificial we could not tell," and the cave mouths were blackened by smoke—perhaps they were "the haunts of predatory robbers." An hour after stopping for the daily meridian observations, they came to the confluence with the River Jabbok. It flowed from the northeast and bore sweet water although the stones on its riverbanks were en-crusted with salt—product of the briny wind blowing upstream from the salty lake that now lay only 20 miles away in a direct line. "It was here," Lynch recorded, "that Jacob wrestled with the angel, at whose touch the sinew of his thigh shrunk up. In commemoration of that event, the Jews, to this day, carefully exclude that sinew from animals they kill for food."[4]

Meanwhile, the land caravan was having a stimulating day. Shortly after setting out they negotiated a ravine, beyond which they spied a young camel grazing in the underbrush—a stray, obviously, and one the Bedouins felt was up for grabs. Whooping, they took off after it, and though ungainly, the animal easily outdistanced the horses. 'Akil, though, finally drew abreast of it, and, leaning over, clapped a free hand over the neck of his quarry. The camel, being once domesticated, stopped, knelt, and waited to be taken—and, haltered, it proportionately increased the wealth of the Bedouin.

Past red sandstone mountains and through scrubby plains, they continued south through the valley as the oppressive heat of the sun and its blinding light finally forced them to a midday halt; the Arabs took shelter beneath their cloaks, which they supported on the butts of their spears. In the afternoon's journey when they sighted a cluster of gazelles, they gave chase, but this flurry of excitement was to no avail.

There was good water at a shallow stream in the Wady Nawa'imeh, and a spring at Ain el Hadj, the Pilgrim's Fountain, where they were joined by a few Arabs from Jericho. They thought they could see, in fact, a hint of the distant ruins of that ancient Canaanite city, whose walls it was said had been toppled by the horns of the Israelites, and where Herod the Great had died. But there was no question, looking south down the valley, when they caught sight of the impossibly blue water of the Dead Sea, "and the grim mountains of Moab to the southeast."

In late afternoon, after 5 p.m., having endured 11 hours in the saddle, they halted on the Jordan's bank at the ford of Bethabara. Lieutenant Dale objected to the Arabs' placement of the tents—they were square in the path of the pilgrim route, and with Easter Sunday in the offing, foot traffic could be considerable, even that early in the week. Everyone was too exhausted to debate, much less move the tents, and even when the two lifeboats came down the Jordan and beached, the consensus was to just rest and worry about it later.

The rivermen had their own chase that day when their boats came upon a wild boar swimming across the river, but they were unable to detain it. "Wild and dangerous rapids" encountered in late afternoon gave them a quick fright, but a short way downriver, when from the bow of the copper boat Lynch spotted an Arab skulking in bushes above the bank and he heard a corresponding shot, he ordered his companions to fire at anything that moved in the underbrush. But the Arab had disappeared. They heard other Arabs shouting at them from a hilltop, and, guns and swords bristling, they readied for a fight.

Just then the iron boat arrived with word that they themselves had been responsible for the gunshot—trying to bag a bird—and the terrified Arab hugging the ground beneath the bushes cried out that he was a friend, an emissary. He emerged in a crouch, the guns of two boats including the blunderbuss staring him down, and quickly stammered that he had been sent to Lynch by the sheikh of Huteim, the tribe near Jericho, to welcome them and present gifts. Still nervous, he handed over a small hoard of oranges, which the boatmen devoured with gratitude, and cakes made from flour, syrup, and sesame seeds, which the Americans found too alien to enjoy.

They took the emissary aboard and pressed on into the gathering twilight. As dark fell so did the temperature—the laboring oarsmen continued, not uncomfortable, but the others in the boats began to shiver from wetness and chill. Not until 9:30 p.m. did they reach their day's destination, the pilgrims' ford, "where the Israelites passed over with the ark of the covenant; and where our blessed Saviour was baptized by John."

They moored below the ford out of reverence for the sacred place, and—15 hours after they had first dipped their oars that day, having rowed and floated some 50 miles—they stumbled up to the camp. Immensely moved by the sight of that famous spot on the river, and grateful that thus far they had been blessed with safety and success, Lynch could only sit upon the bank, "my mind oppressed with awe."[5]

View of pilgrims at the baptismal site on the Jordan, considerably more
sedate than the wild tumult that almost trampled the explorers.

Exhausted they all may have been, but it was an impossible night
for sound sleep. First, the sudden crack of a gunshot brought everyone out of tents with weapons ready. A sentry had heard someone
splashing into the river and fired a warning shot without first challenging, a violation of discipline; it was only a poor *fellahin*, a peasant,
on his way home, and fortunately he was uninjured. Everyone went
back to sleep. Then, at 3 a.m., they were aroused again by a shout:
"*THE PILGRIMS ARE COMING! GET OUT OF THE WAY!*" As they
rushed out into the night, a full moon low over the mountains, the
ground was shaking.

"Rising in haste, we beheld thousands of torchlights," wrote
Lynch,

> with a dark mass beneath, moving rapidly over the hills. Striking
> our tents with precipitation, we hurriedly removed them and all
> our effects a short distance to the left. We had scarce finished,

when they were upon us: men, women, and children, mounted on camels, horses, mules, and donkeys, rushing impetuously by toward the bank. They presented the appearance of fugitives from a routed army. Our Bedouin friends here stood us in good stead, sticking their tufted spears before our tents, they mounted their steeds and formed a military cordon around us. But for them we should have been run down, and most of our effects trampled upon, scattered and lost.

Of course among their effects were the precious scientific instruments. "Strange that we should have been shielded from a Christian throng," mused Lynch later to his parochial American audience, "by wild children of the desert—Muslims in name, but pagans in reality. Nothing but the spears and swarthy faces of the Arabs saved us."

Sailors had been quickly sent down to the boats to row them out of the way of the tumult, and the expedition members had only a little time to absorb the spectacle taking place, and certainly no opportunity to resume their slumber—when it became clear that the mass of humanity that had disturbed them was only "the advanced guard of the great body of the pilgrims." Just at dawn, heralded by a great noise from behind the crest of a high ridge, they poured over

in one tumultuous and eager throng. In all the wild haste of a disorderly rout, Copts and Russians, Poles, Armenians, Greeks and Syrians, from all parts of Asia, from Europe, from Africa and from far-distant America, on they came; men, women and children, of every age and hue, and in every variety of costume; talking, screaming, shouting, in almost every known language under the sun. Mounted as variously as those who had preceded them, many of the women and children were suspended in baskets or confined in cages; and, with their eyes strained towards the river, heedless of all intervening obstacles, they hurried eagerly forward, and dismounting in haste, and disrobing with precipitation, rushed down the bank and threw themselves into the stream.

They seemed to be absorbed by one impulsive feeling, and perfectly regardless of the observations of others. Each one plunged himself, or was dipped by another, three times, below the surface, in honor of the Trinity; and then filled a bottle, or some other utensil, from the river. The bathing-dress of many of the pilgrims was a white gown with a black cross upon it. Most of them, as soon as they dressed, cut branches either of the *agnus castus*, or willow; and, dipping them in the consecrated stream, bore them away as memorials of their visit.

Back in the time of the Crusades, also around Easter time in, it is thought, the year 1173, the visiting German cleric Theoderich had stood at the same vantage point, wondrous at the sight of 60,000 pilgrims swarming into the sacred river, "almost all of them carrying candles in their hands—all of whom could be seen by the infidels from the mountains of Arabia beyond Jordan." Among the pilgrims seen by Lieutenant Lynch were three Britons, "a lady among them," three French naval officers, and even two Americans, who were startled but gladdened to see the stars and stripes fluttering above that camp in the Holy Land. The throng began to disappear after an hour, and in a few more hours, marveled Lynch, "the trodden surface of the lately crowded bank reflected no human shadow." They were again left alone in the wilderness. "It was," said Lynch, "like a dream."[6]

A heavy cloud stood over the western hills, bringing forth "sharp lightning and loud thunder, followed by a refreshing shower of rain."

The ancient village of Jericho lay a few miles away—a collection of huts on a hillside dominated by the square tower of an old Saracenic castle. It was dotted with ruins from its many destructions, from the siege of the Israelites elaborated in the book of Joshua—"*And it shall* be," the Lord said to Joshua, "*that when they make a long blast with the rams' horn, and when ye hear the sound of the horn, all the people shall shout with a great shout; and the wall of the city shall fall down flat, and the people shall go up every man straight before him*"—to the ruinous march of Pompeius Magnus, Julius Caesar's rival, to the sacking by the young Herod the Great. It was also a place of a celebrated miracle, where Jesus healed two blind beggars, according to the apostle Matthew, who hailed him as he and his followers passed by.

But there was no time to see the village for the weary Lieutenant Lynch and his men after discovering that no fresh provisions could be dislodged from the unhappy villagers. The Americans were sick of the salt-cured meat and other food they had been consuming since leaving Tiberias—they had delicately spurned most of the mutton and vegetable stews of their Arab escorts—so upon hearing that the larders of Jericho were bare, Lynch decided to send someone to Jerusalem, a journey of several days on a well-established route—to pick up the bread and provisions he had sent ahead. Dr. Anderson volunteered to go, and Lynch asked him to make a geological reconnaissance along the way.

Before the doctor departed, Lynch scrawled out a report to be sent back to Washington and Naval Secretary John Y. Mason. In a few paragraphs, he sketched their progress from Tiberias across the lower Galilee and down the circuitous and often hazardous Jordan with its "frequent and most fearful rapids" into which they were forced, "placing our sole trust in Providence," to plunge "with headlong velocity down appalling descents." The men in his command drew high praise for their courage and positive attitudes, as did their "efficient and faithful" Bedouin allies, and he reported that though the river had destroyed the wood-frame boat he had purchased for 500 piastres in U.S. Navy funds ($25), the *Fanny Mason* and the *Fanny Skinner* though "severely bruised" could soon be repaired.

He touched on one of the celebrated scientific puzzles that had sent them on their mission. "The great secret of the depression between Lake Tiberias and the Dead Sea," he wrote, "is solved by the tortuous course of the Jordan. In a space of sixty miles of latitude and four or five miles of longitude, the Jordan traverses at least 200 miles." They were preparing a topographic drawing of the river course, he added, and when the secretary saw it, he would "perceive that its course is more sinuous than that of the Mississippi."[7]

By 1:45 p.m. Dr. Anderson had ridden southeastward toward Jericho and Judea; Lieutenant Dale and the Bedouins led the camels down the valley trail; and Lieutenants Lynch and Aulick and their crews pushed off into the waters of the Jordan for the last leg of their journey to the Dead Sea. Several minutes later, an Arab hailed them from the riverbank: he was the sheikh of the local tribe who wished to accompany them.

The river widened from 30 to 50 yards with a muddy bottom 10 feet below their oars, with a current steadily slowing from 6 to 5 knots and water very smooth and light colored, still sweet to the taste. They filled their gum elastic water beakers. They bore southwest, northwest, southwest, north by northeast, west by south, south by west, east by southeast, and on and on, past low red clay banks supporting now mostly dead canes, and they flushed herons, ducks, pigeons, snipes, gulls, and bulbuls. They passed several camels standing in the shallows, and the beasts impassively watched them float past.

Occasional streams trickled in, with nauseating sulfur smells in the water. High mountains stood to the southwest. The river slowed and widened. They took a last draft of the boats at a lazy stretch. The river widened to 80 yards. Across the red clay flats ahead they caught a sight of deep blue water. Islands appeared.

The river spread out even more, and slowed even more, until it was 180 yards wide and only 3 feet deep. The surface of the water was slightly ruffled. And then, at 3:25 p.m., according to William Francis Lynch's lovingly polished naval chronometer, the copper boat and the iron boat glided beneath their flags out onto the surface of the Dead Sea, overlooked by the mountains of Moab and the cliffs of Judea.

PART THREE

CHAPTER EIGHT

The Western Shore to Engedi

THEY WERE SWEPT OUT ONTO A RISING SEA, THEIR MOMENTUM FROM the Jordan's outflow doubled by a stiff wind from the northwest. The river emptied at the northwestern shore, where a gravelly beach gave way to extensive mudflats with a sandy plain behind—it was "the very type of desolation," Lynch would write. On the high water mark, "branches and trunks of trees . . . scattered in every direction, some charred and blackened as by fire, others white with an incrustation of salt."

Eastward and toward the south along the lake's abrupt margin, bare and rugged mountains rose into the sky, mirrored by the even higher mountains marching down the western shore. "The water of the Jordan is whiter and more of a milky colour than any other water," wrote the pious Anglo-Saxon merchant Saewulf in 1102, traveling in the path of the Crusaders, "and it may be distinguished by its colour a long distance into the Dead Sea."[1]

This the Americans could not verify, and the wind freshened alarmingly, slamming them into increasing waves, the foamy water so densely laden with minerals that as the waves struck the boats, "it seemed as if their bows were encountering the sledge-hammers of the

Northwest shore of the Dead Sea, after a sketch by Lieutenant Dale.

Titans, instead of the opposing waves of an angry sea." Spray struck their hands and faces, causing skin to prickle; cuts, raw calluses, and sunburn to smart; and lips, nostrils, and eyes to sting most painfully. As the wind howled, the boats were in danger of foundering, and as they were swept leeward the sailors emptied their casks of fresh water to lighten the heavily laden craft. Lynch's guest on the copper boat, the hitchhiking sheikh of Huteim, was wide-eyed with terror and clinging to the gunwales, moaning that it was death to go out on the surface of the Sea of Lot. "It seemed," said Lynch, "as if the Dread Almighty frowned upon our efforts to navigate a sea, the creation of his wrath."[2]

Suddenly, though, the wind ceased and the sea calmed, becoming mirrorlike. Coated with a greasy salt, eyes still stinging, their clothes stiffened, the exhausted sailors realized they had been fighting the punishing waves and wind for two and a half hours. Above the western mountains, the sky turned rosy with the sunset. A flock of gulls passed overhead, followed by dark, massive clouds, their edges luminous with

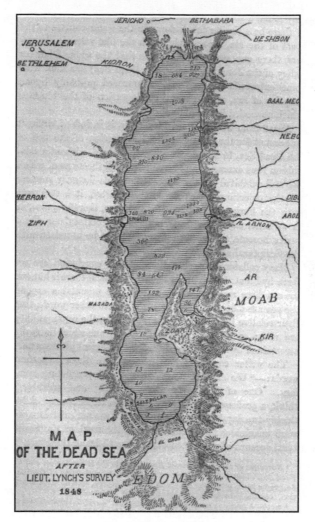

Dead Sea Map, 1848.

raking light. They heard the report and numerous echoes of a pistol
shot somewhere on the northwestern shore, and they began to lean on
their oars and head in that direction, hoping for a rendezvous with
their land party, their way illuminated only by a waning afterglow and
then by emerging stars.

    Several muzzle flashes on the beach, and above, in the craggy
heights, a small fire momentarily gleamed. Muffled shouts. "Divided

between apprehensions of an attack upon our friends and a stratagem for ourselves," said Lynch, "we were uncertain where to land."

But land they finally did, and a mile up the beach in a canebrake, near a brackish spring, they found their friends and their camp. After a miserly supper, "wet and weary," they threw themselves "upon a bed of dust, beside a fetid marsh, the dark, fretted mountains behind, the sea, like a huge cauldron, before us, its surface shrouded in a lead-colored mist." Some hours later, around midnight, they heard the distant and muffled bells of the Christian convent of Mar Saba, calling the faithful to prayer.[3]

In Arabic, it was called Bahr Lut—the Sea of Lot—and in Hebrew, Yam Hamelach —the Sea of Salt; as the latter it was mentioned in the Old Testament books of Genesis and Deuteronomy. Sometimes it was called the Eastern Sea, as in Ezekiel and Joel, or the Sea of the Plain, as in Joshua. The first-century Jewish historian Flavius Josephus referred to it as did the Roman conquerors he embraced as Lake Asphaltites, "bitter and unfruitful," still bearing the marks of the ancient and divine celestial fire sent down to punish the impious five cities of Sodom, Gomorra, Zeboiim, Zoar, and Admah.

Thus, as the traveling German cleric Theoderich wrote about 1173, it was thereafter also known as "The Sea of the Devil" for the wickedness of the five cities, "burned with fire of brimstone from heaven and . . . sunk in this lake, which rose in the place of the aforesaid cities." Moreover, he wrote, "The water of this pool is shocking from its hideous color, and its stench drives away those who approach it. Once a year, on the anniversary of the destruction of those cities, stones and wood and things of other kinds are seen to float on the surface of the lake, in testimony of their ruin."

Or, as his contemporary, the English canon lawyer Gervase of Tilbury wrote in his famous encyclopedia of wonders, *Otia Imperialia*, a burning torch would float on its surface; extinguished, it would sink. So, too, would the noxious waters of the Dead Sea rise over any vessel on its surface, "because of the living people inside it," unless it were coated with bitumen. Beneath those waters, in fact, had to be one of the entrances to Hell, like another portal found by Bishop John of Pozzuoli in a calderean pond near Naples, from beneath which he heard the lamentations of the damned, and, casting oil upon the waters, was "horrified to behold, far down in the depths, the gateway to the infernal regions!"[4]

Sunlight from a new day awakened Lynch on the beach above that sea of death, and he stirred with the sound of the rising wind from the south and the crash of surf. He had intended to let everyone sleep in, but then their sentries roused them all with the alarm that the beached lifeboats were filling with water from the waves. They ran down the flinty beach to secure the boats and dry their belongings, the perpendicular, crumbly and ochre-colored mountains looming a thousand feet over their heads. Dale pointed out a number of small and dark cavern openings high up in the cliffs, seemingly inaccessible from either base or summit—once the hiding places of the children of Israel when the thieving Midianites raided them in the time of the Judges, much later the dens of hermits and of the mysterious sect of the Essenes; 100 years after Lieutenants Lynch and Dale peered up at the caves, powerless to explore them, a young and nimble-footed Bedouin goatherder searching for a lost animal threw a stone into one of those caves at Qumran, and, hearing the shattering of pottery, found, in ancient jars and wrapped in linen, the Dead Sea Scrolls.

At their feet on the beach were scattered numerous oily-looking black pebbles and stones—bitumen, or asphaltum, which when ignited would burn cleanly. Seetzen, the German explorer, had been informed in 1806 that it oozed from certain rocks on the eastern shore, was detached by the wind, and floated upon the surface until gathered. Arabs had told the biblical historian Edward Robinson when he was there in 1838 that earthquakes cast it loose from the bottom, sometimes in huge chunks, and onto the sea and seashore—Josephus and many others over nearly 2,000 years had said that it would "float on the surface, having the form and size of headless oxen," sometimes resembling islands, and that it would soon disappear when local tribesmen found it, chopped it up, and hauled it away to market where it sold for a handsome price. It was called "the stone of Moses" by the Arabs. "I saw pieces of it at the convent of St. John in the wilderness," Henry Maundrell had written after his travels in 1697, "two feet square. They were carved in basso relievo, and polished to as great a luster as black marble is capable of, and were designed for the ornament of the new church at the convent." Most recently, Edward Robinson had found highly polished bitumen rosaries and other articles for sale in Jerusalem.[5]

The Americans heard the song of shore birds and startled partridges into taking flight. That moment they disproved another myth of the sea, that no birds could live near the strand and would die in flight if they strayed into the airspace above the lake. It all bore, as Lynch stood breathing in a sulfurous miasma from the little stream running across the beach, seeing little but bare rock and dead vegetation, "a sad and somber aspect. We had never before beheld such desolate hills, such calcined barrenness." It was a scene "of unmixed desolation,"[6] or, as a later visitor to that flinty shore would echo—the struggling young author Herman Melville, seeking inspiration in early 1857 and scrawling gloomy, self-pitying impressions in his journal: "smarting bitter of the water, —carried the bitter in my mouth all day—bitterness of life—thought of all bitter things—Bitter is it to be poor & bitter, to be reviled, & Oh bitter are these waters of Death, thought I."[7]

It being clear that the Bedouins' horses could not be fed on the salt-encrusted and acrid vegetation drooping over the stream and marsh, 'Akil and his men prepared to leave the Americans the next day, planning to ride at Lynch's behest to visit their tribal cousins in settlements above the eastern shore of Moab; they would make introductions and rendezvous with the explorers later. Sherif Hazza, though, set off with his servant for Jerusalem, two days' ride away, taking extraneous equipment for storage and intending to assist transportation of their food supplies; he also bore a letter from Lynch to the pasha of Jerusalem, asking to borrow a couple of soldiers to guard their depot on the lakeshore while they explored and mapped.

That night, the Bedouins threw a farewell feast, cooking a floury, buttered gruel in a large kettle over an open fire and eating with their hands. The Americans remained aloof from the repast, though all were cordial, and long past bedtime, as they succumbed to sleep, one of the Arabs sang at the campfire in the strange, discordant tones that made the Americans feel far away from home; only at midnight, when again they heard the muffled bell at Mar Saba, did Lynch feel any solace from anything remotely familiar.

The next morning, Thursday, April 20, John Dale and Richmond Aulick pushed off the boats with crews into the lake to compile lines of depth soundings, directly to the opposite shore and also on the diagonal. With the Bedouins departed, Lynch stayed at the camp to record in his journal and prepare the campsite for a move the next day. Meanwhile, every half mile, the boatmen would pause to cast off the weighted line and its vessel, tediously drawing them up from the sea bottom to note the depth and collect the blue mud and sand, and sometimes perfectly square crystals of salt dragged up to the surface. While just out from the western shore, the temperature a pleasant 82 degrees, this was easy, but the sun rose in its "midsummer fierceness," they told Lynch later, and the greasy, mineral-laden water made the rowers' and the sounders' hands "smart and burn severely." Across to the far side, a distance of seven nautical or almost eight statute miles, Aulick would report the greatest depth to be 116 fathoms, or 696 feet, while Dale, heading to the shore on a southeast diagonal, found a nearly level plain with an average depth of 170 fathoms, or 1,020 feet.

At the eastern edge, Aulick took their boat up to a yawning chasm in the high cliffs, down through which flowed a "sweet and thermal stream," which they felt certain was the Wady Zerka Main, the outlet of the famous medicinal hot springs of Callihroe, described by Pliny and where Herod the Great had bathed. Aulick vowed to himself to explore it before they left the sea. It was growing dark as the crews in the separated boats turned to head back to the western shore, and the sea was rising dangerously.

Back at the camp, Lynch kept scanning the water looking for his men, and after sunset he particularly wished them closer when a rag-tag little crowd of Rashayideh Arabs walked into camp, begging to be hired as guides and guardians of the explorers' effects. "They were," recalled Lynch, "the most meager, forlorn, and ragged creatures I have ever seen," and although he could see making use of them as guides he could never trust them around the campsite, and so sent them on their way. They squatted forlornly up the beach, and, realizing he was temporarily outnumbered, Lynch ordered his few companions to strap on weapons until the others returned. They lit signal fires on the beach and around their camp for Dale and Aulick.

By 8 p.m. there was still no sign of the boats. The wind blew strongly from the west. The surface of the sea "was one wide sheet of phosphorescent foam," noted Lynch, "and the waves, as they broke upon the shore, threw a sepulchral light upon the dead bushes and scattered fragments of rock." Not for more than an hour did the copper boat finally struggle in and beach, and the iron boat did not appear until nearly 11, the men exhausted from their long row—a "dreadful pull"—into the waves and wind, and their clothes painfully stiffened from the salt. After they ate and the whole camp was able to relax, they fell asleep to the continuing crash of the surf.[8]

Because the drinking water they had collected from the pure Jordan River was almost exhausted, and the spring near their campsite bore nasty-tasting, possibly unhealthful water, the adventurers, who were permitted to sleep in on Friday because of the late bedtime, bustled after breaking fast to move their equipment to the lifeboats for a move southward to a better spring at Ein Gedi. The ragged Rashayideh hurried over to help with the carrying. "Their astonishing brevity of shirt, and lack of all other covering, save a dirty and faded kuffiyeh [headscarf]," Lynch noted, "rendered them peculiarly interesting to the anatomist." Several were wearing sandals, which Lynch carefully described in his notes for future readers who were unfamiliar with such footgear. The sea was only lightly ruffled with a pale mist above it, and little wind when they pushed off a few minutes before noon. The two boats, though, were so heavily laden that they rode dangerously low in the water and the sailors knew to stay close to shore and that if the wind picked up they would hurriedly beach them. Their remaining camel, similarly laden, was led by their remaining Arabs at a slow, trudging gait down the beach.[9]

They rowed past the outcropping mountainside called Rash el Feshka, and came abreast of the dry Ravine of the Guard, or Wady Mahras, and slightly southward rowed in to look at the Ravine of Fire, or Wady en Nar, bed of the River Kedron. Midway up the ravine would be the Mar Saba convent, which they would see later. At the head of the ravine, Lynch knew, was the valley of Jehoshaphat, which ran to Jerusalem, The mad prophet Ezekiel, from the time of the Babylonian exile, had, after conversing with God on his throne, experienced visions of the waters of that trickling river valley rising to the ankles, to the knees, to the loins, then becoming swimmable, then uncrossable, swirling across desert and down valley and ravine, "into the sour waters, and the waters were to be healed," and then on the shores of the Dead Sea, "the fishers shall stand upon it from Engedi even unto En-eglaim."[10] Now, in the dry season, Lynch stood in the parched, rock-choked riverbed, the sour waters at his back, and fingered some flesh-colored flint and a few freshwater shells from high above.

Resuming, they rowed along a gently curving beach beneath thousand-foot cliffs, in which was visible a large cave about two-thirds up, near the ravine called Wady Sudeir, in which Edward Robinson had reported a sweet-tasting spring. Half an hour later they passed the Wady Ghuweir, its little green fringe of canes and tamarisks something "to cheer the eye" in the otherwise desert brownness.

By 4:30 they were approaching Ein Turabeh, its greenery, including a few ghurra trees and tamarisk bushes, attracting them in for the night's camp, its spring proving to be a warm 75 degrees but clear and sweet. Nearby in the oasis grew a terebinth tree (turpentine tree) in full bloom with white and pink flowers; lily stalks stood along the stream, and they found samples of yellow henbane, wild grape, and the same kind of saline-loving kale found by their fellow American explorer, John Charles Frémont, in 1843 on the shore of Great Salt Lake in Utah.

The Arabs spotted a stray specimen of the shrub-like chickpea plant and presented the unfamiliar-looking peapods to Lynch, calling them, he noted, "hamoos." They also harvested the small crabapple-like fruit of the small Spina Christi tree, or Jerusalem thorn, said to be the source of Christ's crown of thorns at his crucifixion. Though withered, the fruit was quite palatable, and took the edge off the explorers' appetites while the cook prepared their meal—augmented by a large catfish caught by an Arab up in the Jordan and carried down in the hope of a profitable sale.

The next morning, they loaded up the boats and their camel and continued in parallel down the shore through the hazy, overhanging purplish vapor and intense heat, past a number of ravines in the high cliffs, including the Wady Ta'amirah, at the head of which and a day's march away, the lieutenant noted, stood the village of Bethlehem. In the late morning they pulled in to examine some ruins and clambered a little way up the embankment to explore a cavern, its entrance fortified by a rough wall of stones, deep enough to shelter 20 or 30 persons. From the parapet they looked down and southward across the "wilderness of Engedi," the large shoreline oasis created by a free-flowing spring and supporting much vegetation.

The camp at Engedi, western shore.

They rowed a little farther down the beach until they found ground level enough to establish a campsite. Losing little time, after pitching tents they explored the plain, finding evidence of recent cultivation and also ruins of what was thought to be the ancient Judean town of Tamar—fortified by Solomon, and through which the army of the Moabites and Ammonites slipped on their doomed attack on the kingdom of Jehoshaphat.[11] In the year AD 1180, during the First Crusade, the newly crowned king of Jerusalem, Baldwin I, a towering, red-bearded warrior from Boulogne in France, had led an army from Jerusalem across the Judean desert to Hebron and from there down the ravine to the Dead Sea shore at Engedi—the first Crusaders to see the lake—where they ate dates from the oasis and refrained from attacking the local tribe, who seemed so primitive, miserable, and sun-darkened that there was some question among the Franks whether they were human.[12]

Lynch and his men saw that the spring at Engedi was a true fountain, pouring out of a cleft in the mountainside some 500 feet up into a grove of Spina Christi. Through the interpreter, the lieutenant arranged for the Rashayideh tribesmen to carry water down to their camp, a distance of about a mile.

Back at the water's edge, they emptied their battered boats and wrestled them upside down for an inspection of their keels and stern-posts, finding hairline cracks. They could look across the sea to where, perched atop the highest mountain, the stern Crusaders' castle at Kerak stood. Visible on the opposite shore beneath beetling cliffs, was the high-backed peninsula mentioned by many travelers; in the morning's mist it had looked to them like an island, as indeed it had in 1806 when described by the German explorer Ulrich Seetzen.[13] Then they turned their attention to the scientific instruments, recording baro-metrical and thermometrical figures and starting a land survey for a baseline that would stretch from the lakeshore all the way to the Mediterranean.

By then Lynch was worrying about the dwindling provisions, having for several days expected the return of Dr. Anderson and Sherif Hazza with stores from Jerusalem, so he paid some Arabs to climb the pass to the Judean plateau and obtain flour in the market town of Hebron. If anything had happened to the doctor, if anything deterred the Arabs from their mission, Lynch worried, "we should have been in a starving condition." Still, courtesy dictated that when a new and hungry group of Arabs wandered into camp, these from the local Ta'amirah tribe and nearly as ragged and attenuated as the Rashayideh, Lynch directed them to the fire for some leftover cooked rice.

"They had seated themselves round the pot," recounted Lynch, "and were greedily about to devour it, when one of them suggested that, perhaps, pork had been cooked in the same vessel. They rose, therefore, in a body, and came to the cook to satisfy their scruple. I never saw disappointment more strongly pictured in the human countenance than when told that the vessel had often been used for that purpose. Although nearly famished, they would not touch the rice, and we could give them nothing else." Lynch advised them to return to their homes, but they only withdrew a short distance, and he was forced to increase the guards out of caution against pilferage—except the pork, which they had "full confidence would not be touched."[14]

That night, as the moon rose and the warm wind picked up so much that they had to double up the tent stakes and ballast holding down the flapping canvas, Lynch looked up at light clouds coursing above ghostly cliffs, breathed in a disagreeable sulfurous scent, and recalled the words of Sherif Hazza: "I have often heard," he had said, "of the tyranny of the Franks toward each other. But I never thought they would have sent their countrymen to so desolate a place as this."[15]

The next morning was Easter Sunday, and in deference to the Christian holy day marking Christ's resurrection from the dead, the Americans gave themselves a day off from all tasks that could be postponed, though there wasn't much food left for celebration. The heat rose by late morning to the point, noted Lynch, that "we all felt a great oppression about the head, and much drowsiness," though their torpor was briefly relieved by the sight of Dr. Anderson and Sherif Hazza "creeping like mites along the lofty crags descending to this deep chasm." When they and their supplies finally arrived in camp three hours later, the sailors gladly tore into some fresh bread and savored it. Some had pointed out to Lynch more cavern openings high in the cliffs above the fountain; one was even strengthened with a stone arch. But any access paths had long crumbled away, and even though fortified with fresh food from Jerusalem, Lynch noted with regret, "our sailors could not get to them, and where they fail, none but monkeys can succeed."

At sunset, the mountains of Moab shone with a dramatic pink

and orange light and the hulking castle of Kerak stood in sharp contrast against the darkening eastern sky. Lynch was reminded of the last Christian chieftain of Kerak, the brigand Reynauld of Chatillon, who betrayed the peace in 1181 by attacking and plundering a Damascus caravan, provoking the Muslim leader Saladin into the wars of the last Crusade and the ultimate disaster at the Horns of Hattin. Lieutenant Lynch stared at the old battlements, deploring "the folly and rapacity of the 'Lord of Kerak,' which lost to Christendom the guardianship of the Holy Sepulchre."[16]

A meteor blazed brightly that night, streaking from the zenith toward the northeast, and a breeze blew upon them from the north, carrying the unpleasant sulfurous odor from the earth's bowels and shallow, stagnant pools. The lieutenant roused all hands before 5 on the morning of Easter Monday, April 24, while it was still a pleasant 78 degrees, for after a breakfast of fresh bread they faced a long day of hard work. Lynch, Dr. Anderson, and crew headed southeast in the *Fanny Mason*, sounding depths, toward the opposite shore and its bold peninsula. Midshipman Aulick and rowers pushed off in the iron boat, also sounding, to thread a line directly across the lake to the ravine known as Wady Mojeb and its river, known in biblical times as the Arnon. Lieutenant Dale and the rest stayed near camp, setting up their instruments to begin the baseline survey.

Four hours were consumed rowing to the peninsula, the sun beating down on the awning above them and reflecting blindingly off the water and their copper gunwales. Lynch noted as they drew close that the peninsula was bold and broad and between 40 and 60 feet high, crowned by a knifelike central ridge rising a further 20 feet—chalky, perpendicular marl bright in the sun, skirted by a flinty beach strewn with millions of dead locusts. It had first been visited by the English travelers Irby and Mangles in 1818. Now, Lynch and Anderson scrambled up a narrow passage worn by rains through the stone, their perspiration evaporating in the furnace-like heat until they stood at the pinnacle, squinting down at a sheltered bay and up at the towering cliffs.[17]

Meanwhile, Aulick and the crew of the *Fanny Skinner* were enjoying midday in the cool shadow of the Wady Mojeb after their crossing. Its sheer red sandstone walls plummeted from above to the ancient River Arnon, reputed in the revered Hebrew text, the Haggadah of Pesach, to be the site of a miracle saving the Israelites as they fled toward the Promised Land bearing the sacred Ark of the Covenant; the tribe of Moabites lay in ambush for them in ravine caves but were slaughtered when the ark shook the earth and caused the valley to rise and the mountains to fall. Now, in those placid-seeming depths, where little fish darted, Aulick and companions refreshed themselves with cool, fresh water before their return. They had determined that the Dead Sea was slightly more than eight geographical miles wide—or nine statute miles—and that its greatest depth at this midline was 188 fathoms, or 1,128 feet.

The air temperature was still hovering at 92 degrees in a dead calm at 6 p.m. when Lynch's weary party struggled back to the shore below their camp. Aulick's boat beached soon after. Following dinner, their Bedouin escorts entertained them all by firelight in a recitation of Arab poetry—rhyming couplets recounting historic battles. Sherif Hazza, while displaying appreciation for the display, was full of cautions to the Americans about venturing any farther southward. A messenger sent down the lake to prepare the southern tribes for their presence and to hire guides had returned to report that robbers had driven off the peaceable inhabitants and now ruled those mountainous shores. Against Sherif's warnings, Lynch was firm: "We could not leave our work unaccomplished."[18]

The next day, they would leave Sherif in charge of the camp, safeguarded by the four Turkish soldiers, while they performed a boat and shore reconnaissance of the southern part of the Dead Sea, which might take three days. Before they retired they killed a scorpion and a tarantula among their bedrolls, and most of them had trouble sleeping, so oppressive and nauseating was the air around them. Across the dark sea, on the barren and previously uninhabited peninsula, several campfires burned.

CHAPTER NINE

Looking Backward at a Pillar of Salt

THE TWO LIFEBOATS WERE ROWED FROM ENGEDI OUT ONTO THE lake the next morning, leaving Sherif and his Turkish protectors, along with one member of the American party, a sailor too ill to handle an oar. Their seven Arab escorts walked along the cliff-overhung beach parallel to the boats, brandishing their rifles but anxiously casting glances at the explorers and their blunderbuss; they had passed far beyond the southern limits of their respective tribes, the Rashayideh, Ta'amirah, and Kabeneh, and "dreaded an attack from marauding parties," noted Lynch, who kept the boats nearby in case of trouble.[1]

Now, south of the peninsula, they were in an area never seen by their exploring and ill-fated predecessors, Costigan and Molyneux, both of whom had retreated to shore severely ill.[2] The day began hot at 89 degrees, with no clouds nor wind stirring, with Dale and Aulick making drawings as Lynch recorded conditions and a seaman sounded the depth and another kept his eye on the device called a patent log, which, thrown overboard and towed, measured the distance traveled.

Just before 2 p.m., after rowing eight and a half miles, they had

Masada was much as it appeared to Dale and Bedlow when it was photographed several decades later. *(Matson Collection, Library of Congress)*

reason to pause and rest and gape. They had come abreast of the ravine of acacias, Wady Seyal, and, adjacent, "a mass of scorched and calcined rock," the high, flat-topped mountain known as Masada—Herod the Great's fortress, with its ruined cliff-top walls visible from the boats and having, wrote Lynch, "a commanding but dreary prospect, overlooking the deep chasm of this mysterious sea." The Arabs were nervously picking their way across a deep, deltaic beach of sand and broken rock debris. After the boats put in to pick them up, they could only shrug when asked about what stood above: they had heard that "there were ruins of large buildings on the cliff."[3]

But there was work to finish out on the lake—finding a night camp would wait until they saw evidence of fresh water ashore—so the boats continued to row generally southward, sounding often in a search to find an anomaly on the bottom, for there had been several reports, by Seetzen in 1806, for example, of a hidden ford just beneath the surface that stretched across the lake, which local tribes had used to walk directly over to the eastern shore below the peninsula. They found no evidence, however, and later that afternoon, the oarsmen having rowed at least 13 miles, they pulled into a little cove near the Wady Mubughghik.

Further down the lake rose a white promontory, the salt mountain of Usdum. Up in the deep ravine, they found a brook for their camp, and the foundations of ruined buildings constructed of square-cut stones, with what seemed to be a rude canal and a number of terraces for cultivation. An earlier traveler had romantically imagined this the site of the blasted city of Gomorrah. They retired with their guns at their fingertips that night on the sand of the beach, beneath the blunderbuss, with sentries patrolling, as a hot wind sprang up from the northwest, a sirocco so torrid that it was difficult to sleep. "We could not endure even a kerchief over our faces," noted Lynch, "to screen them from the hot and blistering wind."

Several meteors streaked overhead that night. When Lynch awoke early the next morning, it was still very dark and he found a young quail at his side, "where, in the night, it had most probably crept for shelter from the strong, hot wind."[4]

By 5:30 a.m. on the morning of Wednesday, April, 26, the crews were already out in the middle leaning on their oars. Dale piloted the *Fanny Skinner* closer to the coastline, sketching the terrain, while the sailors in the *Fanny Mason* were further out, sounding the dark, muddy bottom in one or two fathoms in a minute search not only for the reputed underwater ford but also for evidence of the sunken and heaven-blasted cities of Sodom and Gomorrah. Nowhere in Scripture could it be found that the cities were plunged beneath the waves, though there was a vague reference in Genesis to "the Vale of Siddim, which is the Salt Sea." But then so authoritative a historian as Flavius Josephus wrote as such in AD 75—"the traces [or shadows] of the five cities are still to be seen . . . which our very sight affords us."[5]

Many visitors and commentators embellished this over the centuries, especially Crusaders and followers such as Bishop Theoderich in 1173—the wicked cities "were burned with fire of brimstone from heaven and were sunk in this lake, which rose in the place of the afore-said cities." Two supposed eyewitnesses, high-level clerics in Jerusalem, told the admittedly skeptical Henry Maundrell in 1697 that "they had once seen one of these ruins; that it was so near the shore, and the waters so shallow at that time, that they, together with some Frenchmen, went to it, and found there several pillars and other frag-ments of buildings." Ulrich Seetzen, however, decided during his brief visit to the seashore in 1806 that the stories "merit[ed] little credit." Though in many other ways in his biblical geography travels in 1838 Edward Robinson weighed in about sites, his time at the Dead Sea shore had been brief and he published no comment, although during their meetings he may have urged Lieutenant Lynch in his search.[6]

Usdum, the land of salt, was not monolithic as they approached, but rather, a range of low, pale, and broken hills beyond the south-western corner of the lake and marching down along the shore about five miles. The boats kept having to retreat from the shoaling water close to the beach, but then, following exclamations, all hands paused in astonishment, when they beheld a high, round pillar of salt standing ashore at the maw of a deep chasm. Lynch hastened them in, and he and Dr. Anderson leaped out to examine it. The words of Genesis on the destruction of the wicked cities were on their mind, as well as those of Flavius Josephus. "But Lot's wife continually turning back to view the city as she went from it," he wrote, "and being too nicely inquisitive what would become of it, although God had forbidden her so to do, was changed into a pillar of salt; for I have seen it, and it remains at this day." Sir John Maundeville, in the year 1322: "the wife of Lot still stands in likeness of a salt stone, because she looked behind her when the cities sunk into hell."

The pillar towered over the two Americans, being about 40 feet high and standing atop a kind of natural, oval-shaped pedestal, round in front but connected in back as if by a buttress to the mountain

Fanciful view of "the Pillar of Salt," a natural formation
on the southern shore of Usdum.

behind. They scraped off a piece, crumbled it, tasted it. It was solid
salt, capped by a carbonate of lime. Lynch knew that the formation
was the result of the action of winter rains, so he could marvel as much
at this vaguely humanlike pillar as at the assertions of a thousand years
worth of visitors viewing and recording similar columns, faithful and
fanciful alike: that inside the pillar of salt, according to Bishop Ire-
naeus in the second century, was imprisoned the spirit of Lot's wife;
that at a certain time of the month, according to a belief in the Middle
Ages, it shed blood; that despite rains, or, in some tellings such as that
of Rabbi Benjamin of Tudela, the lickings of beasts, the rock salt was
always miraculously replenished. When they had finished with their
hammers, the doctor and the lieutenant carried with them generous
samples of Mrs. Lot for the United States government.[7]

* * *

Lynch left the base of the salt pillar, looking first beyond to the salt plains and valleys of Edom where King David of Israel had vanquished the Edomites in his campaign to establish a mighty empire. He squinted then through the blinding glare back at the sea and mountains, which were wreathed in a transparent purple mist, "increasing every moment, and presenting a most singular and awful appearance."

Since they intended to continue the exploration of the southern regions and the eastern shore, Lynch told the Arabs their services were no longer required. Paid off, and seemingly glad not to push any farther into enemy territory, they began their trudge northward along the beach toward home. One Arab from the party, a Ta'amirah, Lynch retained as emissary to the local tribes, but he did not look happy for the employment.

Then, back on the water, Lynch felt a quickening and had the sails lowered, expecting a gust of thunder or an earthquake. Soon "a hot, blistering hurricane" struck them from the southeast, driving the thermometer up to 102 degrees. Waves slamming into the boats made them difficult to control, with the oarsmen forced to row staunchly with their eyelids clamped shut; poor Lynch, at the helm of the copper boat, had to keep his eyes open to steer them toward land, and they blistered from the heat.

They landed the boats on the south side of the peninsula. "Some went up the ravine to escape from the stifling wind," Lynch noted, while "others, driven back by the glare, returned to the boats and crouched under the awnings. One mounted spectacles to protect his eyes, but the metal became so heated that he was obliged to remove them. Our [fire]arms and the buttons on our coats became almost burning to the touch; and the inner folds of our garments were cooler than those exposed to the immediate contact of the wind."

The exposed beach finally became intolerable, and they struggled up the dry ravine looking for water. They found no stream but did happen upon a pool lying beside massive boulders, marked by a dead date palm beneath rising cliffs of red sandstone. They all jumped into the pool, "but the relief was only momentary. In one instant after leaving the water, the moisture on the surface evaporated, and left the skin dry, parched, and stiff."

Out of the ravine they were awed by the sight: "the wind had increased to a tempest," wrote Lynch, "The two extremities and the western shore of the sea were curtained by a mist, on this side of a purple hue, on the other a yellow tinge; and the red and rayless sun, in the bronzed clouds, had the appearance it presents when looked upon through smoked glass. Thus may the heavens have appeared just before the Almighty in his wrath rained down fire upon the cities of the plain."[8]

The temperature was only increasing as the Americans bivouacked there on the peninsula. They were on heightened alert at the sight of campfire smoke from the north end of the peninsula, and they could occasionally hear shouts and laughter. The lieutenant asked their Ta'amirah guide to deliver a message to their unknown neighbors, but he refused, instead squatting down "with his eyes fixed on the streaming smoke," saying that they would be attacked in the night. He did not sleep a wink, and the Americans did not do much better, waking each other by turns to keep watch, tormented by swarms of mosquitoes, and otherwise trying not to obsess about cool water sliding down their parched throats. At 8 p.m. the thermometer stood at 106 degrees. During the night, the breakers calmed. The temperature began to drop, 98 degrees at midnight, 82 degrees at 4 a.m. As they awoke, it seemed almost cool.[9]

It was Thursday, April 27, 1848. A year before, Lynch had been polishing his Holy Land proposal before sending it to the naval secretary. Now he found himself splashing in the pool of a ravine in the mountains of Moab, overlooking the eastern shore of the Dead Sea. Flocks of birds flew overhead. He heard a partridge and spied a dove, and a darting hummingbird. Above him, in the cliffs, he heard voices, and the report of a rifle. Before he could move, grab clothes or his sidearm, his officers burst in on his naked solitude, fearful that he had been attacked, but he told them it was probably only a signal from a lookout and that the local Arabs "in a constant state of civil warfare," were undoubtedly more afraid of the strangers than the strangers were of them.

After he returned to the beach, sailors reported that a group of Arab women had appeared on a plain north of them. The Ta'amirah refused to be deputized, so Lynch appointed their cook and translator from Beirut, Mustafa, to approach them. He could only get within calling distance before they began to draw away, and from that remove the women demanded to know "who we were, how and why we came, and why we did not go away."[10]

It was impossible to tell whether this contact had a good effect or ill, but about an hour later, 40 Arabs approached, singing the song of their tribe. Their leader was armed with a sword, and the rest had assorted guns, lances, clubs, and tree branches. Lynch assembled his 12 comrades in a show of force behind the blunderbuss and then advanced with Mustafa. He drew a line in the sand and had his translator tell them that if they crossed it they would be fired upon.

They squatted down on their side of the line, ready to palaver. "They belonged to the Ghaurariyeh," Lynch discovered, "and were as ragged, filthy, and physically weak, as the tribe of Rashayideh, on the western shore. Finding us too strong for a demand, they began to beg for backshish." Lynch gave them a little food and tobacco, and some money, for which they agreed to take a message to the Americans' Bedouin protector, 'Akil, whom Lynch expected to be waiting to hear from them in the Moabite town of Kerak.[11]

The land of Moab, rising there from the shore of the Dead Sea,

Mustafa, the Arab cook hired at Beirut. Note the Americans'
mounted blunderbuss, their heaviest weaponry.

received its name from the son of Lot, begotten with Lot's elder
daughter after the destruction of the wicked cities and the divine
punishment of Lot's wife for her backward glance. As Josephus had
written, Lot and his daughters stumbled from the catastrophe to exile
at a place called Zoar and, with no provisions or company, "lived
a miserable life." The daughters, "thinking that all mankind were
destroyed, approached to their father, though taking care not to be
perceived." They got him drunk and, pretending to be strangers, slept
with him, "that mankind might not utterly fail. And they bare sons;
the son of the elder was named Moab, which denotes one derived
from his father. The younger bore Ammon, which name denotes one
derived from a kinsman." Josephus did not dismiss this incest at Zoar
as a crime; everyone, he said, had acted with good intentions.[12]

Lynch felt the proximity to Zoar, the one city on the plain that
escaped Jehovah's wrath, though there was no evidence of any habitation beyond the old ashes of campfires. The shallow bay, however,
he would find accurately described in Joshua, and as they pushed the

lifeboats out on the water, with the air temperature rising to 94 degrees at only 8:30, the ragged crowd of Ghaurayieh, who had never seen boats before, asked Mustafa "how the boats could move without legs." "Wait a while," he replied with a smile, until they got themselves going, and "they would see very long legs." And the throng did marvel at the sight.

The sailors sounded the muddy bottom straight across the lake to the western shore finding it to be about two fathoms' deep, and after several hours Lynch sent the *Fanny Skinner* back over to the peninsula to conduct meridian observations while the *Fanny Mason* crew continued to run a depth line parallel to the western shore. Signs of another sirocco in mid-afternoon had them pulling furiously toward the cliffs. Presently it struck with singular violence.

They beached in a good-sized bay, soon joined by Dale and his boat, and, despite the worry of finding no water source there at the foot of the desolate looking Rubtat el Jamus (Tying of the Buffalo), the Americans prepared to wait out the night, hoping for moderating heat and no insects. Their Arab escorts rejoined them from their trudge up the western shore, and shared some dhom apples, the fruit of the *Spina Christie*, or Thorn of Christ, "which amazingly helped out the supper," wrote Lynch. "I do not know what we should have done without these Arabs; they brought us food when we were nearly famished, and water when parched with thirst. They acted as guides and messengers, and in our absence faithfully guarded the camp. A decided course tempered with courtesy, wins at once their respect and good will. Although they are an impetuous race, not an angry word had thus far passed between us. With the blessing of God, I hope to preserve the existing harmony to the last."[13]

The torrid wind gushed all night.

The next morning, with no provisions and no water, the Americans were back on the lake before 6 with only a few mouthfuls of coffee to get them going. Again, they rounded the great prominence of Masada, seeing more tantalizing stone hints of ancient human activity against those bright, high cliffs. The lieutenant looked across the water to the iron boat, pulling up behind them, and thanks to the refraction of light it seemed to be not just riding high in that saline body but actually elevated above it, even floating over intervening land. His compass glass was encrusted with salt. Despite the high wind, he said, "the tendency to drowsiness was almost irresistible. The men pulled mechanically, with half-closed lids, and except them and myself, every one in the copper boat was fast asleep. The necessity of steering and observing all that transpired, alone kept me awake."

It was like a stupor, almost as if the becalmed lake was beginning to pull them in. Evaporation had produced a thin and transparent but purplish vapor; they seemed to inch through it, and looking far up the lake where purple vapor and blue lake water seemed to blend before the eye, it looked like smoke from burning sulfur. "It seemed," thought Lynch, "a vast cauldron of metal, fused but motionless." He struggled to stay awake, his men drooping over their oars or gaping and unconscious against the gunwales.[14]

But then they were drawing in sight of the white tents of the camp against the unaccustomed lush greenery of Engedi. Lynch saw a camel lying on shore, and two Arabs lounging nearby, and when the Arabs spied the mariners they "rose quickly and came towards the landing, shouting, singing, and making wild gesticulations," said Lynch, "and one of them stooped and picked up a handful of earth and put it upon his head." In his resplendent robes, Sherif Hazza appeared to greet the now roused sailors with joy and relief on his face.

Fresh water and food revived them. Their shore party of Arabs staggered in, finally, although one of their number, having fallen behind, had to be rescued by a horseman bearing a water flask.

A packet of letters forwarded to Beirut via Jerusalem, from American vice-consul Jasper Chasseaud, bore sad tidings, in a Maltese newspaper clipping—it reported the "death of the American president." With no name supplied in the dispatch, explorers incorrectly assumed that President Polk must have expired. Crushed, they lowered their flag to half mast, "and there was a gloom throughout the camp." Lynch scratched some depressed thoughts in his journal, noting that "on that sea the thought of death harmonized with the atmosphere and the scenery, and when echo spoke of it, where all else was desolation and decay, it was hard to divest ourselves of the idea that there was nothing but death in the world, and we the only living." Percy Bysshe Shelley's words from a poem of 1820 slid unbidden into his mind: "Death is here, and death is there, / Death is busy everywhere."[15]

Actually, the reported demise referred to the former president of the United States, John Quincy Adams, who had died of a stroke suffered at the U.S. Capitol just before he was to address the House of Representatives. The 80-year-old sixth president had long been a hero to the enlightened for taking his presidential oath on a law book, instead of the Bible. Despite his one term manacled from a meaningful legacy by Congress, Adams served 17 years in the House as a champion of abolitionism, humane treatment of the native Americans, and the advancement of education and science, particularly astronomy and oceanography. Stricken on February 21, he had lingered for two days in the Speaker's Room before whispering, "this is the last of earth. I am content," and passing on. Had Lieutenant Lynch and his crew known that one of their most sympathetic supporters in Washington had now permanently vacated his Capitol desk, they would have doubly mourned the memory of the president who had envisioned America's astronomical "lighthouses of the sky." Back home, Matthew Maury attended Adams's state funeral and continued to dedicate himself to Adams's memory. For his part, President Polk—accounts of his death having been greatly exaggerated, as Twain would someday say—had barely a year of life left to him and would die from cholera only three months after leaving the White House.

Even under the misapprehension, Lynch would not retain the mood for very long after ordering the blunderbuss to be fired 21 times—"echoes reverberat[ing] loudly and strangely amid the cavernous excesses of these lofty and barren mountains."[16] Going through the dispatches and Vice-Consul Chasseaud's letter, he absorbed the latest news of the revolutions sweeping the capitals of Europe—the abdication of the French king Louis Philippe in favor of his grandson and the declaration of the Second Republic; revolutions igniting the Rhineland, Vienna, Berlin, Milan, Venice; the Austro-Hungarian Empire perhaps beginning to pull apart: the bloody backlash from the old regimes; the inevitable counterforce; as de Tocqueville would comment, "Society was cut in two—those who had nothing united in common envy and those who had anything united in common terror."

"The great Being who wisely rules over all," Lynch wrote exuberantly,

> is doubtless punishing the nations for their sins; but, as His justice is ever tempered with mercy, I have not the smallest doubt that when the ordeal is passed, the result will be beneficial to the human race. The time is coming—the beginning is even now—when the whole worthless tribe of kings, with all their myrmidons, will be swept from their places and made to bear a part in the toils and sufferings of the great human family; when, not in theory only, but in fact, every man will be free and all men politically equal; then, this world will be a happy one, for liberty, rightly enjoyed, brings every blessing with it.[17]

Henry Bedlow, whose life in less than three decades had admitted the study of medicine, law, and literature, but whose sole professional post had been in the august diplomatic reaches of the American ministry at Naples—how easily membership in the Social Register and whom one knew admitted one to the State Department!—was avid to comb all the dispatches and newspapers for word on the political situation in Europe. Revolutionaries all but controlled the island of Sicily after kicking out the troops of the Bourbon king Ferdinand II, while in Naples, Bedlow would have noted, large public demonstrations had forced Ferdinand to appoint a more liberal government. Then and there at Engedi, Bedlow began to compose a long poem about the Revolutions of 1848, with which he would tinker for decades. "Mid palms and cacti bivouacked," he would write about the oasis of Engedi, "Reclused from worldly clark and care / A din of conflict freights the air / And cloistral calm with tumult racked." Writing on a fertile green slope above a bitter sea in the Holy Land, Bedlow would equate the local tales of miracles that inspired one of the world's great religions with the messages of democratization spreading from America and France eastward across Europe: "When freedom like a power divine / Turning the dew that wets the plain/Red with the blood of votaries slain / The water once more changed to wine." Inspired, he would continue to work on the poem at odd moments for the rest of the expedition, when not compiling field notes and impressions for Lieutenant Lynch. The latter would find their way into print considerably before the poem, which would not be issued until Henry Bedlow entered his ninth decade.[18]

Dr. Anderson and young Francis Lynch, the nominal herbalist of the team, went out to collect specimens of a notorious local cork-like sapling with oval leaves, identified as ocher, better known as the Apple of Sodom. It was "fair to the eye and bitter to the taste." Josephus had described ocher most vividly as a reminder of what had happened to the once happy land "both for the fruits it bore and the riches of its cities," when after the destruction those fruits ever after had ashes growing in them, and though the apples "have a color as if they were

fit to be eaten, but if you pluck them with your hands, they will dissolve into smoke and ashes."

That account had been a magnet for visitors for nearly 2,000
years, most of whom had been spiritually awed by the aptness of
nature's metaphor. More recently, the Reverend Edward Robinson had
found the fruit at Engedi—when squeezed even slightly "it explodes
with a puff, like a bladder or puffball, leaving in the hand only the
shreds of the thin rind and a few fibers," seeds attached to silklike
threads the Arabs twisted together as matches, being very combustible.
The samples he bore away self-destructed before he even got to
Jerusalem. Dr. Anderson and Midshipman Lynch gingerly filled four
jars with the specimens, put up in spirits of wine; those jars would
arrive intact for storage at the Patent Office in Washington. The Arabs
told them that the milk of the ripe fruit was a cure for barrenness.[19]

After dinner, feeling the need for a bath, the Americans hiked up
the rough-bottomed ravine, soon slowing to crane their necks toward
the overhead cliffs, where they spied the most intriguing habitations
thus encountered, a number of caves with carefully wrought arched
openings, and, in other places, stone-cased sills and lintels. They were
probably the abodes of the Essenes, or of hermits, or of David, who
dwelt in the wilderness of Engedi while hiding from his jealous royal
father-in-law, Saul, or of Matheno, goatskin-garbed hermit of Engedi
and teacher of John the Baptist. The arched openings compelled
them. "We were at a loss how to obtain an entrance," said Lynch, "for
they were cut in the perpendicular face of the rock, and the lowest
more than fifty feet from the bed of the ravine." More than a century
later, archaeologists would discover a Chalcolithic temple complex
between two springs, built around 3500 BC, and though the nearby
Engedi caves yielded little but broken pottery, in one cave seven miles
away was a horde of ceremonial copper objects—maceheads, scepters,
and crowns sophisticated in their metal workmanship.[20]

Though they began to speculate how they might rig a ladder,
they were distracted by the nearby sound of burbling water and has-

tened ahead. "Far in among the cane," said Lynch elaborately, "embowered, imbedded, hidden deep in the shadow of the purple rocks and the soft green gloom of luxuriant vegetation, lapsing with a gentle murmur from basin to basin, over the rocks, under the rocks, by the rocks, and clasping the rocks with its crystal arms, was this little fountain-wonder." Indeed, "Diana herself could not have desired a more secluded bath than each of us took in a separate basin."[21]

Later, back down at the campsite above the beach, they drank coffee and lemonade, and thought themselves in a kind of paradise. Around sunset, partially for amusement and partly answering the call of science, they led a horse and donkey down to the water's edge to try the flotation experiments done by seemingly every previous visitor to the Dead Sea. One of the most notable occurred in the year AD 68, according to Josephus, when his patron, Emperor Flavius Vespasian, ordered three men who said they could not swim taken out in a boat and, with their hands tied behind them, thrown overboard. Entering the water, instead of sinking they shot upward "as if a wind had forced them upwards" and thereupon the helpless nonswimmers floated, hopefully right-side up.

Much more recently, in 1835 the bestselling travel writer John Lloyd Stephens, whom Lieutenant Lynch had consulted in New York, had written of immersing himself in the Dead Sea. "We lay like a parcel of corks upon its surface," Stephens said, and a horse forced into the water "was afloat, and turned over on his side; he struggled with all his force to preserve his equilibrium, but the moment he stopped moving he turned over on his side again . . . kicking his feet out of water, and snorting with terror."

Nearly two decades later when on his *Innocents Abroad* excursion to the Holy Land, Mark Twain would call it "a funny bath . . . no position can be retained long; you lose your balance and whirl over, first on your back, and then on your face." After an hour in the water, he emerged not only dripping but so encrusted with salt that he shone like an icicle. For the Navy's horse and donkey experiment in 1848,

Lynch's sailors could not see the equines turn over; they floated turned a little to one side. But "a muscular man floated nearly breast-high," noted Lynch, "without the least exertion."[22]

That night there was a salubrious breeze from Judea in the west, but closer to morning, the wind hauled to the north, carrying with it the disquieting smell of sulfur.

CHAPTER TEN

Exploring the Fortress of Masada

In the year 37 BC Herod the Great survived a coup and was restored to rule over Judea by the Roman legions—and named king of the Jews by none other than Mark Antony in Rome. As Herod reestablished his power in Jerusalem, he took the precaution of building a retreat fortress on a mountaintop overlooking the Dead Sea and the border of his ancestral homeland, Idumaea, or Edom, extending southward from the lake. A century earlier the promontory had first been fortified by Jonathan Maccabee, high priest and leader of Judea, who called the stronghold Masada.

In the year 40 Herod had used the Maccabean redoubt to shelter his family when he was forced to flee to Rome to secure protection. Sitting on a plateau some 1,300 feet above the shore, as envisioned by Herod, this thickly walled, towered refuge, with palaces, barracks, armory, storehouses, a temple, baths, and amply engineered water supply and storage, was reachable only by three dangerous and zigzagging, narrow paths—"half goat tracks, half ladders," in the words of one commentator— overlooked by towers and terminating in heavily fortified gates. During the 34-year reign of Herod the Great, it stood as a symbol of his power, and he stayed there often in a sumptuously appointed palace. Far below, the salt sea yielded its oily black asphaltum, and the king shared a monopoly over its extraction with Cleopatra of Egypt—the Egyptians used it to waterproof its fleet.

Masada continued to be garrisoned by Herod's heirs and successors, but in AD 66, as the Jews warred against Rome, a splinter force of Judaic rebels called Sicarii overpowered and slew the Romans and seized the mountaintop fortress. Their numbers grew under the command of Elazar ben Ya'ir, and they were sustained by a large amount of food stored in the warehouses and by cisterns and channels for rainwater, and strengthened by the Roman armory, which was said to be enough for 10,000 soldiers.

In the year 72, though, the Roman governor of Judea, Lucius Flavius Silva, brought his army to Masada and laid siege. Silva had a wall built around the upper periphery of the fortress to keep the Jews from escaping and raised a towering rampart for catapults and other siege machines, and caused an earthen assault ramp to be stretched up along a natural rocky spur, giving the legion and its battering ram a fearsome, 375-foot-high path to the base of the fortress walls. Even so, after three months of battle against the massive force, the Sicarii put up a stalwart resistance, until the legionnaires ignited their last defense line and prepared a final assault.

The next morning, according to the historian Josephus, the Romans strapped on their armor and toppled ladders and bridges against the walls, "but saw nobody as an enemy, but a terrible solitude on every side, with a fire within the place as well as a perfect silence. So they were at a loss to guess at what had happened."

Soon enough, they had their answer. Under Elazar's exhortation, the 936 Sicarii defenders had chosen mass suicide for all, men, women, and children—with heads of households to murder their families, and then 10 officers chosen by lot to slay them, and so on, until finally the one remaining killed himself. The Romans found a small group of survivors who had hidden themselves in a cistern rather than succumb to their fellows' swords—two women and five children—who described the bloody night—and inside Herod's palace they "met with the multitude of the slain," wrote Josephus, "but could take no pleasure in the fact, though it were done to their enemies. Nor could they do other than wonder at the courage of their resolution and the immovable contempt of death, which so great a number of them had shown."[1]

In 1838, as the biblical scholar Edward Robinson was preparing for his monumental exploration, his collaborator, the Reverend Eli Smith of Beirut, revealed his ardent belief that the deserted ruins overlooking the Dead Sea, unvisited by any Westerners and barely any Easterners, and known by local Arabs as Sebbeh, might in fact be the storied Masada chronicled by Flavius Josephus.

When the pair finally got to Engedi, none of the local inhabitants had any direct knowledge of the mysterious and inaccessible place, although one of their Rashayideh guides claimed to have once been there. Robinson could only scramble to the cliff top above Engedi and train his telescope on the ruins, but he devoted several pages in his popular 1841 book to retelling the Josephus account. This inspired an American missionary, the Yale- and Andover-trained Samuel W. Wolcott, and an English artist, William J. Tipping, who was to illustrate a new translation of Josephus, to climb the mountain and minutely explore the ruins in 1842. The first printed account of the ghostly Masada appeared in Robinson's little theological journal.[2]

Of course, Dr. Robinson's exhortations were still in Lieutenant Lynch's ears on the morning of Saturday, April 29, as they arose from their bedrolls at Engedi. They might have been thus far stymied from peering inside those inaccessible caverns of David and the Hermit of Engedi, but Lieutenant Dale and Dr. Anderson had studied the cliffs from the lake surface and were eager to go to Masada. With his perennially weak ankle, there was no question of Lynch making the ascent, a frustration to the 47-year-old officer whose every fiber of being was attached to the expedition of his lifetime.

The fortress explorers—Dale, Anderson, and the adventurous young New Yorker, Henry Bedlow, who since Beirut had served, for want of an alternative, as the poet in residence for the expedition— headed south down the beach astride horses, accompanied by a few Arabs leading a camel bearing a supply of drinking water. Bedlow's journal would be the primary source for Lieutenant Lynch's account of the day's journey.

Their path down the strand was so rough that Bedlow and Dale decided that only Arabian horses could have negotiated the chaotic debris fields of rocks, sized from pebbles to packing crates, which had tumbled from the cliffs above; any other steeds would have broken their legs, or thrown their riders down to sure injury among the sharp rocks. They reached the ravine called Wady Sebbeh just after 8 a.m., and were surprised to find their path down the beach smoothed by an old Roman road, some 15 feet wide and bordered by parallel rows of stones, which allowed for easy traveling for at least a quarter mile. By 9 they had come to the ravine called Wady Seyal and could go no further with the horses, which they left picketed and guarded by one of the Arabs outside the entrance to a low cave.

Masada's mountain rose from their feet into the sky. Lieutenant Lynch considered the massif from his copper boat, and his description similarly struck Bedlow, Dale, and Anderson standing at the foot, craning their necks in preparation for the climb: "There was that peculiar purple hue of its weather-worn rock," Lynch noted, "a tint so like that of coagulated blood that it forced the mind back upon its early history, and summoned images of the fearful immolation of Eleazar and the nine hundred and sixty-seven Sicarii, the blood of whose self-slaughter seemed to have tinged the indestructible cliff for ever."[3]

Then, in rising heat, they addressed the heights, climbing hand over hand up a serpentine pathway, gaining a purchase for feet in numerous holes in the rocky cliff, resorting often to hands and knees. Bedlow, who had primed himself on the old Jewish history, identified

Ancient Hebrew fortress of Masada, from Lieutenant Dale's
sketch, showing the explorers' boats with sails raised.

the route as "the serpent path" mentioned by Josephus—"resembling," the historian had written, "that animal in its narrowness and perpetual windings; for it is broken off at the prominent precipices of the rock, and returns frequently into itself, and, lengthening again by little and little, hath much to do to proceed forward, and he that would walk along it, must first go on one leg and then on the other; there is also nothing but destruction, in case your feet slip, for on each side there is a vastly deep chasm and precipice."[4]

Finally they gained the shoulder of the mountain. The Americans and their Arab escorts were then perched on the edge of Jeshimon—the Old Testament word meant devastation—the blasted crags and waste of the Judean desert, with the salt sea a thousand feet below them, reflective heat climbing to engulf them. There from the brink they found a knifelike, chalky ridge that led them through painfully glaring light further upward from the height of the Seyal ravine up the perpendicular face of Masada's head—one writer would remark that

"Masada is the Gorgon's head magnified to a mountain."[5]

They were now 1,300 feet above the sea. From its northernmost crown, ruins of Herod's casemate wall, originally consisting of a line of vaulted chambers within fortified parallel walls, ran along the edge of the summit, enclosing the plateau, with evidence of tower emplacements. A gateway with a Byzantine pointed arch beckoned, its keystone and voussoirs of carefully hewn stone, "curiously marked with Greek delta-shaped figures," they noted, "and others resembling the planetary symbol of Venus, some upright and some reversed, and others again with rude crosses and the unfinished letter T." Through the gateway they passed, and emerged into the bright light of the open fortress, the enclosed plateau for the most part blasted bare and sterile-soiled, some three-fourths of a mile long north to south, and a quarter-mile east to west.[6]

At the northernmost edge of the summit, they stood atop the rubble of a great palace, with administrative chambers, long and narrow storerooms, and elaborate underground Roman baths and sweat rooms not to be uncovered for five quarters of a century. What they could see were "fragments of walls with circular recesses of tessellated brickwork, arched doorways, and mullioned windows, partly surrounding an enclosure which was perhaps the courtyard or quadrangle of the castle." Now it was "filled with rubbish, fragments of marble, mosaic, and pottery." There, looking down the cliffs into dizzying depths, they were struck by the sight a hundred feet below on a trio of inaccessible ledges, of ruins of what would be identified as Herod's personal quarters, or winter palace—"ruins of a round tower," Bedlow noted in their report, "and forty or fifty feet below that, on another ledge, the foundation walls of a square enclosure, with a triangular wall abutting with the angles of its base upon the walls of the circular tower, and the west side of the square enclosure." Window openings had been cut into the bare face of the cliffs in several places, later revealed to be above deep cisterns.

Their steps on that plateau took them to the western edge, past footings of towers and the ruins of a synagogue facing the direction of Jerusalem. Nearby were the walls of a Byzantine Christian church built by monks in the fifth century AD, with a striking arched window opening. They could not resist clambering up to peer through it, realizing then that they had seen the arch passing in the lifeboats. "From thence," they noted, "the sea could be seen throughout its whole extent, its northern and southern extremities clearly defined, even through the haze which overhung them. The configuration of the peninsula lay distinctly . . . and bore some resemblance to an out-spread wing."

Beyond the church was the tumble of stones of yet another large palace, with apartments and administrative rooms; ruins of several small palaces lay still farther on. On the brink of the western edge, looking down below the cliff they could clearly see the circumvallation wall erected by the Roman engineers of Flavius Silva at the beginning of their great siege of the zealot holdouts, and the rectangular ruins of several legionnaires' camps, and the extraordinary line of the assault ramp raised on a natural promontory, upon which the Roman battering rams had been dragged for the final assault. "It was," said the Reverend Samuel W. Wolcott, the first Westerner to explore Masada only six years earlier at the behest of Edward Robinson, "also a stupendous illustration of the Roman perseverance that subdued the world, which could sit down so deliberately in such a desert, and commence a siege with such a work . . . and which could scale such a fortress."[7] Dale, Anderson, and Bedlow stood now in about the same spot, awed by the view so well described by Wolcott and Flavius Josephus, equally able to imagine the Jewish slaves toiling on the siege ramp, the campfires and torches of the besiegers, the catapult-launched boulders, the swish of incendiaries arcing through the night, as any of the thousands of pilgrims who more than a century later would stand in awe at the idea of the fierce legionnaires and the even more determined zealot holdouts. And the story would continue to compel. In nine years, the broken and disheartened Herman Melville, feeling that a literary pilgrimage to the Holy Land might repair his ailments, would stir the waters of the Dead Sea and write these lines of Masada ("until late, but hawk and kite / Visited the forgotten site") for his greatest failure, the 118,000-word epic poem, *Clarel*:

> *The Maccabees' Masada true;*
> *Stronghold which Flavian arms did rend,*
> *The Peak of Eleazer's end,*
> *Where patriot warriors made with brides*
> *A martyrdom of suicides.*[2]

Near the southern edge they followed "a perilous track along the face of the rock, which could not have been less than 1,000 feet in perpendicular height above the chasm," and descended upon a wide shelf or platform with a great litter of masonry and rubbish tumbled from the cliff overhead. They found a cave-like entrance, and, descending a flight of stone steps, beheld what could only be a large cistern hewn into the rock, fed by narrow aqueducts and measuring 30 feet long, 30 deep, and 15 broad, all its surfaces still covered with a white cement. Josephus had written that Herod's royal engineers "had cut many and great pits, as reservoirs for water" collected at the heads of the ravines in the rainy season, "out of the rocks, at every one of the places that were inhabited, both above and around the palace and before the wall; and by this contrivance, he endeavored to have water for several uses, as if there had been fountains there." It would be estimated that hundreds of thousands of cubic meters of water could have been stored atop Masada, enough for a large garrison and royal retinue, sufficient for nearly 1,000 zealots during a months-long Roman siege. Untended, the waterworks were now dry as one would have expected in such a desert region.

Near the entrance they found another, smaller flight of steps, which did not quite reach a window opening hung high on the wall. Greatly intrigued, they notched places in the stone for hands and feet and edged up to clamber inside a low cave; a window opened out onto the stomach-wrenching view into the depth of the Wady Senin. Rough crosses were splayed on the walls with red paint. Tracks of cloven feet crossed the dusty floor—that of a small wild goat.

Back outside, they tried to keep on a zigzag descending path along the southern edge of the fortress, but the rocks underfoot kept dislodging and bouncing away and out into "the fearful dizzy depth below." They turned around and carefully climbed back. Six years before, a more confident Samuel Wolcott inched his way down the path to the bottom and found himself at the entrance to a ravine, "walled in on three sides by rocky ramparts, their somber craggy peaks frowning above, while torn and disjointed masses from them strewed the bed of the valley." Wanting to circle the great rock, he continued to explore for the next hour but was suddenly "arrested by the shouts of our Arabs on the cliff behind me, calling and beckoning to me to return. The reason I soon discovered in the appearance of three wild Bedawin with clubs, whom they had noticed, who accosted me with a demand for a *bakshish*, which however they showed no disposition to enforce. This of course put an end to farther observations in that quarter."[10] Wolcott not only wrote well of his adventures; during his long ecclesiastical career in New England and the Midwest, he would write some 200 hymns, including "Goodly Were Thy Tents, O Israel."[11]

After the Americans retreated from the hazardous path, they headed back following the eastern casemate wall past more cisterns, and what later, more educated study would show to be the ruins of a ritual bath, or *mikvah*, and towers, and dwelling houses; a small disorder of walls and rubble visible almost in the center of the plateau would be revealed as a Roman columbarium, the garrison's funerary repository for burial urns. Finding little shade on that blasted mountaintop, they stopped to sketch the sea and take a number of instrument bearings in a deathly silence broken only by the sound of wind. Young Henry Bedlow, scion of New York and Newport privilege, who for decades would live in his own castle, Malbone, gently scented by the salt breezes of Long Island Sound, and would three times deign to serve as mayor of Newport, would never forget the sights he recorded while picking his way over the rubble of Herod's palace and pausing at the scarred and pockmarked fortress wall, enveloped by the Judean heat and the Dead Sea's glare.[12]

Then they retraced their way down the serpent path to the boulder-strewn coastal plain. As they rejoined their Arab guides and mounts at the cave, the escorts asked if the day's expedition had been "acceptable." "These people believe," Lynch would explain, "that we come here to search for treasure or to visit places we consider holy."

The exhausted fortress explorers got back to the camp at Engedi at sunset, to find Lieutenant Lynch and their companions refreshed from the furnace heat by a bath up in the oasis pool and satisfied from a day in which his men had continued their soundings of the sea floor from the *Fanny Skinner* and he had caught up on his journal. "This Sea is wondrous," he had scrawled, "in every sense of the word; so sudden are its changes, and so different the aspects it presents, as to make it seem as if we were in a world of enchantment. We were alternately upon the brink and the surface of a huge, and sometimes seething caldron."[13] He had also written several letters destined for the outside world, including one to the patron of that wondrous expedition. In a detailed letter to Navy Secretary John Young Mason, his first since the explorers were finishing their descent of the Jordan, Lynch said that they had made a number of scientific discoveries of undoubted interest and import, and refuted a stack of myths, though, he added, his "hopes had been strengthened into conviction, and I feel sure that the results of this survey will fully sustain the scriptural account of the destruction of the cities of the plain." As was common even to many enlightened men, he worked backward from scientific observations to arrive at a predetermined goal—measuring, then, to a seemingly precise and eminently satisfying point of faith.

Mindful of the dangers experienced by his predecessors, they had remained on guard, but Lynch wanted to honor the deaths of the Irishman Costigan and the Englishman Molyneux by naming the two extreme points of the peninsula (to his knowledge never named by the local people) after them. He would also name the deep bay between the northern tip of the peninsula and the eastern shore "Mason's Bay," in honor of the U.S. naval secretary who had supported his expedition.[14]

But thank goodness, he wrote to Mason, "with the Arabs, we are on the most friendly terms," and no doubt due to their presence, save for two false alarms, they had been undisturbed by the local tribes. "I scarce know what we could have done without the Arabs," he added. "They bring us food when nearly famished, and water when parched with thirst. They act as guides & messengers, and in our absence faithfully guard our tents, bedding & clothes. A decided course, taken upon with constancy, wins at once their respect & good will. Although they are an impetuous race, not an angry word has thus far passed between us. With the blessing of God, I hope to preserve the existing harmony to the last."[15]

CHAPTER ELEVEN

The Eastern Shore of Moab

SUNDAY, APRIL 30, LIEUTENANT LYNCH LET HIS PARTY SLEEP IN, in recognition of the Sabbath. It would be another hot day: he recorded a temperature of 84 degrees at only 6:30 a.m.. When the sun's heat and glare and the flies finally stirred the men from their bedrolls, they saw that the night's wind and surf had driven their boats broadside, higher on the beach.

Given the morning off, most retreated into the shade of the ravine, but the lieutenant could not rest his own apprehensions. "Thus far all, with one exception"—a sailor had been incapacitated for a few days with an intestinal complaint—"had enjoyed good health, but there were symptoms which caused me uneasiness," Lynch would write. "The figure of each one had assumed a dropsical appearance"— an almost disfiguring retention of fluids, or edema—in which "the lean had become stout, and the stout almost corpulent; the pale faces had become florid, and those which were florid, ruddy; moreover, the slightest scratch festered, and the bodies of many of us were covered with small pustules. The men complained bitterly of the irritation of their sores, whenever the acrid water of the sea touched them." Lynch would have been alarmed to know that about the only disease that featured edema, pustules, and skin ulcers was cutaneous anthrax—the sixth plague in the book of Exodus—as theoretically they had been at risk since landing, given their exposure to the number of goats and sheep, meat, and hide products like blankets and Bedouin tents. Luckily for the lieutenant, the thought of a scourge of anthrax did not occur to him, for had that been the case many of the sailors would never get to see their home shores again—Dr. Pasteur was at that moment teaching physics in Dijon and more than two decades from finding a vaccine for anthrax (as well as smallpox and rabies). For the American sailors, Dr. Anderson and possibly Henry Bedlow with his limited medical training might have sought out purgatives or diuretics for the swellings of dropsy, but there was nothing nearby. The local Ta'amirah people told them that 10 years before, the short-lived conqueror Ibrahim Pasha had sent legions of Egyptian peasants to colonize the Ghor Valley, with at least 3,000 being settled on the shores of the Dead Sea. "Every one died within two months," Lynch heard, hoping the story was exaggerated. "Dejection of spirits, and scarcity of food, must have been the great destroyers." The flock of myths about a Dead Sea miasma seemed to be exactly that—mythological. In any case, seeing that all the men had good appetites, Lynch and his medics decided to wait and see, hoping for the best.

The arrangement with their Bedouin protectors, made 10 days before when 'Akil left them on the northwestern shore and led his men on a diplomatic mission to see their cousin tribe in Kerak, was that 'Akil would contact them on that day, so it was necessary to cross the lake once again. "I felt sure," said Lynch, "that he would not fail us." Shortly past noon, the explorers gathered on the beach and pushed off in the two lifeboats. Noble Sherif stayed with their equipment, horses, and camels at Engedi, with his small retinue and with the two Turkish soldiers, who tended toward invisibility but seemed to keep marauders at bay. Sherif would begin to move the campsite back up shore to a new rendezvous at Ein Turabeh in three days and wait for Lynch there. Once the boats were out from the beach, the

Warrior of the Ta'amirah tribe, guides of the south-western shore.

sun and intense heat enveloped them; feeling a light breeze from the south, Lynch decided to give the oarsmen a rest and ordered the canopies taken down and the sails hoisted. They glided forward, with

a light tapping of the ripples at the bow, and a faint line of foam and bubbles at her side [said Lynch, at the tiller of the copper boat] were the only indications that the boat was in motion. The *Fanny Skinner* was a mile astern and all around partook of the stillness of death. The weather was intensely hot, and even the light air that urged us almost insensibly onward had something oppressive in its flaws of heat. The sky was unclouded, save by a few faint cirri in the north, sweeping plume-like, as if the sun had consumed the clouds, and the light wind had drifted their ashes. The glitter from the water with its multitude of reflectors,

247

for each ripple was a mirror, contributed much to our discomfort, yet the water was not transparent, but of the color of diluted absinthe, or the prevailing tint of a Persian opal. The sun, we felt, was glaring upon us, but the eye dared not take cognizance, for the fierce blaze would have blighted the powers of vision, as Semele was consumed by the unveiled divinity of Jove.

The black chasms and rough peaks, embossed with grimness, were around and above us, veiled in a transparent mist, like visible air, that made them seem unreal, and, 1,300 feet below, our sounding-lead had struck upon the buried plain of Siddim, shrouded in slime and salt.

In the two boats, everyone but Lynch in the *Fanny Mason* and Lieutenant Dale at the tiller of the iron boat had fallen into a deep stupor. Lynch was filled with awe and dread:

As I looked upon the sleepers, I felt the "hair of my flesh stand up," as Job's did, when "a spirit passed before his face," for, to my disturbed imagination, there was something fearful in the expression of their inflamed and swollen visages. The fierce angel of disease seemed hovering over them, and I read the forerunner of his presence in their flushed and feverish sleep. Some, with their bodies bent and arms dangling over the abandoned oars, their hands excoriated with the acrid water, slept profoundly; others, with heads thrown back, and lips cracked and sore, with a scarlet flush on either cheek, seemed overpowered by heat and weariness even in sleep; while some, upon whose faces shone the reflected light from the water, looked ghastly, and dozed with a nervous twitching of the limbs, and now and then starting from their sleep, drank deeply from a beaker and sank back again to lethargy. The solitude, the scene, my own thoughts, were too much; I felt, as I sat thus, steering the drowsily-moving boat, as if I were a Charon, ferrying, not the

Lisan, the Dead Sea peninsula on the eastern shore, several decades after the expedition. (*Matson Collection, Library of Congress*)

souls, but the bodies, of the departed and the damned, over some infernal lake, and could endure it no longer.

He had to shake himself free of the dread as well as the creeping lethargy. "Breaking from my listlessness," Lynch said, "I ordered the sails to be furled and the oars resumed—action seemed better than such unnatural stupor." His shout roused the men in both boats. "Prudence urged us to proceed no farther, but to stop," he noted, "before some disaster overtook us. But the thought of leaving any part of our work undone was too painful, and I resolved to persevere—but to be as expeditious as possible without working the party too hard."[2]

Off the newly named "Point Costigan," the northern tip of the peninsula, at 4:45 p.m., a sounding found the depth to be 24 fathoms with a hard bottom. The boats steered across the little bay toward the shore fringed with low cane and scraggly bushes, overhung by the beetling red sandstone mountains of Moab. They spotted a few Arabs, and, preparing for hostilities, made directly for them, hoping they were friends. To his relief, Lynch recognized one of his Bedouin party,

Jum'ah, of the tribe El Hasseé, accompanied the explorers.

Jum'ah. The Americans established a bivouac on the beach near a shallow stream emerging from the Wady Beni Hammad while Jum'ah related their story via the Syrian interpreter, Ameuny.

The sheikh's party had only arrived at Kerak the previous day, having had its share of troubles. Camping on the way to Kerak with the allied tribe of Beni Sukr, they had a surprise attack in the night by a force of a hostile tribe, the Beni 'Adwan, and, being strongly outnumbered, 'Akil ordered a retreat, losing his baggage and a camel to the raiders. But more friends from the Beni Sukr showed up, and 'Akil led a retributory attack. Fighting grew fierce over a couple of hours. Some 22 of the Adwans were wounded or killed, including the son of that tribe's sheikh, whose highly prized rifle was awarded to one of 'Akil's force, young Sherif Masa'ad, nephew of Sherif Hazza, "for his gallantry in the action." Two of 'Akil's men were injured—the Nubian took two wounds, one from a sword and one from gunshot—and 10 of the Ben

Sukr comrades were also hurt. But the victory had been sweet, and the Bedouins were in an improved mood as they finished their ascent to the mountaintop fortress of Kerak and a feast in their honor.[3]

Listening to Jum'ah as the adventurers established their camp, scouted for firewood among the acacias, and erected tents and awnings as shelter from a sirocco, Lynch was light-headed and nauseated from heat prostration, "the sun having been pouring on my unsheltered back for some hours while steering the boat." But after he picked his way up the Wady Beni Hammad to find a pool, this sheltered by fragrant oleanders three times a man's height and in full bloom, he was "wonderfully refreshed."

Afterward, he learned much from Jum'ah about the local situation in Moab. There was an Arab village, Mezra'a, a few miles away, being, it was thought, close to the ruins of the biblical city of Zoar, the sole survivor of the five cities of the plain of Siddim, where Lot and his daughters took shelter in a cave. Lynch thought that the "curse" of ancestrous lineage seemed evident in these *fellahin* Moabites, who were generally considered to be of the Ghaurariyeh tribe; darker-complected and more wiry-haired, of shorter and sparer builds, they had "low receding foreheads, and the expression of countenance is half sinister and half idiotic."

Abd' Allah, the Christian sheikh of Mezra'a, "mild even to meekness."

The sheikh of the village paid a call on Lynch, while villagers offered sour milk from apparently unwashed goatskins and some palatable flour made of the dhom apple. The sheikh told Jum'ah that when he saw the two boats being rowed across the upper bay, he gathered all his followers and began to work them up to an attack on the Americans but changed his mind when he saw the strangers hail Jum'ah as a friend. "It would have been a matter of regret," noted Lynch, "had they fired upon us; for, although we would most certainly have defeated them, there must have been blood shed, and it was my most earnest wish to accomplish the objects of the expedition without injury to a human being." Jum'ah warned the lieutenant that these people of Mezra'a were dangerous and bore watching through the night.[4]

Less threatening was a deputation of four men from the fortress of Kerak. Led by a young man named Sulieman, son of the sheikh, they surprised the Americans with the singular news that they were fellow Christians and seemed delighted to meet brothers in faith. In Kerak there were two tribes, one Christian and one Muslim, with the latter outnumbering the former and treating them with cruelty. "It was a strange sight," thought Lynch,

> to see these wild Arab Christians uniting themselves to us with such heartfelt cordiality. It would be interesting to trace whether they are some of the lost tribes subsequently converted to Christianity; or the descendants of Christians, who, in the fastnesses of the mountains, escaped the Muhammedan alternative of the Koran or the sword; or a small Christian remnant of the Crusades. At all events their gratification at meeting us was unfeigned and warmly expressed. They felt that we would sympathize with them in the persecutions to which they are subjected by their lawless Muslim neighbors. They had, indeed, our warmest sympathies, and our blood boiled as we listened to a recital of their wrongs. We felt more than ever anxious to visit

Three of the
Christian Arabs at
the Kerak fortress
above the eastern
shore.

Kerak, and judge for ourselves of their condition. Their mode
of salutation approaches nearer to our own than that of any
other tribe we met; they shake hands, and then each kisses the
one he had extended.[5]

Whether this tribe truly looked different than the Arabs of
Mezra'a, or whether Lynch imagined it because of the religious affin-
ity, he noted that "their features are fuller and more placid in expression, and they seem more vigorous, manly, and intelligent than the
Raschayideh and Ta'amirah of the Judean shore." He asked one of the
tribesmen to fetch mounts for his party to visit Kerak. In the night,
with guard doubled, he had the thermometer checked hourly, as the
temperature surprisingly dropped from 82 degrees down to 70, when
"the air felt uncomfortably cold, so much had we been relaxed by the
sirocco." In the sky above the cliffs of Moab, meteors plummeted
from the zenith northward, but one, peculiarly, "seemed to drop

directly down, with less than the usual velocity," noted Lynch. "It was very bright, and resembled falling fire-flakes from a discharged rocket."[6]

The Americans gleaned more information about the tensions between the Muslim and Christian Arabs of Kerak the next day, Monday, May 1, when deputations rode down the mountain with horses and mules for the visitors. The parties were first spied by Lynch, who had gone up to the ruins of Zoar, refuge of misery, ignominy, and incest for the grieving Lot and his daughters, where he picked across mounds and rubble, foundations and pedestals without columns hidden within thickets of cane and tamarisk; the area corresponded to that mentioned by the British Royal Navy officers, Irby and Mangles, some 30 years earlier in their published journal of travel through the Arab world. Lynch had seen acres of tiny pottery shards, and pocketed a worn old hand mortar, when he saw the line of horses and mules threading downhill, so he awaited them on the plain. A dark Muslim with long black hair, beard and moustache, and fiercely bright, shifty eyes, told him he was Muhammed, son of the sheikh of the Kerakiyeh—about 30 years of age, and in Lynch's quick estimation, arrogant and overbearing. His older companion, the Christian sheikh Abd' Allah, was stocky and "mild even to meekness," giving clear evidence of "a long series of oppression on one side and submissive endurance on the other," thought Lynch. 'Akil had sent a note, apologizing for not welcoming the Americans himself due to fatigue of the Bedouin's own mounts, urging the explorers to the hospitality of his brother sheikh in the mountaintop town.

Down at the campsite, the newcomers were dumbfounded, even agitated, by the sight of the beached metal boats, shining in the sunlight though now considerably corroded below the waterline. To show them off, one was carried down to the shore and the prospect of rides proffered; the haughty Muhammed showed much interest in the craft until he understood the invitation, at which point he stonily refused, so several of his companions tentatively climbed aboard. "I was disposed to think that he was a very coward after all," the lieutenant commented. Sailors rowed the boat a little distance out into the lake before returning, and when the Arabs had hastily disembarked, noted Lynch, "they stuck plugs of onions into their nostrils, to counteract the malaria they had imbibed from the sea. They call it 'the sea accursed of God,' and, entertaining the most awful fears respecting it, looked upon us as madmen for remaining so long upon it."[7]

The ride up to Kerak being steep and difficult, they resolved to depart early the next morning, leaving several of the party to guard the boats and gear, including the American sailor who seemed perpetually in frail health. After sunset from afar they heard the wild ululation of the mountain Arabs—a song of welcome or of defiance depending on the context, which Lynch likened to the yodels of the Swiss Tyrol—and soon more Kerakiyeh bearing rifles and 18-foot tufted spears rode proudly into camp, still singing the war cry. Kinsmen of the sheikh, they nodded, dismounted, and made themselves at home around the campfire.

The wind had quickened after nightfall, bearing tidings of another sirocco along with a dew so heavy that it collected on the two boat awnings strung over the recumbent Americans and began to drip through. Lynch, however, could neither relax nor sleep. "The conduct of Muhammed," he wrote,

> amounting almost to impudence, filled me with distrust. He had come down with about eight men, his brother with fourteen more, and by two and three at a time they had been dropping in ever since, until, at 9 P. M., there were upwards of forty around us; and, if disposed to treachery, there might be many more concealed within the thicket. It seemed as if Muhammed considered us as already in his power, and it occurred to me at times, that

it was my duty, in order to save the lives for which I was responsible, to depart at once.

But he knew he would not give such an order. First, he did not want these local tribes to decide that Americans, "people from another world, of whom they had never heard before," should be held in contempt, endangering any Westerners "who might hereafter sojourn among them." Second, there was his loyalty to the loyal 'Akil, who had undertaken such a hazardous journey around the north and east of the sea in territory of tribes with whom he might have only a tenuous connection; he had offered protection and vouched for the Americans. Certainly he would lose face if they were to take their boats and depart. Finally, Lynch was worried more about his men's health in that punishing climate: they would benefit from even a single day in mountain air at Kerak, he figured. "I preferred," he decided, "the risk of an encounter with the Arabs to certain sickness upon the sea, with its result, unaccomplished work."[8]

The wind calmed before daybreak and the temperature cooled somewhat. Lynch woke everyone at 4 a.m. for a frugal breakfast and an early start. Looking uneasily at the enlarged number of Kerakiyeh, one of the Christian Arabs, the son of their sheikh, sidled over to the lieutenant and whispered a confirmation he had not dared to make at night: the Muslims had indeed planned to attack the Americans and had at least 20 more warriors surrounding them in the darkness waiting for a signal—60 antagonists in all. But the explorers were too well armed, with breech-loading, rapid-fire carbines with bayonets, some swords, and those evil-looking pistols with bowie knives attached to the barrels, not to forget the blunderbuss with two sailors and an officer on watch through the night. Lynch warned his men not to let up their guard during the journey. Minus those detailed to watch the boats, the Americans had 14 in number, along with the interpreter and the cook, and their escort of 12 mounted Bedouins and 8 footmen. Also on their side was the base cowardice and braggadocio of the Arab leader Muhammed. One look at the mountains frowning overhead had told him that there was a rough climb in front of them, and they would have to be on guard from ambush every step of the way as they headed toward perhaps the most impregnable fortress in the Holy Land.

Kerak was closely identified with the Crusaders, freed of their control in the successful siege by the Muslim forces of Saladin in 1189 after the arrogant and perfidious Christian lord Reynauld of Chatillon had broken treaties, raided caravans on the nearby King's Highway from Damascus to Egypt, and dared to threaten the holy city of Mecca itself. The tall, imposing castle had been erected in the 1140s above

Kerak, the Crusader Castle in Moab, as photographed decades after the Lynch party's visit. (*Matson Collection, Library of Congress*)

ancient Moabite and Nabatean fortifications by the French Payen le Boutellier, or Pagan the Butler, courtier to King Baldwin II of Jerusalem and lord of the province of Oultre Jourdain (Trans-Jordan).

Three thousand seventy feet above the level of the Mediterranean Sea on a mountaintop plateau, a day's journey north from its predecessor capital, Montreal, Kerak stood to enrich its lord by commanding tolls on the King's Highway as well as tribute from the scattered Bedouin goatherders of Moab. Successors to Payen had added projecting towers and gouged deep rock trenches and a moat to the north and south. These fortifications had seemed sufficient to repel Saladin's army in 1183 during his first attempt to punish Reynauld, though that assault on Kerak had not been total; Saladin had learned that the castle was sheltering newlyweds, Isabella of Jerusalem, the 11-year-old royal half-sister to Baldwin IV, and Humphrey IV of Toron, Reynauld's 16-year-old stepson. Rather than disturb such a well-connected honeymoon suite, Saladin had chivalrously directed that his siege machines hurl their boulders at other parts of the castle, and he had withdrawn as Baldwin's army approached. But after decimating the Crusader army at the Horns of Hattin in 1189, and having his personal retribution on Reynauld by beheading his defiant prisoner, however, Saladin could at his leisure mount a most satisfying and successful attack on the Kerak castle Christian holdouts, who were said to have been forced by siege conditions to sell women and children into slavery, for food. For the next six centuries Kerak had stood, imperturbable under Muslim rule, strengthened by lords such as the fierce thirteenth-century Mamluk sultan Baibars of Egypt and Syria. Not until 1840, when the Egyptian general Ibrahim Pasha struck at the Ottoman Empire in Syria, did the walls of Kerak suffer any substantial damage from invaders.

The route to Kerak for Lynch's party lay southward along the base of the cliffs for some two miles before turning inland up the deeply cut, dry ravine known as Wady Kerak, "the steepest and most difficult path," commented Lynch, "with the wildest and grandest scenery we had ever beheld. On one side was a deep and yawning chasm, which made the head dizzy to look into; on the other beetling crags, blackened by the tempests of ages." A light rain had begun falling, but the sliver of sky visible directly overhead quickly blackened with storm clouds and, pelted with heavy rain, they were nearly deafened by thunder claps and reverberations, the cliffs illuminated by lightning, and, far below, a sudden, foaming torrent cascaded down the bed of the wady, carrying gigantic rocks and debris and even whole trees with it. "It was a wild, a terrific, but a glorious sight," wrote Lynch, "and I rejoiced to witness this elemental strife amid these lofty mountains." In his venturesome life he had seen many wonders—had climbed Mounts Etna and Vesuvius, looking "over its brink into the fiery caldron beneath," and had once launched a skiff into the tumult at the base of Niagara during a thunderstorm, "but I never beheld a scene in sublimity equal to the present one."

The rain subsided; the heavy clouds moved off toward the mountains' crest; and their view improved. Now they could see more of the heights ahead and the bottom of the deep ravine just steps away from their very steep, narrow, and zigzagging path—"it pained the eye to look into its dizzy depths," said Lynch. The mountainside was bare, black, and blasted, fossiliferous limestone worn into fantastic shapes and a multiplicity of hollows and caverns—no foliage evident, although as their mounts strained upward and they crossed several tributary streams and paused at a spring, they began to see more and more greenery—large broom bushes, purple hollyhocks, oleanders just beginning to bloom, and scarlet anemones—and also more animal life, including a profusion of doves and partridges, and darting hawks. As they continued upward, they spied tiny patches of cultivated wheat, and the occasional fig or olive tree, which, higher, proliferated into more appreciable groves. At one rest stop, the Kerakiyeh showed off their shooting prowess by firing rifles in turn at a mark; though standing close, within pistol range, they usually missed, and their "powder was so indifferent," the lieutenant wrote, "that one of our sailors contemptuously remarked that a gazelle could run a mile between the flash and the report. They were perfectly astonished at the execution of our rifle."[9]

Finally, as they neared the top of Wady Kerak, the ravine branched into two, and from their place on the trail they could see, perched on the heights between Wady Kerak and Wady Beni Hammad, the hulking sight of the walled town flanked by the stark, towering Crusader castle and the ruins of Sultan Baibar's fortress, all darkly weathered stone standing against the sky, taking the breath away from onlookers. Another half hour consumed by the continuing climb, the castle loomed taller, threateningly, as they neared, appreciating the ease with which it could be defended, and they paused to crane their necks from the base of an escarpment, eyes running up along the dun-colored limestone wall, before trudging the length for some 150 yards, thinking how defenders might drop rocks upon anyone approaching. The path turned directly under the walls into an arched tunnel, at least 30 feet high by 12 wide. Passing deep below Kerak, blundering in darkness for some 80 yards, they finally emerged, blinking and grimacing, into the sunlight-washed market of the town, impressed by the idea that with the exception of the two British officers Irby and Mangles, the German Seetzen, and the Swiss John Lewis Burckhardt three and four decades before, they believed themselves the first Westerners to enter the fortress since the collapse of the Third Crusade, more than six centuries earlier.

Crowds of people stopped and gathered in streets and yards and on housetops, gaping at the sight of the sunburned and blotched Franks from far away, naval uniforms the worse for wear. Lynch would learn that the population of the walled town was about 300 families, three-fourths of them Christians—the men mostly wore sheepskin coats and the women dark-colored gowns with uncovered heads and unconcealed faces, some tattooed; the women and children were "squalid and filthy," Lynch thought, perhaps partially due to the fact that their tiny stone huts bore no windows or chimneys breaking their flat mud-terrace roofs, with interiors blackened by smoke. When the Americans were escorted to their quarters in a council house normally used as the Christian Arabs' schoolroom, they found it to be similarly without comfort or adornment, being empty of furniture, floored in stone and ceilinged with mud, no glass or shutters on the windows and a broken door, which swung open incessantly as curious children pushed inside to stare at the strangers; others jostled at windows.

No food was offered to the hungry travelers, whether from poverty, ignorance, or rudeness, despite the obvious abundance of hundreds of sheep outside the town. Later, the lieutenant learned that the Christian settlement had endured seven years of locust plagues and worse than usual heat waves, and, being greatly outnumbered by the Muslim Arabs, were constantly bullied and shaken down for food and cattle, often going hungry when the nomadic tent-dwelling Bedouins came to town, squatted in the Christians' huts, and devoured all in sight. "Already," Lynch learned, "a great many have been driven away, poverty alone keeping the remainder." He would see ample evidence that to them the local Muslim tribesmen would, in the absence of *bakshish*, barely veil their suspicion and hostility. Famished, the Americans prevailed upon the Christian sheikh and the priest from the church across the way, and obtained enough chicken eggs to make a plain meal.[10]

When they were done, the lieutenant gave leave for all to see what they could of the fortress town, provided some of their number remained with their baggage, so they began tours by turns, guided by the priest, somber in his black turban and gown. His little church was still under construction, the walls rising 12 feet with six pedestals laid for pillars. Inside, a dark, low-vaulted room decorated with a picture of St. George fighting the dragon, and a few partial columns of red granite dragged over from the castle ruins. Lynch found a shop nearby—it seemed to be the only such establishment—and was amused to find the only things for sale were "thin cakes of dried and pressed apricots, and English muslin!"

But what remained of the Crusader castle was truly "magnificent," even "astonishing." Square and squat, of closely laid, hard volcanic stone broken frequently by narrow slits for archers, protected by the gouged-out ravine and entered by five fortified gates, the interior vaulted chambers rose high toward ceilings still decorated with fragments of frescoes—one seemed to be of a female saint. Pilastered and columned walls contained sculpted ornamentation, in places Christian religious symbols bearing chisel scars from Muslim successors, elsewhere floral designs, still elsewhere the figure of a celebrated past warrior (later identified as a relic of the Nabatean kingdom, a century before the commencement of the Christian era). Reached by a circular staircase, there was a Crusader chapel with its altar only partly demolished by invaders, and there were seven storehouses with arched ceilings, and seven deep wells and cemented cisterns, and subterranean kitchens and bakeries amid a warren of subterranean passages, assembly halls, offices, barracks, and crypts. Through a narrow embrasure they could look down the Wady Kerak, "green with fields of grain and grass, and the shrubbery of oleanders, and upon part of the sea in the distance."

They also walked through what was left of Sultan Baibars's fortress astride the northwest corner of the Kerak plateau. This limestone monument of the former Turkish slave—who had revered Saladin and with a cruel, conniving brilliance had united Egypt and Syria against the remaining Crusader kingdoms of Syria and Jerusalem in the thirteenth century—had not withstood the ravages of time as well as the Frankish fortress, despite its 27-foot-thick lower walls—but nevertheless it was imposing. Penetrated by loopholes and with an open ledge running all around, it was supervised by a corniced tower Lynch deemed "handsome," still containing its staircase. From the pinnacle, it would have had a commanding view, most satisfying to that tall sultan of six centuries before, destroyer of Antioch and conqueror of Armenia, assassin of monarchs, whose name was feared far beyond the Syrian mountains and the Mediterranean waters visible from that potent tower.[11]

In the evening during a long conversation, 'Akil was uneasy, filled with apprehension about the Americans' safety on the Moabite plateau. Lynch had hoped to take a curving route back down to the Dead Sea, circling over to the head of another of the eastern shore's great ravines, Wady es Safieh, and descending to its verdant delta. But the sheikh warned against it. "The southern tribes were in a great state of excitement, and were all coming up," Lynch was told, "while those along the coast were gathering together, and . . . a general outbreak might be expected." Something ominous was up—'Akil and his men had already ridden into the hornet's nest—and things were not helped by the fact that the peasantry of the mountains were about to commence their grain harvest, and the local Bedouins were already working themselves up to a fighting frenzy to begin their raids "to sweep it off" from the laboring *fellahin*. The Christian Arabs of Kerak were already feeling doomed over the immediate future. But there was also perceptible discord about the hated Ottoman rule. Lynch sensed that 'Akil was eager for some kind of alliance from the Americans—with him that evening was the prince of his brother-tribe, the Beni Sukr— and 'Akil may have been led into this hope by Lynch's fervent assurance that they were grateful for the Bedouins' intercession, and would have advanced, guns and blunderbuss blazing, had they known that their friends had been attacked earlier by the hostile Beni 'Adwan warriors. But the lieutenant felt he had to make it plain that in the larger scheme of things regarding tribal alliances and relations with the faraway Turkish government, the naval explorers had to remain scrupulously neutral. It was one thing, he decided, to publicize the predicament of the Christian Arabs of Kerak and their pleas for outside funds to finish their humble house of worship, but another to venture deeper into politics. In any event, he assented to the sheikh's caution—even 'Akil planned to return to his home terrain by the roundabout pilgrim route well away from the stirred-up Moabite mountains and Jordan Valley, and not head back west to home until he reached the latitude of the Sea of Galilee. This caution from such a brave and gallant warrior was nothing but impressive.[12]

That night, the Americans stood a board against the door of the council room and lay down with their firearms in their hands, "with a feeling of uncertainty as to what the morrow might bring forth." The Muslim sheikh's unpleasant son, Muhammed, had growled at them all day, wanting "cloaks, a double-barrelled gun, a watch," and so on, noted Lynch, claiming that previous outsiders coming up from Egypt had always given presents. "Where did *you* come from," Muhammed complained, "thus out of the sea?" Looking ahead to the next day, 'Akil with only four followers, seemed to be running out of diplomatic resources. Militarily, there were more than 700 fighting men nearby in the encampment next to the castle walls, and the outnumbered Christians would be of minimal help. But Lynch, as an official representative of the American government, was firm on the point that they would pay for food, time, equipment, and rentals, but never purchase "forbearance," whether friendship or mere safe passage, really the equivalent of tribute.

They arose stiff from sleeping on the stone floor on a cold mountain-air night—"the north wind whistling through the casement with a familiar sound of home," Lynch wistfully wrote. They were covered with itchy flea bites. The general sentiment was, "we should have stayed on the beach," but the lieutenant was still glad for the healthier, cooler and thinner air on the plateau, sure that it would help restore his dulled and bloated men. Eggs and rice on that Wednesday morning, May 3, put them in a good mood. Then the unsavory Muhammed shouldered in, complaints already spilling out, but Lynch was running out of patience and just pointed the way back outside, to 'Akil. "We would have liked to remain another day for the benefit of the mountain air and to make some examination of the neighborhood," he wrote, "but we were unanimously of opinion that it would be unsafe, the prospect of difficulty with this insolent people increasing with the lapse of every hour." As they rolled up blankets and gear, the surly Muhammed could be seen just below their window at the head of a growing crowd, shouting and gesticulating violently.

It took an inordinate time for their horses to be gathered. The Americans emerged from the building in battle array, carbines unslung, pistols with bowie knives bristling on belts and ammunition bandoliers. 'Akil, his few followers, and the Beni Sukr prince were nearby, as was the kindly old Christian sheikh. Muhammed swaggered up close to Lynch. "I will not go with you," he blurted, and with a sneer asked what the strangers would do if they found 100 men in their path.

"We will take care of ourselves," Lynch countered. The lieutenant longed "to seize him and carry him with us by force as a hostage, but he was surrounded by too many armed and scowling Arabs."

Only the Christian sheikh and three or four villagers were with them when they rode away from the walled town, with Lynch instructing Lieutenant Dale to take the lead while Lynch kept with the rear, keeping the men from lagging behind lest they be cut off. They had barely covered a mile when the volatile Muhammed and some other horsemen thundered up. "I was never more delighted in my life," recalled Lynch, "for we had now the game in our own hands." He ordered an officer and a seaman to stick close by the sheikh's surly son, paying no attention to his comrades, "and shoot him at the first sign of flight or treachery."

Muhammed did not notice the strategy, so intent was he in demanding a watch, then a double-barreled gun, and then various possessions of the westerners, and flinging insults when he was ignored. But reality dawned on him—"whether he rode ahead or tar-

ried behind," Lynch remembered, "he had ever the same companions," and "if he stopped, the march was arrested, and the whole party
stopped also." Realizing he was a hostage, his demeanor went from
being aggressive and importunate to polite and then markedly submissive. As their trail took them downward toward the coastal plain,
and the sea became visible with its blanket of thin mist, Lynch stayed
near Muhammed to keep an eye on him. The party stopped for a
quarter-hour to rest the horses, and, noted Lynch, "when we were
about to remount, he had become so much humbled, that perceiving
my saddle-girth loose, he hastened forward and drew it tight for me.
In the morning he would have cut my throat rather than have performed a menial office."

The sight of frustrated Muhammed, shore-bound and empty-
handed, who would likely remember westerners as stingy and rude as
Lynch would remember the Arabs of Kerak, receded as the two metal
boats put out onto the lake and steered down the bay and then northward along the barren coast, beneath high perpendicular cliffs of red
sandstone. Occasional ravines, some supporting small growths of
cane, appeared, but the general view as they pulled through the hot
afternoon, a slight breeze with them, was slightly forbidding. One of
the seamen, George Overstock, felt increasingly chilled as they neared
the gorge of the River Arnon; "we feared," commented Lynch, "that
the fever which had heretofore attacked all who had ventured upon
this sea, was about to make its appearance." Dr. Anderson began treating him for cholera.[13]

A large brown vulture rode the thermals above the deltaic beach
just outside the Arnon gorge and there they pulled in for the night, at
half past 5. Dale, Aulick, and Lynch went up to take measurements
while the seamen raised canvas on the beach and their Arab cook
readied food. The stream was 82 feet wide and 10 feet deep as it

Wady Mojeb, the
River Arnon of the
Old Testament,
from Dale's sketch.

flowed out of the high red cliffs in a canyon some 97 feet wide. Lynch
was impressed by the variegated appearance of the towering rock,
"worn by the winter rains into the most fantastic forms, not unlike
Egyptian architecture. It was difficult to realize that some were not the
work of art." The riverbank up the canyon was covered with animal
tracks—camels (they found the nearby remnants of a Bedouin camp),
gazelles (the carcass of one stretched out alongside their path), and a
tiger—and they saw castor plants, tamarisks, and cane. To hear the
reverberations, Lynch fired his pistol into the air, which launched
flocks of birds into alarmed flight, swirling above their heads as the
sun declined toward the cliffs over Engedi, on the opposite lakeshore.
Most of the Americans bathed in the cool waters of the River Arnon,
ancient northern borderline of the Moabites; they drank tea and ate
some rice, and slept comfortably on the beach below bright stars.

CHAPTER TWELVE

From the River Zerka
to Ain Feshka

IN THE 37TH YEAR OF HIS REIGN (4 BC), KING HEROD THE GREAT, builder of the second temple of Jerusalem, of Masada, of the Judean mountain fortress of Herodium; and "slaughterer of the innocents"— referring to the baby boys in the village of Bethlehem as he sought the life of Jesus, feared infant-king of the Jews—as well as executor of his own sons, wives, mother-in-law, brothers-in-law, courtiers, allies, and subjects; and war-maker against Nabatea and other neighbors; being in the terminal stage of a loathsome disease, which seems to have been chronic kidney disease complicated by gangrene and scabies, whose corpse-like breath would soon cease at Jericho, was conveyed to the eastern shore of the Dead Sea, a short distance from his lavish mountaintop palace and stronghold, Machaerus, where in some desperation he was lowered into the medicinal baths of the hot springs of Callirhoe, above the River Zerka Ma'in, though the waters—fortunately—had no effect.

His son and heir of the lands of Galilee and Perea, Herod Antipas, lived in emulation of Herod's ambition and paranoia, building his capital at Tiberias, fortifying Machaerus so it could support 500 for a five-year siege, ruling as fiercely and lusting nearly as ardently as his father, casting aside his first wife in preference for his half-brother's spouse, a kinswoman named Herodias, with whom he repaired to lofty, splendid Machaerus overlooking the salt sea. Learning that his marital gambit was being publicly condemned as against Jewish law by John, son of Zachariah and Elizabeth, preacher and baptizer on the lower banks of the River Jordan, and prophet of the ascension of Jesus of Nazareth as messiah, Antipas arrested John the Baptist, fearing as always a fomented rebellion, and imprisoned him in the dungeons of Machaerus. There, encouraged by new wife Herodias and her dancing daughter Salome, Antipas had the Annunciator, as John was also known, beheaded.[1]

Nearly two millennia later, at the foot of the blasted, ruin-strewn mountain of Machaerus, a handful of American sailors waded up the River Zerka Ma'in for about a mile from its outlet on the Dead Sea, their commander, Lieutenant Lynch, periodically dunking a thermometer. The stream was 12 feet wide and 10 inches deep, rushing quickly southward, and it was 94 degrees; the lake they had just left was only 78 degrees. The further upstream they walked, past date palms and canes, the warmer it got, approaching the temperature of human blood. Had the Lynch party ascended high enough, as did, for instance, the British explorers Irby and Mangles in 1818, or, indeed, their countryman, the intrepid Canon of Durham H. B. Tristram in 1872, the sailors would have found the 10 hot springs of Callirhoe, some tumbling right out of the cliff face and cascading down yellow towers of sulfur deposits into successive pools, 130-degree water mixing with the Zerka to the place where a scabrous, worm-ridden potentate could be eased into the stream without being parboiled. Lynch would have seen a large amount of broken tiles and pottery scattered beneath the hot springs, Herodian relics, but he and his companions saw enough to satisfy them where they were, standing below cliffs some 80 feet high, and then immersed themselves in the tepid clear water. "I could not," he said, "with my feet against a rock, keep from being carried down the stream; and, walking where it was but two feet deep, could, with difficulty, retain a foothold with my shoes off." The sulfury water soothed their many sores.[2]

The Bedouins of Kerak had warned Lynch that he and his men were in danger every time they sallied forth on the pestilential waters of the Sea of Lot. As they had rowed and sailed up the northeastern shore early that morning, the lieutenant feared for his men, not only the feverish George Overstock, but seaman Hugh Read; he seemed to be slipping down that same slope of indisposition, in his case a painful fistula that Dr. Anderson could only treat topically against the eventual need for surgery.[3] Indeed, all one had to see was that all the men, bloated, scabby, blistered, burned, and peeling, inhaling the evaporative lake mists, the light in their eyes being overwhelmed by blasting sun and over 100-degree heat, were beginning to fail.

Even toward the end of the day, when all had reassembled on the beach but Lieutenant Dale and several rowers sent across the lake to sound depths to the opposite shore at Ein Turabeh, spirits were only momentarily eased with recreational bathing, first in the lake and then again in the soothing waters at the outlet of Zerka Ma'in, "a most delicious transition from the dense, acrid water of the sea, which made our innumerable sores smart severely, to the soft, tepid and refreshing waters of Callirhoe." Lynch again tested the buoyancy principle of the Dead Sea, with difficulty keeping his feet down, and when floating on his back and drawing up his knees, immediately rolling over like a barrel.

But his spirits plummeted again a little later when the men huddled over their evening fare, which had dwindled down to half a cup of tea, "to which we were limited from scarcity of sugar." Most of his men, so carefully chosen for their hardiness and upright moral character back home, "submitted cheerfully to privation," he noted, "but a few looked discontented at our scanty fare. This selfishness was painful to witness. If ever there was an occasion requiring a total exemption from it, this was surely one." His own weakened emotional state magnified the moment and he sank into gloom and beleaguered self-righteousness that later transferred to his journal notes, and to his narrative. "In low minds," he would observe, "this [selfishness] trait betrays itself in matters of the stomach and the purse; in those less sordid, but equally ungenerous, in the gratification of sensual love; and, in minds more aspiring, but no less unrestrained by principle, in matters of ambition." Before long he was comparing a few exhausted and malnourished seamen to the biblical Esau, who sold his birthright for a mess of pottage, and to traitorous apostle Judas, to King Charles II, not to forget even Napoleon. His perspective all but gone, at least for that night, Lynch fell asleep in the cooling air, while, on the lakeshore opposite, a large fire burned beneath cheerless cliffs.

It was a short night. Lieutenant Lynch awakened his party at 2 a.m., wanting to take advantage of the slightly cooler night and thus avoid the furnace-like day. He had hoped to climb the mountain to the hilltop ruins of Machaerus, some 3,070 feet above the level of the Dead Sea, encircled by deep ravines. His copy of the book by Irby and Mangles claimed they had in 1818 examined the ruins—later travelers would find tumbled walls of a huge fortress, in the center of which were the remnants of a large palace some 200 feet long by 150 wide, with subterranean passageways leading to underground cisterns and dungeons, where Josephus reported that John had lost his head, and where later explorers would find the scars of iron staples that anchored prisoners' chains. They might also find the Roman siege walls from the time of the First Jewish War in AD 66–72, when the occupying Zealots surrendered to governor Lucilius Bassus. Lynch felt drawn to the mountaintop, where he wanted to excavate one of the tombs mentioned by his British predecessors, but these hopes were lost as he watched his worn-out men breaking their fast and realized such exertions as mountain climbing were now impossible—"the increasing heat of the sun, and the lassitude of the party," he noted, "warned me to lose no time."

As his chronometer moved past 3:30, he made ready to call all hands to duty, and shortly thereafter they were once again afloat on the lake in the copper boat. They sounded the bottom in a straight line aiming at Ein Turabeh across the water, to connect with the diagonal line set by Lieutenant Dale the previous morning. At the distance of a furlong, or 220 yards, from shore, the sounding was 23 fathoms, or 138 feet. Subsequent casts at five-minute intervals showed a dramatic deepening, as much as 218 fathoms (1,308 feet), muddy bottom interspersed with rectangular crystals of salt.[4]

At 8 a.m., in the middle of the lake, a boat materialized out of the thick mist—Dale in the *Fanny Skinner*. They rafted the two lifeboats on the still water, "which looked stagnant and greasy," Lynch said, and he had Dale clambered across into the *Fanny Mason*, to be replaced by Midshipman Aulick, Dr. Anderson, and the cook, Mustafa, along with provisions. Aulick and Anderson were to complete the circle along the northeastern and northern shores, continuing their measurement and mapping of the strand and mountain topography; when they again reached the outlet of the Jordan River, Lynch required precise figures, locations, and drawings. Into the intensely growing heat, no breath of wind stirring, the galvanized boat pulled away and faded into the glare.[5]

Lynch's men rowed their craft across still water toward Ein Turabeh on the western shore while Lynch and Dale took water temperature readings with a self-registering thermometer, finding the surface to be 76 degrees and the lake bottom, 174 fathoms (1,044 feet), 62 degrees. Remarkably, as they had lowered the instrument through the depths, they registered a stratum of slightly colder water, 59 degrees at 10 fathoms (60 feet). Water from the depths was preserved in a bottle for later analysis. By then, it was 10:30 a.m. and the cliffs above Ein Turabeh loomed, where, 10 years before in that same month, Lynch's adviser Edward Robinson had stood, 1,300 feet above the beach, looking down at the "deep green" sea and across to Machaerus and Kerak, making notes for his *Biblical Researches* opus. Now Lynch saw they were nearing the green-fringed Ein Turabeh, where stood their white canvas tents overseen by the noble Sherif Hazza, with whom they were soon reunited on the beach.

"Sherif had heard of the fight between 'Akil and his friends with the Beni 'Adwans," Lynch learned. The older man told him "that several of the Beni Sukrs had since died of their wounds, and that the whole tribe had suffered severely." It was good to have put the width of the sea between them and those disagreeable tribes. Lynch dispatched two of Sherif's Bedouins up the beach with instructions to look after Midshipman Aulick and companions at the mouth of the Jordan, and they trudged off northward toward the outlet of the Kedron and the mountain of Rash el Feshka.[6]

It had been too hot to do anything but rest and plan the closing phase of their time at the Dead Sea, and the next morning—though still oppressive with the temperature measuring 100 degrees in the shade at 9 a.m.—the sailors began dismantling the copper boat for transport by camel to Jerusalem. Lieutenant Dale and six men started with rod and transit to record the horizontal distance and vertical height of a line they would trace over the mountains and the wastes of Judea toward Jerusalem, and soon they were clambering up the pass, above the purplish mist hanging over the Dead Sea, ascending through "wild and awful" cliffs toward thin and misty clouds. They would manage to crawl up 600 feet that day, making measurements and notes. By 11 a.m., Aulick and Anderson and Mustafa rowed in to shore, the galvanized boat bearing bags of numerous geological specimens the doctor had quarried along the way, while Aulick took his bearings and drew the shoreline and elevations of the northern Moabite reaches, including Mount Nebo, towering nearly 4,000 feet above the level of the Dead Sea; traditionally assigned as the spot where Moses was granted his glimpse of the Promised Land. It was also said by some to be the place where his bones rested alongside the Ark of the Covenant. The ancient city of Madaba, its rich trove of mosaics to remain undisturbed beneath the soil another 50 years, lay nearby.

Lynch sent Aulick out into the boat again, to repeat his various experiments with the self-registering thermometer; the water temperature readings would be identical. With that, and Aulick's notes on the northern Dead Sea, with bearings and observations done at the Jordan's mouth, Lynch pronounced that "the exploration of this sea [is] now complete."[7]

Feeling that sense of finality settling in, by dinnertime the entire crew was back at the oasis campground, flattened with exhaustion, with sleep not far removed. "Light, flickering airs," Lynch noted in his journal, "and very sultry during the night."[8]

Everyone was grateful for the day of rest ahead on Sunday morning, May 7, with the temperature starting out even hotter than the day before—106 degrees at 8:30. "The clouds were motionless," Lynch noted, "the sea unruffled, the rugged faces of the rocks without a shadow, and the canes and tamarisks around the fountain drooped their heads towards the only element which could sustain them under the smiting heat." Humans of all backgrounds could feel themselves drooping also. "The Sherif slept in his tent, the Arabs in various listless attitudes around him," said Lynch, "and the mist of evaporation hung over the sea, almost hiding the opposite cliffs." In late afternoon, another sirocco tore in, blowing down the tents and breaking their siphon barometer, "our last remaining one," noted Lynch. They could not imagine feeling more unwelcome, there on the western shore of the Dead Sea. "All suffered very much from languor, and prudence warned us to begone," wrote Lynch, planning just one more day of significant labor before they could be released from the spell he had wrought.

The sky pressed down the next morning, cloudy and sultry, but they were awakened to the musical notes of a bird singing in the thicket near the spring—the Arabs told Lynch it was a bulbul—like a kingfisher, brown-and-blue-plumaged with a red bill, which the Americans had seen numerous times but never identified the song. The lieutenant thought it sounded like the nightingale of Italy. As the leveling party lugged their instruments up the pass to continue their line survey, sailors on the shore began hammering wood together into a passable, large-sized float, to which they attached a tall staff. By the time of the daily meridian readings at noon, the thermometer had climbed to 110 degrees, and Lynch called off the rest of the work. The wind picked up in the afternoon, and when the line surveyors trudged back into camp around 4, they reported that the afternoon wind had been too brisk for much work, although they had managed to crest the pass and work their way 300 feet out into the Judean desert before breaking to eat, crawling under a tent they had erected against the sun. The wind blew down their tent; they finished their repast under the shadow of a rock and gave up on getting anything else done that day.

Lynch's last full day on the Dead Sea shore began at daybreak, Tuesday May 9, when he was awakened by the Muslim call to prayer. Dale and the Syrian interpreter, Ameuny, took charge of the two sick seamen, George Overstock and Hugh Read, and they made their way up the pass toward the Mar Saba convent in the Ravine of Fire, where the patients would seek medical care.[9] Lynch and rowers took their remaining boat, the *Fanny Skinner*, and towed the float they had constructed out to the still misty center of the lake, where they moored it in 80 fathoms of water, far out of reach of the local Arabs; on the top of the high staff they fixed an American flag to mark their achievement, trusting that the angry forces of the sirocco, which several times had nearly drowned them and which had always defeated beach-based tents and other equipment, would respect the Stars and Stripes.

Back on the beach, a light northeast wind stirring the colors visible out in the water, Sherif sidled up to Lynch to report on the sheikh of the ragtag Rashayideh Arabs, who had been helping with small tasks while they waited for the *bakshish* that the Americans had said would be given when their scientific work was finished, and not before. Impatient, the sheikh had muttered to Sherif that if it wasn't for Sherif's presence at the camp, he would have found a way to get what he wanted, "intimating," said the lieutenant, "by force." When called out and told to leave immediately, the sheikh instantly became sorrowful and repentant, and with Sherif's stern but generous intercession, the Rashayideh was allowed to remain, though warned that the slightest negative remark and he would be expelled from the camp. There was plenty to do: the galvanized boat was taken apart and packed, with the dismantled copper lifeboat, on some of the camels that had arrived the day before. That small caravan finally embarked for Bab el Hulil—the Jaffa gate at Jerusalem, their bells tingling, mingling with an occasional metallic *thunk* from a boat part, up the incline toward Judea.

Dale and the interpreter tiredly rejoined them at the campfire at 8:30 p.m., the two sick seamen having been welcomed into the care of the monks of Mar Saba. Before the Americans retired, they bathed one last time in that salt sea. Lynch went to his bedroll, satisfied with the new body of scientific knowledge they had amassed—"we have carefully sounded this sea," he would reflect, "determined its geographical position, taken the exact topography of its shores, ascertained the temperature, width, depth, and velocity of its tributaries, collected specimens of every kind, and noted the winds, currents, changes of the weather, and all atmospheric phenomena." He was thankful for the history that he and his men had written, and even for the spiritual comfort of believing that with all of man's science, they had settled not only a great and long-standing mystery as to the depth in the earth of the Dead Sea, the lowest place on the planet, but they had actually, he believed, verified an ancient story of sin, divine punishment, and violent conflagration. Since the surrounding mountains were older than the sea, he reasoned, "there can scarce be a doubt that the whole Ghor has sunk from some extraordinary convulsion; preceded, most probably, by an eruption of fire, and a general conflagration of the bitumen which abounded in the plain." "Upon ourselves, the result is a decided one," he would note in his reports to Secretary Mason and Congress as well to a vast and interested reading public. "We entered upon this sea with conflicting opinions. One of the party was skeptical, and another, I think, a professed unbeliever of the Mosaic account. After twenty-two days' close investigation, if I am not mistaken, we are unanimous in the conviction of the truth of the Scriptural account of the destruction of the cities of the plain."[10]

Science was truly a wonder, even when used, in his case, to justify a tenet of faith. "We have done our best," Lynch would write the American consul at Malta, "but if the health of the men had permitted it, I would have gladly remained a month longer on the Dead Sea & its shores, to have made the observations at leisure." He hoped the work would help advance knowledge. "Possessing no pretensions to science," he would add, "I can only present facts, the result of our joint labors, for others, better qualified, to draw conclusions."[11]

At midnight he awoke from a light sleep, and, staring out at the still waters, it seemed eerily like their first night upon that beach, with

> the tents among the tamarisks, the Arab watch-fires, the dark mountains in the rear, the planets and the stars above them, and the boats drawn up on the shore. The night was serene and beautiful; the moon, now beginning to wane, shone on a placid sea, upon which there was not the slightest ripple. The profound stillness was undisturbed by the faintest sound, except the tread of our sentinels.[12]

It was warmer now. Camels for tomorrow's journey lay nearby. "The night passed away quietly," he noted, "and a light wind springing up from the north, even the most anxious were at length lulled to sleep by the rippling waves, as they brattled upon the shore."[13]

* * *

Aulick, Bedlow, and young Francis Lynch were the first to leave, climbing the dim path up the Fire Wady out of the Ghor at first light and bearing the party's chronometers, which they would carry to Jerusalem to check their rate.[14] The leveling party, led by Lieutenant Dale, followed at 7 a.m., and by 10 a.m., tents struck and all packed, the rest of the American adventurers and their Arab escorts began their ascension with the camels bearing their belongings. "From Sodom in her pit dismayed," Melville would write of the vale in *Clarel*, "Westward they wheel, and there invade / Judah's main ridge, which horrors deaden—Where Chaos holds the wilds in pawn, / As here had happed an Armageddon."[15]

Did they hesitate to look back, as they climbed?

They did not. "Winding slowly up the steep pass, we looked back at every turn upon our last place of encampment, and upon the silent sea," noted Lynch. "We are ever sad on parting with things for the last time. The feeling that we are never to see them again, makes us painfully sensible of our own mortality."

But there was something stirring him—as he moved higher above that blasted and lifeless sea of Lot, of Herod, of the Essenes and the Maccabees, of Crusaders and pilgrims, of doomed adventurers, of ragged and noble Arabs, of fearful myths and only partially solved mysteries—and he would scrawl in his journal at a rest, struggling with words about the achievement, the realization of his dreams. "We turned to look upon our flag, floating far off upon the sea"—he blotted out some words to get it right. Then, "the only flag of freedom in the world." That had somehow gotten him there. And for last words that had to do.

PART FOUR

CHAPTER THIRTEEN

From Mar Saba and Jerusalem
to the Jordan's Source

IN THE YEAR 473 OF THE CHRISTIAN ERA, A CAPPADOCIAN-GREEK monk, Sabbas, having spent more than half his life in orthodox monasteries of Palestine, took up hermetic residence in a craggy cave high in the valley of the Kedron, some 18 miles up the blasted Fire Wady from the shore of the Dead Sea. Sabbas, living simply with prayer, the singing of Psalms, and the weaving of baskets, was said "to live an angelic life so far above nature that he seemed no longer to have a body."[1i] In subsequent years many tonsured followers joined him, hollowing out their own holes in the valley walls and embracing physical denial, pain, and prayer. There were tales of miracles—many involving the invocation of water, whether in miraculous rains ending periods of drought, or when Sabbas erected a tower on the right bank of the Kedron, striking the bare rock with his staff and praying until a spring bubbled forth. Another tale, related by a western visitor to the monastery, involved a lion and the holy man's rocky den. "Sabbas," the traveler recounted,

> on entering his grotto one day, found it tenanted by a lion. The
> saint betook himself to repeating his prayers as hard as he could;

but the lion, quite regardless of this pious proceeding, dragged him out twice. Nothing daunted, the saint came in again; and at last a modus vivendi, or mutual arrangement, was arrived at, the lion undertaking to keep to his own corner.[2]

By 484 a great Lavra, or monastery, was established, in which the younger monks lived in community while their elders clung to the hermetic way. By 491, Sabbas and his monks had constructed a church inside a large hollowed grotto, blessed and dedicated by the Patriarch of Jerusalem as he also ordained Sabbas as a full priest. The teachings and writings of Sabbas figured largely in the development and liturgy of the Greek Orthodox Church, and by the time of the death of Sabbas, in 532, his monastery had already begun to grow, perched like a swallow's nest high on the canyon face. A century and a half later the monastery, by now memorialized for St. Sabbas as Mar Saba, was the residence of the venerable Arab Christian monk and priest John of Damascus, defender of the veneration of holy images or icons, his monastic home the site of the prayerful and miraculous restoration of John's right hand, which had been chopped off in Damascus by order of the caliph, fearing a Christian revolt. After his death in 479 the body of St. John of Damascus was interred at Mar Saba; St. Sabbas's bones, however, were plundered by Crusaders in the twelfth century and removed to Rome, where they would be held for centuries until repatriated by Pope Paul VI in 1965 as a friendly gesture to the Greek Orthodox Church.[3]

Mar Saba was a fortress astride a steep mountain wall, its only entrance a heavily armored gateway door, which was opened from within after depositing identification in a basket lowered by rope from a high window in the wall. But to Christians it had a tradition of welcoming pilgrims and the occasional friendly Arab—though no women were allowed inside, for fear of polluting monks' thoughts. As Mark Twain would write after being admitted to Mar Saba, "Some of those men have been shut up inside for thirty years. In all that dreary time they have not heard the laughter of a child or the blessed voice of a woman; they have seen no human tears, no human smiles; they have known no human joys, no wholesome human sorrows. In their hearts there are no human memories of the past, in their brains no dreams of the future. . . . They are dead men who walk."[4] They ate little but bread, salt, and water, but, as Lieutenant Lynch and his party learned, they were generous to strangers.

The Americans and escorts reached Mar Saba on Friday afternoon, May 12, having measured at a crawling pace across rocky, bare, furnace-like terrain for two days; at night they shivered in those desert heights as the nighttime temperatures dropped to 60 degrees. The impressive sight of the monastery stunned Lynch—"a perpendicular cliff, of about 400 feet," he noted, "has its face covered with walls, terraces, chapels, and churches, constructed of solid masonry, all now in perfect repair. The walls of this convent, with a semicircular-concave sweep, run along the western bank of the ravine, from the bottom to the summit."

They toured throughout, down flights of stairs and through passages, flagstone courts, a small, round chapel containing the remains of St. John of Damascus and the now-empty tomb of St. Sabbas, and into the church, "gorgeously gilded and adorned with panel and fresco paintings, the former enshrined in silver, and some of them good; the latter, mere daubs. The pavement was smooth, variegated marble; there were two clocks, near the altar; and two large, rich, golden chandeliers, and many ostrich-eggs, suspended from the ceiling." Passages led downward to catacombs and burial chambers, one filled with stacked human skulls from a long-ago Muslim raid and massacre of the innocents. In one old chapel the walls were carved with the names of many seemingly Greek pilgrims; the oldest written date found was from the seventeenth century. Roofs gave way to more stairways of cut stone, leading to monks' cells—dry burrows in the rock. Lynch was told there were 70 wells and a number of cisterns, filled with gathered rainwater. About 30 monks quartered in the convent, "good-

At the Mar Saba convent, the Greek Archbishop posed for the Americans.

natured, illiterate, and credulous," thought the lieutenant; apparently the rich tradition of Mar Saba as a center for the copying and illuminating of manuscripts, known as far back as the eighth century, was a lost cause. With the exception of a few Russians all were Greek, and the archbishop, from Jerusalem, impressed the visitors with his bearing and his pontifical attire.[5]

In an apartment reclined the recuperating George Overstock and Hugh Read, both improving under the monks' care, though apparently suffering from a rash of itchy bites. The explorers politely refused similar accommodations inside; "dreading the fleas," Lynch admitted, "we preferred the open air." His adviser and earlier visitor to the monastery, John Lloyd Stephens, had not been so delicate, when offered a divan and a large pile of coverlets. "I thought of the bush in which I had lodged the night before," Stephens wrote, and thankfully spread out a few of the coverlets and crawled in among them, "and in a few moments the Dead Sea, and the Holy Land, and every other land and sea were nothing to me."[6]

Camping outside away from the fleas, the Americans endured a thunderstorm and rain, the thermometer standing at a still chilly 58 degrees at midnight. For a few days they would rest and reconnoiter. The officers searched for a leveling route out of the valley; Dr. Anderson picked botanical samples for scientists at home, such as familiar-looking chicory, white henbane, dyer's weed, dwarf mallow, and the caper plant, gathering seeds from a palm supposedly planted by Saint Sabbas, and he dislodged some unidentified fossils from the rock.

It was no trouble feeling dislodged from time and space at Mar Saba, as one inhaled the dry air and allowed the eyes to sweep up across fortifications, towers, dome, and canyon walls, trying to reconcile the actual mileage in the Holy Land against the formidable breadth of religious imagination, as Mark Twain would when he tramped abroad in many of Lynch's footsteps. Despite their crawling pace, they were less than a half-day's normal ride to the Dead Sea. Indeed, about an equal distance in the opposite direction lay Jerusalem. Science, though, required continuing the measured crawl across the Judean desert, trailing the pack camels, squinting through instruments into the epochal glare.

Resuming the westward walk very early on Monday, May 15, accompanied now only by their translator, cook, guide, and a few men to tend the camels, the Americans saw more evidence of human habitation the further they followed the dry Kedron across the desolate, ash-brown plain toward the cultivated valleys and Jerusalem. As before, Dale ran the surveyors' level. At a large cistern hewn out of solid rock, as big as a cottage inside with four feet of water below green, slimy walls, they began to fill their water bottles when they realized there were two Arabs wedged fearfully into corners from where they had been bathing themselves. Shrugging, the explorers finished what they were doing, and left the bathers to their ablutions. Later, a patch of tobacco, and then small fields of wheat and barley ready for harvest, the figures of *fellahas* (peasant women) against the sky, a cluster of black Bedouin tents, a local sheikh who tried to shake them down for passing through his territory, and then, after refusal, for at least some *bakshish*. Further on, they passed goats and sheep grazing, and a Bedouin in a sheepskin robe leading a she-camel and foal, and then, "standing by the roadside," Lynch noted, "was a *fellaha*, with a child in her arms, who courteously saluted us. She did not appear to be more than sixteen."

The explorers were clearly mindful that they had not encountered women so closely in a long time, not since they left New York. Later along the road, they met an older woman and her attractive daughter who came over to sell them some *leban*, or sour milk; their guide woefully confided to Lynch that he knew them well, and for a year had courted the daughter only to be turned away by her father, who demanded a dowry twice what the young man could afford. Lynch wrote that the young woman was "lightly and symmetrically formed, and exceedingly graceful in her movements. The tawny complexion, the cheek-bones somewhat prominent, the coarse black hair, and the dark, lascivious eye, reminded us of a female Indian of our border." He encouraged the guide to tell him other tales of Syrian romance and woe in Judea, and copied them down for the benefit of his future readers.

Henry Bedlow, 28, a poet and romantic, might have been feeling his own stirrings. Back home, he would marry in less than two years (to a De Wolf, likewise on the Social Register), have two coddled daughters, and settle into a dabbling scholarly and artistic life in Newport. Many years later, though, the image of a beautiful Syrian girl bearing a jug and a basket of fruit would inspire a collection of poems he would publish elaborately, with romantic drawings accompanying each poem—the depiction of the young man is plainly that of the youthful Henry Bedlow.[7] The last gave voice to thoughts perhaps experienced on that road across the Judean plain:

I dreamed of kisses sweet as wine,
Lips cooler than Siloam's water;
Clasped in her arms, which like the vine,
Gave love, for strength that did support her;

Decades after his adventure, Bedlow memorialized an Arab woman seen at Judea, in his illustrated book of romantic poems.

Below, Bedlow's fancy, as imagined for his poems of Palestine.

Finally, the party moved on westward, Lynch and Bedlow with their own literary thoughts, their young guide casting back rueful glances toward his unattainable love.

Lieutenant Lynch came into sight of Jerusalem late on the second day out of Mar Saba. Leaving the surveyors to continue in the path of their camels and drivers, he rode to the summit of a hill and took in the stirring sight of the ancient city. "Mellowed by time, and yet further softened by the intervening distance," he noted, "the massive walls, with their towers and bastions, looked beautiful yet imposing in the golden sunlight; and above them, the only thing within their compass visible from that point, rose the glittering dome of the mosque of Omar, crowning Mount Moriah, on the site of the Holy Temple. On the other side of the chasm, commanding the city and the surrounding hills, is the Mount of Olives, its slopes darkened with the foliage of olive-trees, and on its very summit the former Church of the Ascension, now converted into a mosque."[8]

Their campsite was established for the night on a terrace below the Zion Gate, near the lower pool of the Gihon, the source of water for Jerusalem, and as tents went up Dale and Lynch hammered a surveyor's benchmark into the rock at the northwest angle of the high Jerusalem wall. Over the next several days, as Dale reconnoitered for his leveling measurements down the Jaffa Road toward the sea, their interpreter, Ameuny, repeatedly heard comments from onlookers and passersby: "the Franks are preparing to take possession of the Holy City."[9] Fortunately, the comments would not become a widespread rumor, and the Americans encountered no trouble, whether camping and reconnoitering or exploring the ancient city, which they did in turns. On the 18th, they were reunited with the noble Sherif Hazza, looking for something to do while he waited impatiently for the Ottomans to issue him his back pay and expenses. Sherif gladly took charge of the dismantled boats, which were conveyed on camelback from the Jaffa Gate to the terminus of the road and the Mediterranean.

It was also on May 18 that Dr. Anderson wistfully parted company from his fellow Americans, "his business calling him in another direction," as Lynch noted. "Although not required to do so, he had, while with us, generously persisted in bearing his portion of watchfulness and fatigue; and by his invariable cheerfulness, his promptitude and zeal on all occasions, proved, independently of his professional services, a most valuable auxiliary." Anderson "won our esteem," Lynch would continue, "and carried with him the fervent good will of every member of the party." His modest bill for services was $168, just $3 per day. Young Henry Bedlow, the onetime medical student who had competently assisted Anderson, agreed to take the doctor's place.[10]

Henry Anderson would continue to lead a venturesome and exciting life, spending enough time at home in New York to be elected a trustee at Columbia College and appointed emeritus professor of mathematics and astronomy; he also served for years as president of the Catholic Society of St. Vincent de Paul in its mission serving the poor, and founded the Catholic Protectory in nearby Westchester, noble pursuits for a late convert. He also took many trips abroad, most notably his final one, in late 1874, when he volunteered to join the U.S. naval expedition dispatched by the U.S. Navy to the South Seas to observe the extremely rare transit of the planet Venus across the face of the sun. Upon completion, Dr. Anderson traveled from Australia to India. While exploring the Himalayas, he contracted cholera and died, at Lahore, northern Hindustan (present day Pakistan), in 1875, at the age of 76. After his body was transported home, his funeral at New York's St. Patrick's Cathedral was the most attended for any person in the laity, and he was interred in a vault below the Church of the Madonna in Fort Lee, New Jersey, near his old home on the Palisades.[11]

For nearly a week the Americans camped outside the Jerusalem walls, moving once to the western side of the city. The British consul for Jerusalem and Palestine, James Finn, a well-published writer and historian with a scholarly interest in Jewish communities, made them welcome at his home and office and extended financial courtesies.[12] Oddly enough, not one other resident of the small Western community in Jerusalem would have anything to do with the explorers. This Lynch ascribed to their "toil-worn and shabby appearance," having occupied only the clothes on their backs (with a change of underwear), hand-washed infrequently, since arriving at the shore of Galilee on April 6, well over a month before. Some trousers and a few jackets being to the point of transparency in places, they found a cheap tailor to sew some "indifferent" replacements, to no discernible improvement of their social status. Only the throngs of beggars in the city seemed initially gladdened at their appearance ("the war-cry of the Syrian pauper: *bakshish! bakshish!*") as the Americans in turn visited as many revered historical sites as could be crammed in a week's time and a miserly budget—among them, the Tombs of the Prophets; the Church of the Holy Sepulcher, said to be built above the briefly inhabited tomb of Jesus; the still-verdant Garden of Gethsemane, site of his Passion; the Mount of Olives, where it was believed he taught, wept, and ascended.[13]

The view from the summit of the mount was "magnificent," wrote Lynch. "On the one hand lay Jerusalem, with its yellow walls, its towers, its churches, its dome-roof houses, and its hills and valleys, covered with orchards and fields of green and golden grain," he continued, "while beneath, distinct and near, the mosque of Omar, the Harem (the Sacred), lay exposed to our infidel gaze, with its verdant carpet and groves of cypress, beneath whose holy shade none but the faithful can seek repose."

The lieutenant's gaze shifted toward an axis they now knew firsthand, "the valley of Jordan, a barren plain, with a line of verdure marking the course of the sacred river, until it was lost in an expanse

Tomb of Absalom,
near Jerusalem.

of sluggish water, which we recognized as the familiar scene of our recent labors." It seemed almost a storybook remove. "The rays of the descending sun shone full upon the Arabian shore, and we could see the castle of Kerak, perched high up in the country of Moab, and the black chasm of Zerka, through which flows the hot and sulphureous stream of Callirohoe."

Standing there on ancient Olivet, to which David had fled from Absalom, and upon which King Solomon had built altars, and upon which Jews had mourned and marked Sukkot after the destruction of the Temple, Lynch continued his reverie. "No other spot in the world," he said, "commands a view so desolate, and, at the same time, so interesting and impressive. The yawning ravine of Jehoshaphat, immediately beneath, was verdant with vegetation, which became less and less luxuriant, until, a few miles below, it was lost in a huge torrent bed, its sides bare precipitous rock, and its bed covered with boulders,

Tombs in the Valley of Jehosephat.

whitened with saline deposit, and calcined by the heat of a Syrian sun. Beyond it, south, stretched the desert of Judea; and to the north, was the continuous chain of this almost barren mountain."[14]

There was even time during this recuperative stay for a day trip to Bethlehem, revered as Jesus's birthplace and only two hours distant. On the way they once more caught a glimpse of the Dead Sea through gorges in the Judean mountains. On Monday, May 22, they settled their accounts in Jerusalem, broke camp, and Lieutenant Dale began laying a direct level line from the benchmark outside the city walls down the Jaffa Road toward the Mediterranean, some 33 miles away. With mules hired to replace their camels, the route would take them on a "frightful" road along precipices, past ruins, stone-cut mountain-side terraces containing olive, fig, and apricot groves, and vineyards. They camped for the night near the stone-arched bridge over the dry Kulonieh River, awoke the next morning enshrouded in mist, and pressed on across a succession of hills and mountains, ever seaward.

Their camp Tuesday night was near the village of Beit Nakubeh, where they slept in sight of a ruined castle of the Maccabees; howls of jackals creeping in a ravine punctuated their rest.

The next morning, descending a ravine into the vale of Jeremiah, they had leveled to that biblical prophet's birthplace, 'Kuryet el 'Enab. For a while they were detained by a rough-talking sheikh, who demanded tribute to permit them to cross his territory, and he seemed hardly swayed by the sultan's firman granting them all official courtesies, but finally backed off, muttering curses and imprecations. From his village, though, came a piercing cry of an old man—"*O ye Muslims, come forth and see the Christians searching for treasures concealed by their forefathers in this country.*"—and soon the little detachment of Americans were swamped by curious though friendly Arabs. "All desired," Lynch wrote, "to look through the telescope, and even little children were held up for a peep." They moved on, the locals satisfied.[15]

Finally, the Americans reached the summit of the last ridge between them and the sea, and "we beheld the blue, the glorious Mediterranean," wrote Lynch. "Not the soldiers of Xenophon cheered more heartily than we did when we beheld its broad expanse stretching towards the west, where lay our country and our homes." The afternoon's heat rose as they picked their way down a steep road, and, seeking shade in a gnarly old olive grove, they established camp, retiring early.[16] Their caravan continued in the morning, Dale trailing with his instrument, freshened and beckoned by an ocean breeze as they reached the coastal plane and moved on, passing the palm-fringed walls of Ramleh, its minarets towering over the town of small, mud-plastered stone houses, the air perfumed by cooking fires of camel dung, and they camped for two days just off the Jaffa Road, reminded by the sight of passing Christian pilgrims of the passage of baby Jesus and his parents on that road during their flight to Egypt.

The following morning, Monday, May 29, beyond the village of Yazur, they followed the old "Frank road, the one on which Napoleon marched to and from Gaza," and a few miles later the adventurers passed through sand hills, then dunes, and Lieutenant Dale planted his level on the foaming beach, just south of Jaffa, and their measuring task was completed for the world. Lynch exulted in his journal: "We had carried a line of levels, with the spirit-level, from the chasm of the Dead Sea, through the Desert of Judea, over precipices and mountain-ridges, and down and across yawning ravines, and for much of the time beneath a scorching sun," he wrote. "It had been considered by many as impracticable. It has, however, been accomplished; and with as much accuracy as, I believe, it can be done."

Their figures would in time be entered in the world's record books, satisfying all scientific congresses, and standing, uncorrected, until satellites soaring in the skies over the ancient land measured and improved Lieutenant Dale's calculations by a few centimeters. The surface of the Dead Sea was a little over 1,300 feet below the level of the Mediterranean; Jerusalem's altitude, Lieutenant Lynch would add, was "very nearly three times that of this difference of level, while, at the same time, it is almost the exact multiple of the depth of that sea, of the height of its banks, and of the depression of its surface." He relished, as one might have predicted, this exquisite symmetry.[17]

For several days the Americans rested in the comfortable country house of the American consul at Jaffa, Jacob Serapion Murad, an Armenian native of Jerusalem and of long service to the foreign interests.[18] Lynch set two of the sailors to reassembling the metal lifeboats, and otherwise the Americans were free to explore ancient Jaffa, where, supposedly, Noah had built his ark, where the cedars of Lebanon had been landed for the building of the great temple, where the first of Jesus's apostles had dwelt, where the first of the Crusaders had landed, and where the footsteps of other invaders from Napoleon to Ibrahim Pasha had sounded. Lynch occupied himself with filling descriptive pages of his journal, including some pointed thoughts about the position of women in the Arab world, which gave him reflection on history of the Old and New Worlds, and, unerringly, to the plight of women everywhere in that modern year of 1848. "All over the world, civilized and savage," he noted, "women are treated as inferior beings. In what is esteemed refined society, we hold them in mental thralldom, while we exempt them from bodily labour; and, paying a sensual worship to their persons, treat them as pretty playthings."[19] Timely thoughts: interestingly, in another month, in July 1848, a convention of women led by Lucretia Mott and Elizabeth Cady Stanton would voice similar opinions in a "Declaration of Sentiments" at Seneca Falls, New York.

Lynch also worked on his correspondence, sending a new report to Naval Secretary Mason and a polite but urgent letter to the *Supply* officer Pennock, then at Malta, a thousand miles to the west, regarding their transportation home. Lynch was worried about the building heat of the summer season, and its accompanying miasmas and galloping plagues, and the health and safety of his men. "Let me urge you therefore," he underlined to Pennock, "to lose no time in coming here." Lynch sent word to the Mediterranean fleet officer, Commodore George C. Read, via Consul Winthrop at Malta.[20]

Early Tuesday morning, June 6, Lieutenant Dale took command of the land party, which started northward toward Acre; Lynch embarked late in the day with the rest of his men in a chartered Arab brigantine, upon which were tethered the two lifeboats, with the Stars and Stripes fluttering above on the mast. At the outer limit of the harbor, the evening darkening as the moon rose, they had a good view of the many-terraced town of Jaffa. The night breeze being light, the brig did not gain much headway up that coast of sand hills and cliffs until after midnight, but with a rising they then made good progress. Anchoring off Acre, approximately where the *Supply* had moored the night before the expedition first made landfall, they waited for dawn and the last facet of their mission—following the Jordan northward to its source. Unfortunately, their notes were to be highly descriptive but bereft of scientific measurement, their three barometers being broken with no opportunity found in Jerusalem for either repair or replacement, and the boiling water apparatus too cranky for reliance.[21]

In Washington, John Young Mason had for some time been working two jobs for President Polk—his official post as Navy secretary, and a filling-in at the head of the Army Department for Secretary William Learned Marcy during the ex-governor's protracted absences from the capital. "We believe," commented one newspaper, "that in the course of his career in the cabinet he has at one time or another discharged the duties of Attorney General and Secretary of War, in addition to that of Secretary of the Navy. Indeed, his capacity fits him for any station in the nation. In addition to his distinguished talents, we can truly say that he is one of the most amiable gentlemen in the whole country."[22] His many duties were causing a painful marital discord; his wife, Mary Ann, had complained of husbandly neglect throughout the summer from North Carolina, to which she had gone on family duties. "You will be disappointed," Mason wrote her with feeling, "I am sure, when I tell you that I cannot leave Washington while the Navy Appropriation Bill is under discussion." Senators had been making wild, unfounded charges, which Mason refuted after each assault. In the latest exchange, he said, "If I had been absent, I should have been ruined." But their house looked "very desolate without you, my dear wife," he wrote affectionately. Correspondence with their son, serving in the Mediterranean on the *Supply*, worried him, as much for his developing naval career as for all the newspaper reports of continued revolutionary strife in Europe, and the beginning of the dreaded fever season in the Mediterranean basin, particularly in the East.[23]

* * *

At Nazareth, a
Greek Catholic
priest posed for
Dale's sketchbook.

Dale's land party picked its way along a white beach strewn with
shells, passing the ruins of the cliff-top city Apollonia and Herod
the Great's sandstone-walled Caesaria, its massive granite columns
recumbent in the surf ("how beautiful once! how mournful now,"
commented Dale). On the third day's march, as they neared the
ruins of the thirteenth-century Crusader keep, Castellum Peregrino-
rum—last of the Templars' fortresses—one of the American sailors,
Charles Homer, accidentally triggered his shotgun, which was
unfortunately loaded. All 12 of the buckshot tore into his arm near
the wrist, exiting near the elbow, leaving his forearm in shreds, and,
as Dale reported, "the severed artery discharged dark arterial blood
in frightful jets, and the wounded man suffered excruciating agony."
Henry Bedlow leaped to his side, only staunching the blood with
great difficulty. While they found shelter from the sun amid the castle ruins, Dale procured the use of an Arab *felucca* in the harbor, and
Seaman Homer was dispatched under Bedlow's care up the coast to
Acre, which they reached thanks to good winds in six hours. He was
carried to the consul's house, where a surgeon in the Ottoman Turkish army hastened to dress the wound. "I dreaded, however, the heat

of the climate," said Lynch, "and felt it my duty to procure for the unfortunate man the most comfortable quarters and the very best surgical attendance. I therefore sent him, the same evening, to Beirut, under charge of Passed Midshipman Aulick, Mr. Bedlow, and three men." The Sisters of Charity would care for him, and a French surgeon looked in daily.[24]

Back down in Acre, Lynch led the remainder of his party inland on Saturday, June 10, making a stop at the hallowed village of Nazareth, reaching it in a day's ride. "The feelings are inexpressible," noted Lynch, "which overpower one in passing to and fro amid scenes which, for the greater portion of his mortal existence, were frequented by our Saviour. In Jerusalem, the theatre of his humiliations, his sufferings, and his death, the heart is oppressed with awe and anguish; but in Nazareth, where he spent his infancy, his youth, and his early manhood, we yearn towards him unchilled by awe, and unstricken by horror." For part of a day, as pilgrims, not engineers, they visited all the associated sites in that quiet valley town and thought it "the prettiest place we had seen in Palestine."[25]

Ancient associations continued. By the afternoon of the 12th, they were on the summit of Mount Tabor, where they could simultaneously look down below flowered slopes to a battlefield—site of the Book of Judges battle between the Israelite General Barak, commander of the army of the prophetess Deborah, and the Canaanite General Sisera—while standing on the heights where, reputedly, Jesus of Nazareth had been transfigured while speaking to the spirits of Moses and Elijah, and blessed by the voice of God. The Americans could easily see in the east the Jordan, Galilee, and the glittering peak of Mount Hermon, which for the next several days would be the beacon drawing them on toward the Jordan's source. By nightfall, their horseback ride continued, they were camped on the bank of the lower Jordan next to the ruined bridge of Samakh, and they bathed in the river, and they rested.

By mid-morning on June 13 they had ascended the Galilean

At a fountain in Nazareth, the pious Americans paid homage.

shore to Tiberias, planning to resume their survey of the hallowed lake; two months before, having bought the only boat of that lake, they had made arrangements for its twin to be constructed and carried from the seacoast to Tiberias, but to their "great regret," Lynch reported, the delivery would be delayed another two weeks, making their exploration impossible due to "the advancing [hot] season and our enfeebled condition."[26]

Into the forenoon they followed the road overlooking the lake, pausing at the heights above the refreshing 'Ain et Tin (Fountain of the Fig) to look for ruins of the biblical city of Capernaum, to which they were guided by Lynch's biblical geography adviser, Dr. Robinson; although the lieutenant admitted only a "feeble understanding" of the subject, he found a likelier site for the city further up the shore at the Tell Hum, a conspicuous hill at about the middle of the northern shoreline. By late afternoon in oppressive heat they had reached the wide mouth of the upper Jordan, pouring into the Sea of Galilee at its northeast corner, and they camped a short distance upstream, at a safe

301

remove from an Arab camp of the ill-reputed tribe of El Batiheh planted on the eastern bank of the river. Their night, however, was still not peaceful, tormented as they were by fleas, mosquitoes, and the nearby cries of a jackal pack.

With an early start on the 14th, they followed the tumbling and foaming river through clusters of pink oleander overlooked by bowing willows, up ravines into foothills past occasional ruins, beneath an old four-arched bridge, where the Jordan was some 40 yards wide and running extremely fast. They came up and out onto a large plain dotted with tented encampments of Arabs, where once Joshua, successor to Moses, routed the Canaanites. The camp for the night was on an elevated plateau beneath dome-like limestone hills, one commanded by Honin, fortress from Crusader times. In the morning, continuing their ascent toward Banias and the ruins of Caesarea Philippi, including the sacred precinct of Pan with its blasted temples, grottos, and niches, they reached an oak-sheltered cave mouth, its seep-moistened interior as well as deeper subterranean fissures considered one of the sources of the Jordan. Later and still higher, passing by olive, mulberry, and fig groves and fields of grain tended by lighter-skinned and Christian peasants, they collapsed near the stream below the town of Hasbeiya and the looming peak of Mount Hermon, almost too tired from the rough road to erect tents or cook food.

Even after a night's sleep, Lynch gave them a forenoon of rest, June 16, during which many curious townspeople descended to visit. Hasbeiya had, a few years ago, been joined by a tiny enclave of Protestants, who stuck despite numerous persecutions by the local Greek Orthodox church and timid acquiescence from local Druse and Muslim neighbors. Tales of the religious discord triggered a diatribe in Lynch's journal, decrying fanaticism and bigotry. "The persecuted," he noted, "have our warmest sympathies."[27]

That afternoon, however, came the extraordinary sight of the fountainhead of the Jordan, when a local dignitary, Prince Ali Shehab, came down to escort them through a ravine, past numerous groves,

The source of the Jordan, sketched by Dale with Prince
Ali in foreground.

across the tree-lined river on a one-arched bridge, until, minutes later,
"we came suddenly to the source," exulted Lieutenant Lynch, "a bold,
perpendicular rock, from beneath which the river gushed copious,
translucent, and cool, in two rectangular streams, one to the northeast, the other to the north-west." He went on to describe it fully:

> The scarp of the rock was about forty feet high; and the north-
> east branch, being mere back-water, extended only a few hun-
> dred yards; but its banks were fringed with the wild rose, the
> white and pink oleander, and the clematis orientalis, or oriental
> virgin's bower. The north-west branch, at the distance of about
> a hundred yards, plunged over a dam, and went rushing through
> the arch of the bridge below. The hand of art could not have
> improved the scene. The gigantic rock, all majesty, above; its
> banks, enameled with beauty and fragrance, all loveliness, beneath;
> render it a fitting fountain-head of a stream which was destined
> to lave the immaculate body of the Redeemer of the world. Mr.
> Dale, who had the eye of an artist, thought that the scene would

make a more beautiful picture than any he had ever beheld. He sketched it, with Prince Ali in the foreground.[28]

On Saturday, June 17, Lynch and Dale rode to the Litani River valley, the untrammeled stream rushing down from the north between the Lebanon and Anti-Lebanon ridges, and after a rest on Sunday, impatient to hear news from Beirut of their wounded seaman Charles Homer, they learned from a messenger on Monday that he was out of danger and that Richmond Aulick and Henry Bedlow were on their way to rejoin the group. On the 19th, Lynch led the reconstituted group up and along the shoulder of Mount Hermon, over the Anti-Lebanon and through a gorge onto the plain of Damascus; over the next day they continued across that sparsely populated expanse, "a long, dreary ride over the dry plain, under a burning sun" toward the green groves and fields surrounding the walled city of Damascus, perhaps the oldest city in the world. "Before entering the city, we were advised to furl our flag," wrote Lynch,

> with the assurance that no foreign one had ever been tolerated within the walls; that the British Consul's had been torn down on the first attempt to raise it, and that the appearance of ours would excite commotion, and perhaps lead to serious consequences. But we had carried it to every place we had visited, and determining to take our chances with it, we kept it flying. Many angry comments were, I believe, made by the populace, but, as we did not understand what our [interpreter] was too wary to interpret, we passed unmolested.[29]

They remained in the city the rest of the week, touring historical sites and marketplaces until the oppressive heat of Damascus began to weaken them. This was the rare locale where the lieutenant did not recall their being bothered by vermin, but sometime around Tuesday or Wednesday, the 20th or the 21st, they were visited by fleas or lice.

Great Sheikh of the
Anazée tribe.

The transmission vector would not be discovered for another 60 years, but the parasites were infected; they rode out of Damascus late in the afternoon of Sunday the 25th trusting that a change in climate would restore them, but this would not be the case.

Their ride took them over the mountains again to the plain of Bekaa, thence down to Ba'albek and the immense constructed stone plateau and topmost ruins of Heliopolis, the Great Temple of the Sun of the Romans, its columns soaring into the sky. They spent an energetic day exploring its elaborate ruins in punishing heat, but by Wednesday the 28th, most of the men—including Lynch and Dale—began to suffer from backaches and abdominal pain; and then red rashes over the chest and back; a hacking, dry cough; and a climbing, alarming fever. Lynch suffered worse than any except Dale, and he was frightened enough to order an immediate retreat down the Litani valley and a high cut over the Lebanon mountains toward the seacoast, aiming for Beirut and competent medicine. "We seemed to have imbibed the disease which has heretofore prostrated all who have ventured upon the Dead Sea," Lynch noted, ignorant of its true nature.

Ruins of Ba'albek.

"As I looked upon my companions drooping around me, many and bitter were my self-reproaches for having ever proposed the undertaking." It appeared to be what was then called a "low, nervous fever." In modern times it became known as typhus.[30]

By mid-afternoon on the 29th, pausing to rest at the mountain hollow village of Zahle, Lynch sent their interpreter ahead with the mission of reaching the consul in Beirut to ready medical attention, and if their ship had not already arrived—Lynch was expecting it to appear on the first of July—to procure an apartment in which to be treated. Ameuny's horse would die on the way, delaying him. The rest of the party rode higher in the mountains, Lynch and Dale barely able to keep to their saddles, shivering in the wind blowing from the coast; they camped near the summit, at about a 4,000-foot altitude, suffering from the cold and from febrile chills, and one of the party, hastening out of the tent in the dark to answer the call of the illness, nearly stumbled off a ledge down the precipice.[31]

306

The next morning, Dale was worse, and the lieutenant sent him ahead with Bedlow, the mountain flank and summit still wreathed with clouds. Lynch and the rest followed, unable to keep a steady pace on a rough, descending road that occasionally showed the curb traces of Roman builders. Finally in late morning they came in sight of Beirut and the sea. "As we [sighted] the harbor of Beirut, our strained eyes sought in vain for the ship we so longed to see," Lynch would note. "My heart sank within me, as, after many alternations of hope and fear, the only three-masted vessel in the port proved not to be the *Supply*. The end who could foresee!"[32]

When they reached their quarters overlooking the shore, Lynch wrote, "Some of us were unable to dismount, from sheer exhaustion; Mr. Dale, two of the seamen, and myself, requiring immediate medical attendance." That night, and all the next day, July 1, they were nearly all sick, attended by a French physician; fearing, though, for Dale and one other, Lynch sent for an American doctor attached to the Evangelical Mission at Beirut, who reached them on Sunday, July 2. He found a few of them improved, but then one of the two or three well men came down with it on Monday, and another on Tuesday, and Lieutenant Dale was not responding. Those who could went out at noon and, it being July 4, fired their guns 21 times.

"We look anxiously for the *Supply*," Lynch wrote to Naval Secretary Mason on July 6, reporting that since he had written Lieutenant Pennock in early June, with a copy for separate dispatch via the American consul at Malta, the ship should have responded at the appointed time. "In this hot climate, we cannot expect thorough renovation on shore and moreover, our expenses are necessarily very heavy."[33] He sent an urgent note to the American consul at Malta that same day, begging him to notify Lieutenant Pennock of their peril.

On the 10th, with still no sign of the *Supply* out in the harbor, Lieutenant Dale became convinced that he would die in Beirut; he insisted that he climb the mountains to a village called Bhamdun, 12 miles up the bad road but requiring four or five hours on horseback, where he would stay at the house of Reverend Smith of the American Presbyterian Mission, and where another American physician could be found. "We have since looked anxiously for the *Supply*, but each successive day has closed in disappointment," Lynch wrote to Mason on July 14. "The health of the party is slowly improving with the exception of one seaman, on whom the fever hangs tenaciously. I have been advised to remove to the mountains, but do not like to encounter the expense, particularly as the *Supply* may be hourly expected." The doctor had added that far better than the thin mountain air, the best place for the sick was out in the fresh air at sea.[34]

On the 17th, Lynch received word that Dale's condition had turned for the worse, and that Dale was asking to see his friend. "I am now about to start, to get to him as soon as possible," Lynch scrawled in a note to Mason at 2 a.m. on the 18th, adding that a packet reported that a cholera epidemic was burning through Antioch and Aleppo, "and its visitation here may soon be expected. Had the ship been here at the appointed time, the serious illness of Mr. Dale, and perhaps yet more serious consequences, would most probably have been avoided. Should a single death occur, I will deem it my duty, if I live, to ask for a strict investigation into the cause of the detention of the ship."[35]

Lynch reached Reverend Smith's mountain house only to find Dale in delirium from the continued high fever, wracked and blinded by headache and deep muscle pain, the doctors in constant attendance unable to alleviate his infection. In such cases, with no medicine to kill the bacteria in his blood, Dale would have begun to experience kidney failure, stupor, and coma. "My poor friend lingered until the evening of the 24th," Lynch would write, "when he expired so gently, that it was difficult to tell the moment of dissolution."

On the other side of the world, in Boston, Mrs. Dale said to a friend: "I wish you to note this day; my spirits are so oppressed, my feelings are so unaccountably strange, that I am sure some great calamity awaits me—note it, that this is the 24th of July."[36]

* * *

"Determined to take his remains home," Lynch recalled,

> if possible, I started immediately with them for Beirut. It was
> a slow, dreary ride down the rugged mountain by torchlight. As
> I followed the body of my late companion, accompanied only
> by swarthy Arabs, and thought of his young and helpless chil-
> dren, I could scarce repress the wish that I had been taken, and
> he been spared. At times, the wind, sweeping in fitful gusts,
> nearly extinguished the torches; and again their blaze would
> stream up with a lurid glare, as we made our way through
> chasms and hollows, enveloped in a dense and palpable mist.[37]

Back up the hill in his mournful house, Reverend Eli Smith
wrote to his friend Edward Robinson in New York. "When one thinks
of Costigan, and Molyneux, and Dale," Smith wrote, "he is almost led
to imagine there is a fatality attending all attempts to unveil the mysteries of the Dead Sea."[38]

In Beirut Dale's body was placed inside three nesting coffins, two
wooden and one metallic, and stored in a vacant building. The other
Americans continued their vigil looking out to sea for the storeship,
grief in their hearts. Lynch wrote a letter intended for his friend's
widow in Boston and enclosed it with a long missive to Secretary
Mason, asking him to immediately "direct a strict, thorough, and sift-
ing investigation of this matter." By then, he said, he had heard from
the American consul at Malta, who said that—incredibly—the *Supply*
was reported to still be in Italian waters, heading only to the port of
Spezia on the northwest coast with a full load of naval supplies for the
fleet there. If true, the *Supply* was still 1,700 miles to their west—and
they would not be rescued for at least a month.[39]

By then news arrived that cholera had overtaken the ancient city
of Aleppo to the north, and the panic level in Beirut was rising because
refugees from Aleppo had been admitted into the gates of Beirut just
the previous day. Lieutenant Lynch otherwise would have faithfully

abided by Secretary Mason's original instructions to re-embark upon the *Supply*, but now he felt duty-bound to see to his men; he chartered a small, two-masted brig from a Frenchman to take the Americans, including the body of Lieutenant Dale, along with their battered lifeboats and equipment, to Malta, a thousand miles to the west. He left letters for Lieutenant Pennock of the *Supply* with the consul and harbormaster, warning him not to venture ashore and fall into quarantine, but to follow them without delay to Malta.

Horribly, as Dale's coffin was being moved onto the ship, it was dropped and overturned. The glimpse of the decomposing body was all the superstitious crew and their French captain needed to see, and they refused to let it be taken aboard. Reluctantly, sorrowfully, the Americans conveyed the coffin back to dry land, and at sunset, "as the Turkish batteries were saluting the first night of the Ramedan," noted Lynch,

> we escorted the body to the Frank cemetery, and laid it beneath a Pride of India tree. A few most appropriate chapters in the Bible were read, and some affecting remarks made by the Rev. Mr. Thomson; after which, the sailors advanced, and fired three volleys over the grave; and thus, amid unbidden tears and stifled sobs, closed the obsequies of our lamented companion and friend.[40]

It was "a sad, sad adieu," commented Reverend Thomson after burying Dale and then saying goodbye to the explorers as they embarked on the ship. "I have rarely had my sympathies more deeply awakened than in this case of Dale." These words, written to Edward Robinson in New York, would soon be reprinted in Robinson's journal, who mourned that Dale "had hardly reached the age of thirty-five; he was a man of fine appearance and elegant manners" with great experience and engineering skills. "His loss will doubtless be greatly felt in making up the report of the expedition; the end of which he was permitted to behold, but not to participate in its fruits, nor to enjoy its rewards."[41]

La Perle d'Orient struggled westward across the Mediterranean for 38 days, touching at Cyprus and Rhodes for water and running so low on food that the convalescing Americans and crew were on half rations for most of the voyage. "But every evil has its antidote," Lynch would write Secretary Mason on September 10, 1848, from a *lazaretto* to which they were quarantined upon arrival at Malta, "and the sea air, and the necessarily low diet proved our great physicians."[42]

But with several men still on the sick list, and the raw memory of Dale's death abrading him, Lynch did not want to forget the question of why the *Supply* had not been waiting for them at Beirut on July 1—why, as he had learned from William Winthrop, the American consul at Malta, the *Supply* had not left Malta until August 9. He suspected that the blame would lie with the Mediterranean fleet officer, Commodore Read. Indeed, as he would learn on September 12, when the storeship finally appeared at Malta, the *Supply* had not reached Beirut until August 25, 50 days after the appointed time.

Lieutenant Pennock, its temporary skipper until Lynch rejoined the ship, was, along with his officers, remorseful over the loss of poor Dale. Lynch learned the *Supply* had been ordered by Commodore Read to stay with no duties at Mahon for half the month of July, then to take on supplies to the fleet in Spezia before being released to head toward the Syrian coast and the Lynch expedition.[43]

But then Lynch was infuriated to be shown a letter from Read, in which the fleet commander seemed to be trying to shift responsibility to Lynch: he asserted that he and Lynch had verbally agreed back in early February that Lynch could order the *Supply* to wait along the Syrian coast, off Acre or Jaffa, for the expedition to take its three-month course from Acre to Tiberias, from the Jordan to the Dead

Sea, and thence to Jerusalem, the seacoast, Galilee, the Jordan head-waters, and so on. Read even strangely asserted that Lynch had asked for this, thus hinting that by releasing the ship to its duties elsewhere, the tragedy was in the lieutenant's hands; Lynch could not believe his eyes at such an assertion, which had not ever been discussed, and which would have been in direct contradiction of the naval secretary's orders to Lynch, and would have put the ship's crew in danger of disease waiting four months on that "sultry coast" to pick up the explorers. He had copies of all the dated letters that proved the opposite, laying the blame on Read—though "I do not wish respectfully to complain," he wrote to Secretary Mason. It was strange, it was bizarre, it was "nothing short of fatuity," Lynch continued. Commodore Read might think that the interests of the fleet and U.S. policy superseded the needs of Lynch and party where the storeship was concerned, he said, but if he had only been informed that this was the way the wind was blowing, he could have chartered a ship at Jaffa, or Acre, or even Beirut before the men started dropping like flies from the plague, and these "successful measures" would have preserved "a valuable life." Dale might be alive, and all the other sufferings, perhaps even Homer's shotgun wound, might not have transpired.[44]

To these entreaties for an accounting, for an inquiry, there has survived only silence, as if the files were denied any further deposit of letters passing between Lieutenant William Francis Lynch and Naval Secretary John Young Mason on the blame for the untimely death of Lieutenant John B. Dale, husband, father, son of an eminent naval commander. Balanced against that: George Campbell Read, commander of the Mediterranean Fleet, past commander of the African Fleet, past commander of the Philadelphia Naval School, past commander of Old Ironsides, veteran of the pirate wars and the War of 1812, was eminent, too. And Secretary Mason was a politician. And Lieutenant Lynch was an officer.[45]

And there, then, it rested.

* * *

Lynch took back his command of the *Supply* on September 15 and re-embarked his men, his son, a hitchhiking Henry Bedlow, and the lifeboats. Into crates went the equipment, the notes, logs, diaries, charts, sketches, and journals; the surviving specimens in their cages, the rocks coaxed out of the Old World by Dr. Anderson's hammer, the chunk of Mrs. Lot from Usdum, the botanical clippings from the Ghor, and Ein Gedi, and Moab; the vials and bottles of water from the Jordan, the Sea of Lot, Callihroe, the pool of Gihon; the sand from Nazareth, the souvenirs from the souks at Jerusalem, Damascus, and Beirut. Two weeks later Lynch was at Marseilles, in terribly low spirits over the loss of friend Dale and the contretemps over responsibility; feeling himself the cause of the loss and all the suffering, he believed that he would return home disgraced, with long-felt hopes dashed, having let down his service, his supporters, and his country.

The ship had been refused pratique (release from quarantine) and free entry into the ports at Naples and Marseilles, for fear of the contagious diseases by then ruling the eastern Mediterranean coasts. But entirely by chance, before the *Supply* weighed anchor and left Marseilles, someone showed him a weeks-old copy of the *New York Herald*.[46] An article there digested a report from the *Southern Literary Messenger*. The source article was written by Lynch's friend Matthew Maury. It was based on long, detailed letters Lynch had written Maury from Jerusalem and Beirut, and contained a copious number of quotations from Lynch's accounts of their adventures in the Holy Land—the alarming first moments of a boat-swamping storm on the Dead Sea, the mysterious pillar of salt on the Usdum shore, the geologic descriptions of the submerged plains, the chemical analysis of the noxious waters, the myths exploded, the imagery of the Stars and Stripes flapping in the baleful wind of a sirocco. "We hope soon to have the pleasure of announcing his return to the United States," wrote Maury, "and welcoming him and his companions back to country, home, and friends."[47]

In late July Lieutenant Maury had excitedly approached the editor of the *Messenger*, John R. Thompson, offering to publish the first account of Lynch's Dead Sea expedition using his just-received letters from Lynch, but Maury wanted his article to run anonymously. Thompson thought the lieutenant only meant for him to keep quiet about the forthcoming article until the actual day of publication and so published it with prominent credit to the Naval Observatory director as author. To Maury's subsequent complaint, Thompson was obsequious in his apology: "I would sooner have sank the *Messenger* in the bottom of the Dead Sea itself," he hastened to assure Maury, "than to have outraged your confidence. I painfully and sincerely regret it."[48]

The damage to Maury's privacy, however, was done, and in the aftermath both Maury and Thompson felt sour about the matter, the former still so in mid-October when he received an anxious letter from none other than Virginia Lynch, his friend's adulterous ex-wife, writing from Louisville, Kentucky, after reading in local papers of the death of Lieutenant Dale near Beirut in August. The papers reported that the rest of the men were sick, and Mrs. Lynch said she was greatly worried about her ex-husband and their son Francis, whose last letter to her had been dated back on July 18: when, she wondered, were they expected home, and please, could Maury "do all in your power to relieve my great anxiety regarding those so near and dear to me."[49] Maury's answer was peremptory, hardly gallant, but it probably assuaged her fears; he was still obviously pained over the editor's mistake.

But the *Southern Literary Messenger* article attracted a huge amount of attention in the United States and abroad, and was extensively quoted in publications like the *New York Herald* to scholarly numbers like the *American Journal of Science*, and widely abroad. "Lieut. Maury gives a history of this expedition," said the *Herald*, "brief but lucid, and which will increase the anxiety of the public to see the report of Lieut. Lynch, who has made a successful survey, and who, we are glad to learn, is expected to return soon to this country." Edward Robinson also quoted extensively from Maury's article as well as letters from Lynch, in the November 1848 issue of his journal. "What it has accomplished," he said, keenly anticipating the official findings, "it has done well."[50]

Thus the depressed, defeated Lieutenant Lynch felt his mood soar as he read the *Herald*'s digest of the Maury article, and he put pen to paper as the *Supply* sailed toward Gibraltar, to give his friend thanks. "You have proved a true friend in need," Lynch would write to Maury.

> Three weeks since, on our arrival at Marseilles, my spirits were dejected from the loss of poor Dale, and I looked forward to much unkind criticism on our Expedition, which has terminated so unhappily. But at the moment when I was most despondent, I was cheered by a synopsis of your letter on the Expedition which was published in the *S. Lit. Messenger*. The *Herald* the paper that contained it, referred to your letter in the most flattering terms. Acceptable as well earned praise must be to you in common with all other men of laudable ambition. I know that you will be yet more gratified with the heartfelt thanks of an old friend to whose rescue you so gallantly hastened. I hope to live to grasp once more your honest hand and express how much I thank you.[51]

He had no idea that his name had become a household word at home.

Authorities at Gibraltar ordered the *Supply* away—"unclean, unclean!" was the general message, with hundreds dying daily in the cities of the Levant. "Like the dove that could find no resting-place," Lynch would note, "our weary ship then winged her way for home; and, early in December, we were greeted with the heart-cheering sight of our native land."[52] Norfolk and Virginia embraced them; Washington and Secretary Mason greeted Lynch with due honor; and he turned, with reams of blotted, travel-stained, minutely scrawled paper, to write his first book, finally at this late stage in his life feeling he had something to write about.

CHAPTER FOURTEEN

Aftermath: 1848–1865

THE *SUPPLY* CAME TO REST IN VIRGINIAN WATERS ON DECEMBER 8, 1848. As it dropped anchor, newspaper columns in Norfolk and in Washington as well as the rest of the East were struggling to digest the thousands of words of President Polk's last annual address on the state of the union, no less than 41 pages long, as delivered by a clerk to the combined bodies of the House and Senate on December 5.

"The gratitude of the nation to the Sovereign Arbiter of All Human Events should be commensurate with the boundless blessings which we enjoy," Polk had said. "Peace, plenty, and contentment reign throughout our borders, and our beloved country presents a sublime moral spectacle to the world." His war in Mexico was now history; California was conquered, Texas annexed, the Southwest and southern Rockies surrendered; with Oregon Territory acquired, the physical size of the nation had grown by more than a third, its new seacoasts lengthening the total by two-thirds.

To this widely known and celebrated knowledge, Polk flung a thunderbolt, which may have jolted some of the dozing denizens of the Capitol. "It was known that mines of the precious metals existed to a considerable extent in California at the time of its acquisition," he said. "Recent discoveries render it probable that these mines are more extensive and valuable than was anticipated. The accounts of the abundance of gold in that territory are of such an extraordinary character as would scarcely command belief were they not corroborated by the authentic reports of officers in the public service, who have visited the mineral district, and derived the facts which they detail from personal observation."

The harbor at San Francisco was already being thickened by derelict ships "deserted by their crews, and their voyages suspended for want of sailors," Polk continued. "Our commanding officer entertains apprehensions that soldiers cannot be kept in the public service without a large increase of pay. Desertions in his command have become frequent, and he recommends that those who shall withstand the strong temptation, and remain faithful, should be rewarded."

This official declaration giving solidity to widely scattered, often distrusted rumors of the past half-year of a new, true El Dorado, signaled the beginning of a vast tectonic shift in the population and the political power of the United States. Some 80,000 souls would struggle their way to California by land or by sea in the next year, with many more to follow, augmented by more streaming in from an uneasy Europe, and upon arrival themselves feeling the westward gravitational pull. The Navy would need to patrol its seas and protect its new ports, the Army to explore and map, protect wagon routes and garrison the West. Posts, villages, towns, even cities and capitals would sprout as farmers and ranchers made their imprint on the land, as resource exploiters commenced their extractions. The call would rise for better communication and transportation, for a national railroad to span the continent and lasso the new West to the bosom of the East. All this was unknown in the waning days of 1848 as the U.S.S. *Supply* rode the swells of Hampton Bays, and its captain disembarked and transferred to a Potomac packet, and, soon enough, took a tired but triumphant walk into the 17th Street office of the naval secretary—a fervent handshake, a clap on the back, perhaps a cigar but certainly not a brandy, even under such happy and relieved circumstances for the abstemious Lieutenant Lynch.

There were no welcoming parades for the adventurers—the country had had enough of parades for a while, after the Mexican War and then the three-way national election between two old war heroes and a consummate insider the previous fall. But the people had been digesting newspaper bulletins about the Dead Sea expedition for more than a year by then, and the columns were full of notices of their return and speculation about the most interesting report to come from the pen of Lieutenant Lynch.

The storeship crew was discharged until such time as they found another berth, with the exception of seaman Charles Homer with his blasted arm, who was sent for care to the Receiving Ship; the midshipmen given a two-month leave filtered off for home.[1] True to a promise made at the Crusader castle of Kerak, Lynch began a campaign to aid the beleaguered Christian community there with a long letter to the *Washington Globe*, widely reprinted, the cause taken up from pulpits around the country.[2] A grateful Lynch presented two crated, bawling red Arabian calves to Secretary Mason for his home farm.[3] Mason could not accept a personal gift from a subordinate, so the calves were delivered to "the people of Virginia," care of the governor, who chose a suitable Virginian gentleman farmer to raise and breed them. Lynch delivered the boxes of plant specimens and envelopes of seeds to the Patent Office, as expected. Aulick was detailed to take a chunk of salt from Usdum to the Library of Congress together with his sketch of the salt pillar standing out from the highlands.[4] A few ephemeral articles Lynch inadvertently left on board the *Supply*—an Egyptian tent, a Bedouin spear, and a tattered American flag they had carried down the Jordan and across the Dead Sea—fortunately were well stored at the Gosport Navy Yard until he would have time, in a year, to gratefully retrieve them.[5] Lynch, rejoined by Dr. Anderson who had returned to the States on his own, took possession of the crates of samples and resumed work writing the official reports in Washington and Baltimore.[6]

Lynch finished and submitted the official report on February 4 and his journal of travel down the lower Jordan River a few days later, telling Mason that the geological portion would take a few months to complete. Already there had been remarks in Congress about the expedition reports, notably from the Florida senator James Westcott. Vice President George Mifflin Dallas would deliver Secretary Mason's report along with the Lynch documents on the 26th, and it was ordered to be printed.[7] As the *New York Herald* had commented, "Lieut. Lynch's report will be eagerly awaited by the public."[8]

By then, Lynch was already embarked on a narrative version for book publication—"importuned from all quarters for a narrative," he told Mason in asking for official permission to issue such a work with a commercial press. It had become known in early February that someone had signed a contract with the Philadelphia publisher, Carey and Hart, to hastily write a book about the Dead Sea expedition. Initially Lynch thought that it was Dr. Anderson with such competitive literary plans. That was, however, swiftly cleared up and he found it was a crewmember of the *Supply*, the surgeon's steward, Edward Montague, aided by a diary of unknown authorship—capitalizing on the growing public interest in the returned expedition despite having been confined to the storeship for the duration of the season in question. Mason readily granted Lynch permission, adding that it did not seem right for "any other, who had not the responsibility of the enterprise," to rush to publication before Lieutenant Lynch. All the more reason for Lynch to redouble efforts, he thought. That the lieutenant also had pledged to turn over any profits to the family of the late, lamented Dale gave him even more entitlement, said Mason. Lynch would sign with Lea and Blanchard of Philadelphia, publisher of the *Encyclopedia Americana* and of other authoritative tomes such as Grahame's *History of the United States* and James Fenimore Cooper's history of the U.S. Navy, as well as Captain Charles Wilkes's narrative of the United States Exploring Expedition of 1838–42, as well as literary gems by Charles Dickens and Henry Fielding.[9]

Though Lynch worked day and night on the manuscript in Philadelphia, he was interrupted by the sad news that Mrs. Dale had died of consumption[10] on February 16, leaving her two children to be cared for by relatives; he labored from a distance to help "the poor orphan children" in Boston, as he told Mason, importuning the secretary to help him get the widow's pension transferred to the children, which Mason speedily helped him arrange.[11] It would be one of Mason's last official duties, for he would return to private life on March 4, with the inauguration of the Whig candidate General Zachary Taylor, "Old Rough and Ready," war hero of Buena Vista. Mason returned to Virginia to practice law, and during the Buchanan administration, to serve as minister to France. His Navy Department successor was Virginia representative William Ballard Preston, an attorney with little naval expertise— "a strong man, untried," was Matthew Maury's measured estimation. "The Navy—there is no doubt of it—is terribly demoralized. To heal it requires reform & how can reform be reasonably expected from those who know nothing about navy matters; navy wants; and navy ills."[12]

In Philadelphia, Lynch wrote furiously, heeding little of outside events unless they touched on his work. In March, he took a few minutes to send a thank-you letter to the inventor and manufacturer of the lifeboats he had steered through the Holy Land. "If in any way I can serve you," he wrote, "by making known the excellent qualities of your Metallic Life Boats, I feel bound to do so; for with no other kind of boat, however strongly constructed, could the descent of the Jordan have been accomplished, and the Expedition must have been unsuccessful without them." This and other testimonials, notably that of seaman Joseph Thomas, one of Lynch's men, were quickly put to use in marketing Francis' Metallic Lifeboats to the U.S. Navy and merchant shipping lines. "No other kind of boat could have bounded over rocks," said Thomas, "and down such deep and dangerous rapids. To these boats we owe our lives, for, had they failed, as did the one wooden boat we had, we must have been thrown on the shore, and been murdered by the hostile Arabs, and the whole Expedition have failed."[13]

In April he had a few bad days when it seemed that the Congressional Printing Office was releasing his official report before Lynch could correct its lavish typographical errors, but with frantic telegrams and letters shot over Secretary Preston's bow, Lynch was given enough breathing room to clean up the proofs.[14] The Montague book appeared in bookstores around March 30, 336 pages with a small, colored gatefold map of Palestine and Jerusalem, which, at least, was attractive. "Most of the diary was written on board ship," said the author, truthfully, in his preface, though he also claimed to have written "a portion in port, while a part of it was indited [sic] on shore, on horseback, or whilst mounted on the back of the camel." Lynch and some of his comrades wrote to the papers that "Mr. M. was not in the expedition, nor near the Dead Sea while the expedition was there." But the book was well advertised, and featured in most bookshops, and that knowledge could not have sat well with the laboring Lieutenant Lynch.[15] His own publisher rose to the competition by serializing an excerpt from Lynch's narrative—that about the Dead Sea —assault of the sirocco and their near swamping, which attracted encouraging attention in the press.[16]

He probably felt as if he had rounded the corner and was heading home with his narrative in early May when he contacted Preston again on behalf of the Dale orphans. An artist in the city had approached him—he did not identify him to the secretary, but presumably it was young John Banville, a painter who had achieved

worldwide success with his panoramic painting of the entire Mississippi River, done on a monumental, three-mile-long canvas that was
unrolled at a stately pace before theater audiences in the United
States and Europe. Banville's next project would be *Pilgrimage to the
Holy Land*, based on his own extensive travel and drawings. The artist,
said Lynch "is anxious to embody in it the sketches of scenes taken
by the recent expedition to the Dead Sea, and offers a share to the
orphan children of the late Lieut. Dale. . . . Many of the sketches
were taken by Lieut. Dale and as they are not embraced in my official
report, are of no public use whatever." The guardian and the children
supported the idea, and no one else from the expedition would have
any interest in the royalty. He received a quick approval from Ballard's office, the project went forward, and Lynch returned to pen
and inkwell.[17]

Weeks later in May the manuscript of more than 160,000 words
was finally done and lugged to the publisher. Unbound printed sheets
found their way to the office of the *Philadelphia Inquirer*, which found
them "beautifully executed" and bound to extend general knowledge.
And the first copies came out of the bindery late in the initial week of
June. As quickly as they could be crated, they were sent out on the
road. On June 7, anxious for approval, Lynch wrote John Y. Mason.
"With satisfaction tempered by fear," he wrote, "I send two copies of
my narrative. I pray your acceptance of them as a very slight proof of
my fervent and unbounded gratitude." Mason would see that the lieutenant had dedicated the book to him, "tribute to his private worth
and public excellence."[18]

Lea and Blanchard's embossed, gold-stamped edition bulked at
509 pages, with two large foldout maps, and 28 full-page wood
engravings rendered from the original drawings by Lieutenant Dale
and Passed Midshipman Aulick. It looked sumptuous, and a quick flip
through would flash glimpses of Bedouin warriors, ruined temples
and strongholds, hallowed villages and cities, frowning mountains,
unfathomable waters. It fairly flew out of the stores. It would be

printed again, revised, and reprinted in no fewer than nine editions. In England, Richard Bentley of London soon followed with at least six editions, later succeeded by a new and revised edition from James Blackwood that contained an introduction from the noted Irish dramatist James Sheridan Knowles. In Leipzig, Dyk'sche Buchhandlung issued a German translation that went through at least two editions. The next year, Lea and Blanchard released a condensed edition of 332 pages with one double map, which went through several printings and editions.

Lynch's *Narrative* was acknowledged to be a great critical success. "The narrative," pronounced the *Baltimore Sun*,

embracing so much that is entirely new, abounds, of course, with entertainment, while the style of the writer, so peculiarly adapted to invest the most trivial subject with interest, contributes to enchain the attention of the reader and charm and fascinate his imagination. There is an air of habitual truthfulness in the delineation of scenes, incidents and personal affairs, which engages our confidence and delights us with the assurance that the author, while appealing to the imagination, is not imposing upon it. Sensitively affected by the beautiful, the gentle, and the graceful, he is keenly alive to the grand, the majestic and the sublime, and his mind and pen respond alike harmonious to each. But, above all, he is susceptible of other emotions than those originating in the physical variety of the face of nature, and the narrative is imbued with sentiments, springing, as it were, spontaneously from the hallowed associations of the land of Palestine. The book is one that will speedily attain an enviable popularity."[19]

The *New York Commercial Advertiser* called it "a succinct, direct, pleasing account of those scenes which, under shelter of our national flag, he successfully explored. . . . Lieut. Lynch's style is altogether agreeable. It has an imaginative glow and a high poetic tinge, without verboseness or exaggeration—faults which too commonly accompany those qualities." The *New York Tribune* deemed it "a graphic and lively description of his adventures. . . . Our thanks are due to Lieut. Lynch for the gratification and instruction we have derived from the perusal of his very able volume, which bears the most emphatic testimony to his diligence, energy, fertility of invention, and devoted fidelity in the conduct of the expedition, as well as to the modesty, conscientiousness, and religious humanity of his personal character." The *Tribune* also delivered a critical coup de grâce on Lynch's competitor: "a superficial and commonplace narrative . . . wholly unworthy of the honor of print."[20]

From Savannah, Georgia, the *Republican* called Lynch's book "a work that well deserves to be faithfully read, and it should find a place in every library. . . . These pages are written with a good share of the graceful ease which is apt to belong to the narratives of seafaring men, and numerous anecdotal personal adventures enhance their value." The *Missouri Republican* declared that "we confess that we have not met with a book of travels that we have perused with more pleasure than this volume." The *Merchants' Magazine and Commercial Review* called it "highly creditable to the genius and research of the author."[21] "We have found this to be a much more readable book than we had anticipated," allowed the Whig organ, the *New Hampshire Patriot*. "Upon the whole, much new and interesting matter is contained in this work, and it will well repay the perusal."[22]

Weighing in similarly, the grouchy *Boston Daily Atlas* complained that Polk (who died in June of cholera contracted at New Orleans during a farewell tour), "who vetoed as unconstitutional the appropriation of money for the improvement of our own rivers and harbors, but yet could find constitutional authority for dispatching a government vessel and men some four thousand miles beyond our borders, to explore a river without any outlet, and a sea that can never be made available for commercial purpose—has not only passed from power, but from among his fellow men." The editor could not refrain from speaking ill of the dead or of his comatose party, but Lynch, the *Atlas* editor admitted, "has certainly made a very readable book of it, though we should like it much better if he had spared us all his poetic sentimentalism, of which he has altogether too much. . . . He writes as an enthusiast, of course, for none but one could have planned or undertaken such an expedition. It is all the more interesting on that account."[23]

British critics for the most part praised it highly, though a few thought it sometimes too feverish in literary style; those that refrained from critical comment nevertheless devoted many pages to digesting and quoting from the narrative. *Sharpe's London Journal* called it "most interesting and important"; the *North British Review* thought it, though hastily written, "of great value, not only for the additions which it makes to our knowledge, but as the authentic record of an enterprise in the highest degree honourable to all the parties concerned." It considered Montague's competing volume "upon the whole a worthless, trashy book."[24]

The successful author began work, as only seemed natural, on a memoir of his youthful days, *Naval Life, or, Observations Afloat and On Shore: The Midshipman* would be published by the fledgling New York firm of the young publisher Charles Scribner, in 1851, its 308 pages of dramatically written episodes from Lynch's apprentice days at sea padded inexplicably by long, torrid passages of romantic human interest stories collected in various ports of call—that a more judicious editor would have instantly trimmed. Unfortunately for the hopeful author (and his publisher), the protean Scribner editor Maxwell Perkins was not only unborn at the time but some 60 years from picking up his red pencil. It was respectfully but modestly received in the critical and book-buying communities. That was also the year he was awarded a medal from the Geographical Society of France.[25] Around this time, it has been long believed by descendants, Lynch began composing and publishing a series of high-flown, romantic penny novels, all under a pseudonym, which seemed to satisfy him immensely. The only trace of this literary oeuvre, one book-length manuscript, lies in a Virginia archive.[26]

Lynch bought a house in Baltimore and in October 1850 was recorded in the federal census as living there with his son Francis and his ex-wife Virginia, who evidently rejoined the family for a time to keep house; nothing is known about her later life. At some point subsequent Lynch remarried, to Eliza D. Lochhead, a Virginia native who was 20 years his junior, about whom little is known but that she died in 1880 of epilepsy and was buried with her husband.[27]

In between scribbling, and correcting and tinkering with his endless new editions of the *Narrative*, Lynch resumed his daily scanning of the obituary columns, hoping to see the name of a superior officer—any superior officer would do—that would open a space for him and even possibly give him a ship. The news soon came that Captain John Gwinn, a 67-year-old Marylander and former skipper of *The Constitution*, Old Ironsides, known in the service for his fondness for having errant sailors flogged, died either of chronic gastritis or a cerebral hemorrhage while at Palermo, Sicily, in September 1849. In October, Lieutenant Lynch was commissioned a commander; he would be awarded his captain's rank in March 1850.

He was back into the long reduced-pay, naval career torpor of "waiting for orders" after leave and then waiting for release from special duty connected with tying the last knots on his official Dead Sea report and scientific appendices; it would be published in Washington in 1852. Lynch looked for a fitting adventure as he passed his 50th birthday. In November 1849, he publicly responded to a call from the British Admiralty and a reward of 20,000 pounds from the wife of Sir John Franklin, arctic explorer whose ships had been missing in the Northwest Passage off Greenland since 1845. Lynch asked the Navy Department for a commission and ship to rescue Franklin and his men, and declared to the press that "in case the Government will sanction his efforts, he will raise from private sources sufficient to charter, strengthen, and equip a steamer, the Government furnishing such officers and men as choose to volunteer to go." He wrote to enlist Naval Lieutenant Edward Fitzgerald Beale, hero of many escapades in and after the Mexican War, as his second in command. "My reasons for applying to you are twofold," he wrote Beale, "first physical, for my own constitution is weak, while yours, from all I can learn, is a vigorous and hardy one, and secondly, you have the moral qualities, unshrinking courage and indomitable perseverance which are indispensable for such an undertaking." Maury, too, was enlisted to persuade Beale to join Lynch, but Beale, newly married, soon to leave the service to begin surveying the West, demurred.[28] Despite personal indications of encouragement from Lady Franklin, Lynch was not chosen when merchant Henry Grinnell privately outfitted two ships and crewed it with Navy volunteers.

Still, the high public interest in Lynch's Dead Sea and River Jordan Expedition, and the commercial success of his book, helped stimulate the Navy, Congress, and four presidential administrations (Whigs Zachary Taylor and Millard Fillmore and Democrats Franklin Pierce and James Buchanan) into sponsoring a decade of naval exploration that rivaled the land exploration and surveys of the Army in the American West, and far overshadowing them in terms of breadth and depth of scientific value.

Matthew Maury was, of course, instrumental in supporting this time of enlightenment, training at the Naval Observatory most of the young officers who would lead the explorations. Unable to convince Congress to support a land-based system of weather observation, he did succeed in inspiring an international congress to share mainland and ocean-based meteorological data. He also actively advocated the transcontinental railroad for years after 1849, countering Asa Whitney's popular plan for a route between Lake Michigan and the Pacific with a southern route—encountering fewer mountains and no harsh winters—that would link Memphis with the West Coast via Texas.

In 1849, the Navy sent an astronomical expedition to the Southern Hemisphere.

In 1851, Virginian Lieutenant William Lewis Herndon—Maury's cousin and former assistant—backed by Lieutenant Lardner Gibbon, led a large government expedition exploring the Amazon region. His party sailed to Lima, Peru, and they crossed the Andes. Gibbon separated from the main party and took men to explore the Bolivian tributaries, having many adventures, with Herndon leading the rest to the main trunk of the Amazon, and thence all the way to its mouth. His resulting reports and dramatic book (published in 1853) were widely circulated, filled with much geography, natural history, and ethnology. Gibbon also contributed a popular account. Maury, with an intellectual's distaste for slavery but with a Southerner's inability to imagine a world without it, had hoped that the Brazilian terrain could be developed to take off the pressure in the American South by absorbing its slave workers economy, even some of its plantation owners.

Another Virginian naval officer, Thomas Jefferson Page, was assigned in 1853 to take an expedition to Paraguay to explore the widest river in the world, the La Plata, and its headwaters. Equipped with diplomatic treaty powers, Page took a man-of-war, the side-wheel steamer *Water Witch* to South America. For three years Page steamed a total of 3,300 miles on rivers such as the Paraná and Paraguay, and traveled some 4,400 miles by land across Paraguay and the Mato Grosso province of Brazil. His relations with South American politicians hit a snag in 1854, when an "Ugly American" commercial agent, Edward Hopkins, involved Page in a diplomatic fracas. Page's ship was fired upon by Paraguayans. His protests were ignored. Two years later, though, President James Buchanan equipped him for a retaliatory mission; Page took a fleet of 19 ships back to Paraguay. Apologies swiftly greeted him. Page's report of explorations was a masterpiece, detailing contributions in geology, botany, zoology, and mineralogy.

Captain William Francis Lynch had, in fact, proposed the La Plata expedition in 1852 but was passed over in favor of the better-connected Page. Later that year, Lynch was back again, proposing to explore the coast and interior of Western Africa to contribute to the dramatically growing political interest in supporting the colony or protectorate of Liberia, and its neighbors, to settle freed slaves from America. Swiftly approved, Lynch's African reconnaissance occupied some six months, and his 64-page report was widely published and well praised and had a role in strengthening the settlement efforts, which must have personally satisfied the Virginian officer's private abolitionist views.

The next naval effort began in 1853 when Captain Matthew C. Perry, a Rhode Islander, six years older than Lynch and his former superior in the slave trade suppression squadron, was appointed by President Millard Fillmore to open relations with Japan. As is well known by most history students, Perry sailed a bristling armada and anchored in Yedo Bay in 1853, and stayed until Japanese officials agreed to consider the U.S. proposal. While they thought about it, Perry withdrew to the China coast. The "opening of Japan" concluded in early 1854. Perry's three-volume report on the China Seas and Japan began a long popular run in 1856.

Part of Perry's mission had been to extend knowledge about the China Sea, but yet another U.S. exploring expedition set out in 1852 to explore the China Sea, North Pacific, and the Bering Straits, a three-year mission originally proposed by Thomas Jefferson Page after his La Plata River adventures. Page was bypassed in favor of Commodore Cadwalader Ringgold, a Marylander who had commanded a ship during Wilkes's great exploring expedition and had saved much Gold Rush–era shipping by accurately surveying the Northern California coast. Matthew Maury of the Naval Observatory, whose efforts imprinted all the expeditions, designed the North Pacific scientific program. By the time the five ships reached Hong Kong (where the Taiping rebellion was raging), discipline had broken down, drunkenness and brawling was common, and Ringgold was suffering from malaria and a mental breakdown. Commodore Perry arrived on the scene (having just returned from his first sail to Japan), relieved Ringgold of command, and replaced him with Lieutenant John Rodgers. Over the next several years the ships exhaustively charted the China Sea and many of the bordering lands; the seamen had a multitude of difficulties with locals from Okinawa to Honshu and suffered many adventures with pirates, typhoons, and privation. In 1855 the ships sailed northward, dipping over the Korean and Siberian coastlines, and finally skirted the Aleutian chain on their return to the North American coast. They sailed into San Francisco harbor in October 1855. Later, several popular narratives by officers attracted many readers.

When the North Pacific Expedition was at its halfway mark, another naval effort was championed by Maury, supported by President Pierce, and led by Lieutenant Isaac Strain, a science-minded Pennsylvanian whose explorations included Brazil and Baja California; it focused on the Isthmus of Darien (present-day Panama). It was a long and hard eastward march between the Pacific and the Caribbean seeking a canal and railroad route, the sufferings of which resulted in a number of deaths including that of the commander. This harrowing journey was well documented in contemporary accounts, both official and popular.

In those heady years of exploration, during which time he was elected a fellow of the American Philosophical Society at its meeting of January 21, 1853,[29] Captain Lynch briefly commanded the

U.S.S. *Allegheny* in Virginia coastal waters before assuming command of the U.S.S. *Germantown* in November 1853, a 150-foot-long sloop of war that had seen service off Mexico, the Caribbean, and in the African Squadron. Under Lynch, it cruised the South Atlantic in the Brazil Squadron; during political unrest in Uruguay, he twice sent marines ashore to protect foreign commercial interests. Lynch commanded until February 1857, being placed on wait status after home leave.

During the next two years, he continued writing and gave lectures at places like the American Geographical and Statistical Society in New York; the society boosted its lecture series' attendance by holding it at Niblo's Saloon on Broadway, and Lynch's talk had the extra attraction of a ceremoniously unveiled painting, *The Dead Sea*, by the celebrated artist William E. Trove.[30] But of all his public appearances, perhaps the most satisfying was the well-attended talk on "the Commerce of the East"—widely reprinted in pamphlet form and in the press—at the large hall of the Cooper Union Institute. "The lecture will be illustrated by maps, showing the ocean routes, canal navigation and projected lines of railway," reported the *New York Herald*. "To those that have read Capt. Lynch's concise account of the Dead Sea expedition, the mere mention of his name in connection with a lecture would be sufficient to warrant their attendance on this occasion; but to those who have not had the pleasure of reading his fascinating book, we recommend them to go tonight and hear the author treat on this subject. . . . Captain Lynch is represented as a very eloquent speaker. The patriotic object of these lectures is sufficient to warrant a large attendance."[31]

Eleven weeks later, also in the great hall of the Cooper Union Institute, the Republican presidential candidate from Illinois, Abraham Lincoln, would deliver his historic talk on the subject of slavery, the Constitution, the federal union, and the growing threat of secession in the South.

* * *

In the early morning of April 12, 1861, in Charleston Harbor, when a mortar round shot from Fort Johnson on the mainland burst in the air above the besieged Fort Sumter, it signaled 43 Confederate guns ringing the island to begin the bombardment that opened the Civil War. "In a moment," remembered Captain Abner Doubleday, from New York and West Point, "the firing burst forth in one continuous roar, and large patches of both the exterior and interior masonry began to crumble and fall in all directions." Shells began to set the fort afire, and "the balls and shells from the ten-inch columbiads, accompanied by shells from the thirteen-inch mortars which constantly bombarded us, made us feel as if the war had commenced in earnest."[32]

With those first shots the Civil War had indeed commenced in earnest. To the seven states of the Deep South, which had seceded from the Union following the election of Abraham Lincoln on November 6, were added the four states of the upper border—Virginia, on April 17, and Arkansas, Tennessee, and North Carolina over the next month. An invasion from the North was inevitable. Virginia's secession sent a shock wave through the officer corps of the U.S. Army and U.S. Navy, with many of the most gifted in the federal service resigning—270 Army officers, a quarter of the federal leadership,[33] and from the Navy, more than 100 officers in the month of April alone, doubling the number "going south" since election day—16 percent of the Navy's captains, 27 percent of its commanders, 25 percent of its lieutenants.[34]

Commander Maury tendered his resignation in Washington on Saturday, April 20; Captain Lynch wrote his on Sunday, April 21 from Norfolk. Both were accepted.

* * *

Maury, becoming an ardent secessionist, served the Confederacy as Chief of Sea Coast, River, and Harbor Defenses, and spent well-publicized diplomatic time in Europe, securing financial and military support. He also developed an electric torpedo, so effective against federal shipping that the U.S. secretary of the Navy reported in 1865 that the invention had "cost the Union more vessels than all other causes combined."[35] After the war and his federal parole, Maury consulted for Emperor Maximilian of Mexico, helping develop an immigrant community that would include self-exiled Confederates. In 1868 he was one of the founders of the American Association for the Advancement of Science. He was an honorary pallbearer in 1870 for the funeral of Robert E. Lee. He took a chair in physics at Virginia Mechanical College in 1872, but died a semester later, in February 1873, and is buried in Hollywood Cemetery, Richmond, Virginia.[36]

Commissioned a captain in the Virginia Navy and then the Confederate States Navy, William Francis Lynch commanded naval batteries at Aquia Creek, Virginia, and naval defenses along his home state's and North Carolina's coastal waters. In 1862, he took part in the defense of Roanoke Island, North Carolina, and commanded Mississippi River defenses at Vicksburg, and through 1864 led naval defenses of Fort Fisher in North Carolina and again in Virginia. He was paroled at Richmond two weeks after Appomattox. President Andrew Johnson signed a special executive pardon on June 11, 1865.[37]

He moved back to Baltimore, which Lynch had considered his home in the years between the Dead Sea and Fort Sumter, and where he kept many friends in spite of the great, almost unhealing rift that had opened down the middle of America. He resided at his house on East Baltimore Street at the corner of Ann Street and attended St. Andrew's Episcopal Church until his death, on October 17, 1865, at 64. His funeral filled his house two days later, officiated by the Reverend Mr. Henry of St. Andrews, and before his body was borne to the parklike Green Mount Cemetery—which sheltered governors, senators, mayors, military leaders, industrialists, philanthropists, educators, artists, writers, and actors, including John Wilkes Booth—in his last home Captain Lynch's mourners viewed, one hopes, the ephemera of a 42-year career on many oceans, at many ports, including a vial of water, a bottle of beach sand, a Bedouin spear, a folded tent, and a faded, extremely tattered American flag.[38]

Notes

Prelude

[1] Lynch, *Narrative*, 117; Reverend J. P. Newman, *From Dan to Beersheba*, 432–459; *Smith's Dictionary of the Bible*, 2514; Bromley, *Bible Encyclopedia*, 9350, "Ladder of Tyre," http://bible-history.com/isbe/l/ladder+of+tyre.
[2] Lynch, *Narrative*, 115–116.

Chapter One

[1] Lynch, *Naval Life*, 9.
[2] Ibid., 81, 85.
[3] Ibid., 115.
[4] Ibid., 29.
[5] Ibid., 141, 149–150; Lane, "The African Squadron"; Morison, *"Old Bruin,"* 70–76; Alden and Westcott, *The United States Navy*, 117.
[6] Lynch, *Naval Life*, 154.
[7] Ibid., 235; Alden and Westcott, *The United States Navy*, 116–117.
[8] Lynch, *Narrative*, 234–235, 239–241.
[9] Church, "Lafayette's Last Visit to America"; A. Levasseur, *Lafayette in America*; MacIntire, *Lafayette*; Ward, *An Account*.
[10] Levasseur, *Lafayette in America*, 258–259; Church, "Lafayette's Last Visit to America," 339.
[11] Mary Maury Werth sketch of her father, Maury Papers, vol. 42, Library of Congress (henceforth identified as MP, LC); Dabney H. Maury document, January 25, 1872, MP, vol. 44, LC; MFM to Rutson Maury, August 31, 1840, Maury Correspondence, University of Virginia Alderman

Library (henceforth identified as MC, UVAL); Williams, *Matthew Fontaine Maury*, 26–32.

[12] MFM to Rutson Maury, August 31, 1840, MC; Navy Records, *Appointments*, vol. 13, 235, National Archives; Williams, *Matthew Fontaine Maury*, 32–37.

[13] Corbin, *A Life*, 16–17; MFM to Rutson Maury, August 31, 1840, MC; Williams, *Matthew Fontaine Maury*, 43–58.

[14] Levasseur, *Lafayette in America*, 258–261.

[15] *New York Registers of Vessels*, M237, Roll 8, list 97.

[16] *William Francis Lynch Biography*, U.S. Navy chronology compiled March 22, 1935. ZB Files, U.S. Navy Library.

[17] Cooper, 140.

[18] *Lynch Biography*, U.S. Navy Library; *Dictionary of American Naval Fighting Ships*.

[19] *Army and Navy Chronicle* 6, no. 1 (July 5, 1838): 5.

[20] MFM to Blackford, October 2, 1849, Box 3, MP, LC. Also cited by Frances Leigh Williams, Maury's biographer.

[21] *William F. Lynch vs. Virginia Lynch*. FR Divorce. Maryland State Archives, Chancery Court Papers 1845–1846, MSA SSF 512, 1846/01/30, 9234 [Acc, 17,898-9234, MSA S512-11-9519. Loc. 1/38/4].

Chapter Two

[1] John Quincy Adams: First Annual Message, December 6, 1825: http://www.presidency.ucsb.edu/ws/index.php?pid=29467.

[2] The following excellent sources should be consulted about Reynolds, the Exploring Expedition, and Charles Wilkes: William Stanton, *The Great United States Exploring Expedition of 1838–1842* (1975); David B. Tyler, *The Wilkes Expedition* (1968); Nathaniel Philbrick, *Sea of Glory* (2004).

[3] Reynolds's address was republished in *Southern Literary Messenger* (January 1837).

[4] Cong. Debates, 24 Cong., 1 sess., vol. 12, part 2, 1298–1299; part 3, 3467–3478; Stanton, *Great United States Exploring Expedition, 33*.

[5] Jackson to secretary of the Navy, July 9, 1836, Ex. Ex. Letters 1.

[6] W. Patrick Strauss, "Mahlon Dickerson," in Coletta, *American Secretaries*, 155–163;

[7] Williams, *Matthew Fontaine Maury*, 85–88.

[8] Stevens and Smith, "Two Early Proposals," 127–137.

[9] Fasano, *Naval Rank*, 23, 69–75.

[10] Maury, "On the Navigation of Cape Horn," 60–61.

[11] Ibid., 56–61.

[12] Corbin, *A Life*, 25; Williams, *Matthew Fontaine Maury*, 101–102, 105–106.

[13] Williams, *Matthew Fontaine Maury*, 103–109.

[14] *Southern Literary Messenger* 2, no. 7 (June 1836): 454–455.

[15] *American Journal of Science and Arts* 32, no. 1 (July 1837): 208.

[16] Williams, *Matthew Fontaine Maury*, 112–113.

[17] MFM to Ann Maury of New York, September 23, 1836, MC, UVAL.

[18] Reynolds, *Pacific and Indian Oceans*, 310–451, 505–507, 514–515; *New York Times*, July–September 1837, and *New York Courier & Enquirer*, December 1837–January 1838; Tyler, *Wilkes Expedition*, 8.

[19] MFM to Dickerson, October 23, 1837, Ex. Ex., House Exec. Doc. No. 147, 498–499.20

[20] Charles Wilkes to Naval Secretary Samuel Southard, October 5, 1828; Jeremiah Reynolds to Southard, October 28, 1828: Box 28, Folder 11, Collection 250, Southard Papers, Princeton University Library; Philbrick, *Sea of Glory*, 23–24.

[21] Steven J. Dick, *Sky and Ocean Joined*, 12–14, 15–29, 37.

[22] Jones to Dickerson, November 4, 1837: *Exploring Expedition*, House Ex. Doc. No. 147, 503.

[23] Jones to MFM, November 12, 1837, quoted in MFM to Dickerson, November 14, 1837, *Exploring Expedition*, House Ex. Doc. No. 147, 583–585.

[24] MFM to Dickerson, November 14, 1837, House Ex. Doc. No. 147, 583—585.

[25] Jones to Dickerson, November 14, 1837, Ex. Ex., House Exec. Doc. No. 147, 562–564.

[26] Dickerson Papers, Historical Society of New Jersey, Newark.

[27] MFM to Ann Maury of New York, January 25, 1872, MP, vol. 42, LOC; MFM to Ann Maury of New York, April 5, 1838. MC, UVAL; Hawthorne, *Matthew Fontaine Maury*, 60–61.

[28] Adams, *Memoirs*, 491; Stanton, *The Great United States Exploring Expedition*, 62.

[29] W. Patrick Strauss, "James Kirke Paulding" in Coletta, *American Secretaries*, 164–171.

[30] "Harry Bluff" articles appeared in the *Richmond Whig and Public Advertiser*, August 10, 13, 14, 17, 18, 25, 27, 28, September 4, 1838. "Will

Watch" letters appeared in the *Richmond Whig and Public Advertiser*, December 21, 25, 28, 1838.

[31] Williams, *Matthew Fontaine Maury*, 512, note 124; MFM to Ann Maury of New York, April 5, 1838, MC, UVAL.

[32] Paulding to Dickerson, December 3, 1838, Dickerson Papers, Historical Society of New Jersey, Newark.

[33] By far, the best general biography of Maury is Frances Leigh Williams's *Matthew Fontaine Maury, Scientist of the Sea* (1963). An uncritical though valuable resource is Diana Fontaine Maury Corbin's *A Life of Matthew Fontaine Maury* (1888).

[34] *M.F. Maury v. D. Talmadge*, U.S. Circuit Court, Columbus, Ohio, July Session, 1840, in John McLean (ed.), *U.S. Circuit Court*, 157–167; MFM to Ann Maury of New York, November 6, November 17, December 7, December 25, 1839, MC, UVAL; MFM to Ann Maury of New York, December 16 and 17, 1839, MP, vol. 2, LC; Williams, *Matthew Fontaine Maury*, 121–124; Corbin, *A Life*, 29–32.

[35] MFM to Ann Maury of New York, January 26, 1840, October 15, 1842, MC, UVAL.

[36] "Scraps from the Lucky Bag" by "Harry Bluff," No. 1, *Southern Literary Messenger* 6, no. 4 (April 1840): 233–240; No. 2, *SLM* 6, no. 5 (May 1840), 306–320; No. 3, *SLM* 6, no. 12 (December 1840): 786–800; No. 4, *SLM* 6, no. 1 (January 1841): 3–25; "Supplement to Scraps from the Lucky Bag," *SLM* 7, no. 2 (February 1841): 169–170; "More Scraps from the Lucky Bag," *SLM* 7 nos. 5 and 6 (May and June 1841): 345–379.

[37] White to MFM, December 13, 1840: recounted in MFM to Lucian Minor, December 14, 1840.

[38] Williams, *Matthew Fontaine Maury*, 135.

[39] MFM to Ann Maury of New York, June 21, 1841, MC, UVAL.

[40] "Lieutenant M. F. Maury of U.S. Navy," by "A Brother Officer," *SLM* 8, no. 7 (July 1841): 560–563.

[41] MFM to Matthew Maury, October 12, 1840, and MFM to Ann Maury of New York, June 21, 1841, MC, UVAL; MFM to Secretary of Navy George E. Badger, June 10, 1841, MP, vol. 2, LOC; MFM to Ann Maury of New York, July 4, August 14 and October 10, 1841, MC, UVAL.

[42] Secretary of Navy A. P. Upshur to MFM, November 15, 1841, MP, vol. 2, LOC; MFM to Secretary of Navy A.P. Upshur, November 18, 1841, MP, vol. 2, LOC.

[43] Paolo E. Coletta, "Abel Parker Upshur" in Coletta, *American Secre-*

taries, 177–197; Gould, Benjamin Apthorp, "Biographical Notice of James Melville Gilliss," *Biographical Memoirs*, 135–179; Dick, *Sky and Ocean Joined*, 44–60.

[44] MFM to Rutson Maury, February 20 and February 22, 1842, MC, UVAL; MFM to Prof. John B. Minor, January 28, 1856, MP, vol. 5, LOC.

[45] *New York Morning Herald*, June 13, 1842; Stanton, *The Great United States Exploring Expedition*, 278–289; Tyler, *Wilkes Expedition*, 368–385.

[46] See Haskell, *The U.S. Exploring Expedition*.

[47] United States Navy Department, 1842, *Courts Martial Records* 43, nos. 823–826; 44, no. 827.

[48] Stanton, *The Great United States Exploring Expedition*, 282.

[49] Charles Wilkes, "Autobiography and Other Writings," 1374–1380, Wilkes Papers' LOCO.

[50] Gilliss's efforts in outfitting what would become the Naval, or National Observatory are well covered in Dick, 44–60.

[51] MFM to Ann Maury of New York, August 4, 1842, October 15, 1842, MC, UVAL.

[52] Maury, Introduction, *Physical Geography*, vii.

[53] MFM to Ann Maury of New York, February 16, 1843, MC, UVAL.

[54] K. Jack Bauer, "Thomas Walker Gilmer," in Coletta, *American Secretaries*, 203–205.

[55] K. Jack Bauer, "John Young Mason," in Coletta, *American Secretaries*, 207–214.

[56] Dick, *Sky and Ocean Joined*, 44–60.

[57] MFM to William Blackford, November 19, 1843, MP, vol. 3, LOC; Williams, *Matthew Fontaine Maury*, 156–157; MFM to William Blackford, January 1, 1847, MP, vol. 3, LOC; Corbin, *A Life*, 49–50.

[58] MFM to Commodore William M. Crane, October 12, 1844. Naval Observatory—Letters Sent, vol. 1, NARS.

[59] Dick, *Sky and Ocean Joined*, 44–60; Williams, *Matthew Fontaine Maury*, 158–161. "Systematic Review and Exploration": U.S. Naval Observatory, *Washington Observations*, vol. 1, 33.

[60] Once again I am indebted to Bernard DeVoto and his *The Year of Decision: 1846*, in this instance for the first reference to Maury I saw, as a young reader, decades ago: 3–4.

[61] Coletta, *American Secretaries*, 217–229.

[62] Adams, *Memoirs*, XII, 189; MFM to J. Q. Adams, July 28, 1846, Naval Observatory—Letters Sent, vol. 2, National Archives; Williams,

Matthew Fontaine Maury, 160.

[63] Sarah Mytton Maury, 167–168. Note: Mrs. Maury was not a blood relative of MFM but had recently married his cousin William Maury in Liverpool.

[64] MFM to Prof. Benjamin Peirce, Cambridge, Mass., March 20, 1845, Naval Observatory—Letters Sent, vol. 1; Williams, *Matthew Fontaine Maury*, 524.

[65] Williams, *Matthew Fontaine* Maury,167.

[66] MFM to Prof. Elias Loomis, Union College, New York, April 20, 1847, Naval Observatory—Letters Sent, vol. 2, National Archives.

[67] The Walker-Henry-Bache affair is well covered in Williams, *Matthew Fontaine Maury*, 167–175. The German publication was *Astronomische Nachrichten*, (Altona, Germany, 1847) vol. 26. See also: MFM to Joseph Henry, September 20, 1847 and October 20, 1847, Naval Observatory—Letters Sent, vol. 2, National Archives, and Williams's explanatory notes 69 and 72 in her book, p. 527.

[68] Alexander Dallas Bache to MFM, April 14, 1835, quoted in Maury, *New Theoretical and Practical Treatise*, 337.

[69] *Astronomical Observations*, 1180.

[70] MFM to William Blackford, January 1, 1847, MP, vol. 3, LOC.

[71] Sarah Mytton Maury, *Op. Cit.*

[72] MFM to Prof. Elias Loomis of Union College, April 20, 1847. Naval Observatory—Letters Sent, vol. 2, NARA.

Chapter Three

[1] Lynch, *Narrative*, 13.

[2] *New York Review*, October 2, 1837, 351–367.

[3] Lynch, *Narrative*, vi.

[4] Kent, *Biblical Geography and History*, 54. The author continues, "In common with the Jordan valley, this region is richly suggestive of the destructive forces of nature. Life is here grim, severe, and relentless. It is not difficult to detect in Jewish character the deep impressions made by this constant contact with the symbols of death and with these suggestions of the presence of a stern, austere God." John the Baptist: Josephus, *The Antiquities of the Jews*, 18:5:2, Works. Masada: Robinson, 525; Josephus, *The Wars of the Jews*, 7:9:1–2, Works.

[5] Josephus, *The Wars of the Jews*, 4:8:4, Works.

[6] Stephens, *Incidents of Travel*, 336–337.

[7] Robinson, "Depression of the Dead Sea," 77–88.

[8] John Young Mason Papers; Confidential Letters, RG 45, T-829, Roll 359, NARA; Letters Received by Sec. Navy from Officers Below Rank of Commander," RG 45, M-148, Roll 182, NARA.

[9] Lynch to MFM, May 8, 1847, National Archives, RG45, M148, Roll 182, NARA.

[10] MFM to Matthew Maury, Jr., March 3, 1840. MC, UVAL.

[11] Maury, "The Dead Sea Expedition," 549.

[12i] Mason to Lynch, May 27, 1847. M49, Roll 42, NARA.

[13] Battle, *A History*, 503–509; "Address Before the Alumni Association of the University of North Carolina," John Young Mason Papers; *New York Herald*.

[14] *Richmond Enquirer*, June 11, 1847; *Boston Journal*, June 19, 1847; *Niles Register*, June 26, 1847.

[15] *Niles Register*, June 26, 1847; "Taney," "Supply": Chapelle, *History of the American Sailing Navy*, 460, 544; *Report of the Secretary of the Navy*, December 5, 1846; *Bronson's Quarterly Review* 6 (January 1852): 204.

[16] Mason to Lynch, July 31, 1847, RG 45, M325, NARA.

Chapter Four

[1] Lynch to MFM, August 2, 1847, Naval Historical Foundation Manuscript Collection, Box 231, Manuscript Division, Library of Congress.

[2] Passport application, May 29, 1858, Passport Applications, 1795–1905; (National Archives Microfilm Publication M1372); General Records of the Department of State, Record Group 59; National Archives, Washington, D.C.

[3] Lynch, *Narrative*, 14.

[4] Lynch, *Narrative*, 15, 19; Lynch to Mason, August 12, 13, 1847, M335, Roll 181; Mason to Lynch, August 14, 1847, M325, Roll 43, NARA.

[5] Lynch, *Narrative*, vi; *Putnam's Monthly* 1 (January 1853): 64–68; Walter Hubbard and Richard F. Winter, "North Atlantic Mail Sailings 1840–75" (U.S. Philatelic Classics Soc., Inc., Ohio), 1988; "An Hour with Humboldt," *Living Age* 15, no. 180, October 1847: 145–192; Lynch to Mason, November 4, 1847, M148, Roll 182, NARA.

[6] *Bibliotheca Sacra* 19 (August 1848): 34.

[7] Buchanan to Mason, Washington D.C., October 15, 1847; Buchanan to Carr, Washington D.C., October 15, 1847, Moore, *Works of James Buchanan*, vol. 7, 433–435.

[8] Lynch to Mason, October 16, 1847, M335, Roll 182, NARA.

[9] Mason to Lynch, October 18, 1847, M325, Roll 43, NARA.

[10] Lynch, *Narrative*, 15; Mason to Lynch, October 26, 1847, M325 Reel 43, NARA; Lynch to Maury, October 21, 1847, Naval Observatory—Letters Received, NARA; Lynch to Mason, November 15, 1847, M335, Roll 182; NARA; Maury to Dale, October 22, 1847, National Observatory—Letters Sent, RG78, NARA.

[11] Lynch to Maury, undated letter (about November 9) misfiled in Naval Observatory Correspondence—Incoming, Box 3, folder 1 (January–June 1847), LOC; MFM to Lynch, November 11, 1847 (three separate notes), RG78 USNO—Letters Sent, NARA; Arthur Stewart to Maury, November 22, 1847, Naval Observatory—Incoming Correspondence, Box 3, Folder 2.

[12] *New York Herald*, November 20, 1847; *Friends' Review* 1, no. 18 (1848).

[13] Lynch to Mason, November 4, 1847, M148, Roll 182, NARA; Mason to Lynch, November 4, 1847, M325, Roll 43, NARA; Lynch to MFM, undated letter (about November 9) misfiled in Naval Observatory Correspondence—Incoming, Box 3, folder 1 (January–June 1847), LOC; Mason to Lynch, November 11, 1847 (two letters), T-829, Roll 359, NARA.

[14] Lynch to Mason, November 17, 1847, M335, Roll 182, NARA; Mason to Lynch, November 19, 1847, M325, Roll 43, NARA.

[15] Lynch, *Narrative*, 16–17; Lynch to Mason, November 26, 1847, M335, Roll 182, NARA.

[16] Lynch to Mason, Gibraltar, December 19, 1847, T829, Roll 438.

[17] Lynch, *Narrative*, 21–26.

[18] Lynch to Mason, Gibraltar, December 19, 1847, January 22, 1848, T829, Roll 438, NARA; Lynch, *Narrative*, 29; Montague, *Narrative*, 78–79; *New York Herald*, March 23, 1848, 1.

[19] Lynch, *Narrative*, 91–93; Lynch to Mason, Gibraltar, December 26, 1847, January 22, 1848, T829, Roll 438, NARA; Lynch, *Narrative*, 33.

[20] Lynch, *Narrative*, 34–38.

[21] Ibid., 48–55.

[22] Ibid., 56–57.

[23] Ibid.,169; Pelletreau, *Historic Homes*, 111–119; Hill, *Historical Register*, 171–172; *Factors in Columbia County History*, 10–11.

[24] Lynch, *Narrative*, 76–77; *New York Herald*, April 11, 1848, 2.

[25] Lynch, *Narrative*, 91–92.

[26] Ibid., 79.

[27] Lynch to Mason, March 8, 1848. T829, Roll 438, NARA.

[28] Mason to Lynch, Washington D.C., February 28, 1848, March 31, 1848, T829, Roll 359.

[28] *New York Courier*, quoted in *Baltimore Sun*, December 1, 1847, 1; *Baltimore Sun*, December 1, 1847, 1; *Berkshire Whig*, January 6, 1848, 3; *Journal of Commerce*, quoted in *Charleston* (South Carolina) *Patriot*, December 29, 1847, 2; *Maine Farmer*, quoted in *Berkshire Whig*, January 6, 1848, 2.

[30] Lynch, *Narrative*, 113; *New York Herald*, April 15, 1848, 2.

[31] Antonius Ameuny: *Banvard's Description*, New York, 1853, vi.

[32] Molyneux, "Expedition to the Jordan," 104–130.

[33] Ibid., 136–138; Lynch to Anderson, March 31, 1848, T829, Roll 438, NARA.

[34v] Lynch, *Narrative*, 115–118; *Appleton's Cyclopedia* (Henry James Anderson); Lynch to Mason, March 31, 1848, T829, Roll 438; Lynch to Anderson, March 31, 1848, T829, Roll 438, NARA.

Chapter Five

[1] Lynch, *Narrative*, 130–131.

[2] Winthrop to Bancroft, May 4, 1848, T829, Roll 438.

[3] Lynch, *Narrative*, 136. Lynch to Mason, Encampment near Acre, April 3, 1848, T829, Roll 438.

[4] Lynch, *Narrative*, 142–143.

[5] Ibid., 144.

[6] Winthrop to Bancroft, May 4, 1848, T829, Roll 438.

[7] Lynch, *Narrative*, 150.

[8] Ibid., 147.

[9] Ibid., 149–151. Lynch to Mason, Encampment near Turan, April 4, 1848, T829, Roll 438.

[10] Twain, *Innocents Abroad*, 372.

[11] Lynch, *Narrative*, 161.

[12] Ibid., 161, 165.

[13] Ibid., 162; Lynch to Mason, Tiberias, April 7, 1848, T829, Roll 438; Seetzen, 21.

[14] Lynch, *Narrative*, 167–168.

[14] Ibid., 165.

16 Lynch, *Narrative*, 169.

17 Ibid., 171.

18 Ibid., 172–173; Lynch, *Minutes taken during the descent of the Jordan* (hereinafter referred to as *Minutes*), April 10, 1848, Official Report.

Chapter Six

1 I am indebted for phraseology and background to the eminent Nelson Glueck, "The Geography of the Jordan," 719–744; and John D. Whiting, "Canoeing Down the River Jordan," 781–808.

2 Lynch, *Narrative*, 173–175.

3 Ibid., 179; Lynch, *Minutes*, April 11, 1848.

4 Lynch, *Narrative*, 179–180.

5 Ibid., 186–187.

6 Ibid., 188.

7 Ibid., 189–190; Lynch, *Minutes*, April 12, 1848.

8 Lynch, *Narrative*, 192.

9 Ibid., 194–198.

10 Ibid., 199.

11 Ibid., 201; Lynch, *Minutes*, April 13, 1848.

12 Lynch, *Narrative*, 208.

13 Ibid., 208–209.

14 Ibid., 216, 329.

15 Ibid., 211–221; Lynch, *Minutes*, April 14, 1848.

16 Lynch, *Narrative*, 222–245; Lynch, *Minutes*, April 15, 1848.

17 Lynch, *Narrative*, 232.

18 Ibid., 239.

19 Ibid., 240–245; Lynch, *Minutes*, April 15, 1848.

Chapter Seven

1 Lynch, *Narrative*, 247; Molyneux, "Expedition to the Jordan," 120–121, 130.

2 Lynch, *Narrative*, 248–250.

3 Ibid., 251; Lynch, *Minutes*, April 17, 1848.

4 Lynch, *Narrative*, 252–253.

5 Ibid., 254–260; Lynch, *Minutes*, April 17, 1848.

6 Lynch, *Narrative*, 260–263; Theoderich, *Guide to the Holy Land*, 48–49.

7 Lynch, *Narrative*, 262–265.

Chapter Eight

[1] Saewulf, "The Travels," in Wright, *Early Travels*, 47.

[2] Ibid., 267–272; Lynch to Mason, April 29, 1848, T829, Roll 438;

[3] Lynch, *Narrative*, 269–271.

[4] Josephus, *The War of the Jews*, vol. 8, 4, Works, 476–484; Theoderich, *Guide to the Holy Land*, 53–54; Gervase of Tilbury, *Otia Imperialia*, 588–589, 796–797; Wright, *Geographical Lore*, 208–209.

[5] Seetzen, 41; Robinson, *Biblical Researches*, 517–518; Josephus, op. cit., 480–482; Maundrell, "A Journey From Aleppo to Jerusalem, at Easter, A.D. 1697," in Wright, *Early Travels*, 453; Robinson, *Biblical Researches*, 512.

[6] Lynch, *Narrative*, 274–275.

[7] Melville, *Journal of a Visit*, 136.

[8] Ibid., 278–280.

[9] Ibid., 282.

[10] Ezekiel 47, 1–12; Smith, *Historical Geography of the Holy Land*, 509–510.

[11] Lynch, *Narrative*, 290–292; Smith, *Historical Geography of the Holy Land*, 272–273.

[12] Robert Payne, *The Dream and the Tomb*,118; Fulcher of Chartres, *Chronicle*, 79.

[13] Seetzen, 43.

[14] Lynch, *Narrative*, 291–292.

[15] Ibid.

[16] Ibid., 295; *New York Herald*, June 8, 1848, 2.

[17] Irby and Mangles, 390; Lynch, 298.

[18] Ibid., 299.

Chapter Nine

[1] Ibid., 301, 304.

[2] Ibid., 307.

[3] Ibid., 302.

[4] Ibid., 305.

[5] Josephus, *The Wars of the Jews*, Works, vol. 4, 8, 311.

[6] Josephus, *The Wars of the Jews*, Works, vol. 4, 8, 484; Theoderich, *Guide to the Holy Land*, xxxv, 54; Maundrell, 144; Seetzen, 43.

[7] Josephus, *Antiquities*, Works, vol. 1, 11, 203; Maundeville, in Wright, *Early Travels*, 180; White, *History of the Warfare*, 221–235; Lynch, *Narrative*, 307–308.

[8] Lynch, *Narrative*, 313.

[9] Ibid., 315–316.

[10] Ibid., 316–317.

[11] Ibid., 317.

[12] Josephus, *The Antiquities of the Jews*, Works, vol. 1, 11, 4–5; *Genesis* 19:30—38.

[13] Lynch, *Narrative*, 316–319.

[14] Ibid., 324.

[15] Ibid., 320–322; Lynch to Mason, April 29, May 18, 1848, T829, Roll 438. "We have been all gratified to learn that the statement was unfounded," wrote Lynch from Jerusalem of the Polk rumor.

[16] Ibid.

[17] Lynch, *Narrative*, 322.

[18] Bedlow, *War and Worship*, 3, 24. On the title page is this statement: "Convictions Based on Recollections of the Revolts of 1848. While the officers attached to the expedition under the command of Lieut. W. F. Lynch were camped at Ain-Jiddy (En Gedi) on the shores of the Dead Sea, a messenger from Jerusalem brought tidings of the revolutionary state of Europe and the spirit of 'Popular Rule' animating all parties arrayed against the dominant powers. The following verses were suggested at the time and place above mentioned, roughly sketched in Syria, and completed in Palestine and New York. Henry Bedlow."

[19] Josephus, *The Wars of the Jews*, Works, vol. 4, 8, 484; Robinson, *Biblical Researches*, 523–524; Lynch, *Narrative*, 325–327.

[20] Shanks, "Ein Gedi's Archaeological Riches"; Ussishkin, "The Ghassulian Temple," 23–39.

[21] Lynch, *Narrative*, 322–323.

[22] Ibid., 324–325; Josephus, *The Wars of the Jews*, Works, vol. 4, 8, 477; Stephens, *Incidents of Travel*, 393; Twain, *Innocents Abroad*, 445.

Chapter Ten

[1] Josephus, *The Wars of the Jews*, Works, vol. 7, 8–9.

[2] *Bibliotheca Sacra* (February 1, 1843): 54–60.

[3] Lynch, *Narrative*, 302.

[4] Ibid., 302.

[5] Ibid., 302.; Smith, *Historical Geography*, 513.

[6] Lynch, *Narrative*, 331; Smith, *Historical Geography*, 514. Lynch's account, drawn from notes and journals of Dale, Anderson, and Bedlow, may

be compared to the account of Samuel W. Wolcott (the first Western visitor to Masada, in 1842) as published by Edward Robinson in *Bibliotheca Sacra* 1 (February 1, 1843): 54–60. [The Wolcott account is reprinted in *The Jewish War of Flavius Josephus* (London: Houlston and Stoneman, 1851), cxi-cxiv, albeit erroneously attributed to Wolcott's co-explorer, William J. Tipping, illustrator of the edition.] In recounting the naval officers' exploration, I have tried to identify the things they saw and identified as well as the remains they traversed that were not identified until the modern era, beginning in the 1960s with Yigael Yadin and his successors.

[7] Wolcott, "Researches in Palestine," 57.

[8] Melville, *Clarel*, 243, xix.

[9] Lynch, *Narrative*, 333; Josephus, *War of the Jews*, Works, 849.

[10] Wolcott, "Researches in Palestine," 58.

[11] Bailey, *The Gospel in Hymns*, 502–503; John Irving Erickson, *Sing It Again!* Chicago: Covenant Press, 1985, 429; Charles S. Robinson, *Annotations Upon Popular Hymns*. New York: Hunt & Eaton, 1893, 40.

[12] *New York Times*, May 31, 1914.

[13] Lynch, *Narrative*, 328.

[14] Lynch to Mason, April 29, 1848, T829, Roll 438.

[14] Ibid.

Chapter Eleven

[1] Lynch, *Official Report*, Sunday April 30, 1848, NARA; Lynch, *Narrative*, 335–336; Blackall, John, *Observations of the Nature and Cure of Dropsies* (London: Longman, 1813), 277–283, 292–337.

[2] Lynch, *Narrative*, 337–338.

[3] Ibid., 339. H. B. Tristram, in his book *The Land of Moab* (New York: Harper and Brothers, 1873), contributes vivid descriptions of the Moabite terrain and the mores of the tribes there.

[4] Lynch, *Narrative*, 340–342.

[5] Ibid., 339–343.

[6] Ibid., 343–344; Lynch, *Official Report*, April 30, 1848.

[7] Lynch, *Narrative*, 345–348.

[8] Ibid., 348–349.

[9] Ibid., 352–355.

[10] Ibid., 355–357, 359; Lynch to Mason, May 18, 1848, T829, Roll 438; Lynch, *Official Report*, May 2, 3, 1848; Tristram, *Land of Moab*, 82–85; Libbey and Hoskins, *Jordan Valley*, 319–321.

[11] Lynch, *Narrative*, 358–359; Tristram, *Land of Moab*, 86–94.

[12] Lynch, *Narrative*, 359–361; Lynch to Mason, May 18, 1848, T829, Roll 438.

[13] Lynch, *Narrative*, 368; Lynch, *Official Report*, May 3, 1848: Anderson to Lynch, May 15, 1848, T829, Roll 438.

Chapter Twelve

[1] Josephus, *War of the Jews* 7, Works, 6.2/177; Josephus, *Antiquities of the Jews*, 18, Works, 5.1/111–112; Josephus, *Antiquities*, 18, 5.2/116–119; George A. Smith, "Callirrhoe and Machaerus," PEFQS 37 (1905): 228.

[2] Irby and Mangles, *Travels in Egypt and Nubia*, 144; Claude Reignier Conder, *Heth and Moab*, 151–152.

[3] Anderson to Lynch, May 15, 1848, T829, Roll 438.

[4] Lynch, *Narrative*, 372–373.

[5] Ibid., 374.

[6] Ibid.

[7] Ibid., 375.

[8] Lynch, *Official Report*, Monday, May 8, 1848.

[9] Lynch to Mason, Jerusalem, May 18, 1848, T829, Roll 438.

[10] Lynch, *Narrative*, 377–380.

[11] Lynch to Winthrop, May 25, 1848, T829, Roll 438.

[12] Lynch, *Narrative*, 287.

[13] Ibid., 380.

[14] Lynch's *Narrative* (381) initially names only Aulick and Bedlow for this mission, but later he includes the unnamed "youngest member of our expedition" (403) which was not the 27-year-old poet and diarist Bedlow, but of course 16-year-old Midshipman Francis Lynch.

[15] Melville, *Clarel*, 278.

Chapter Thirteen

[1] Guerin, *Les Petits Bollandistes*, 67-77.

[2] Kean, *Among the Holy Places*, 103.

[3] Walsh, *Butler's Lives of the Saints*, 403.

[4] Twain, *Innocents Abroad*, 447.

[5] Lynch, *Narrative*, 385–387; Gil, *History of Palestine*, 451.

[6] Stephens, *Incidents of Travel*, vol. 2, 216.

[7] Bedlow, *White Tsar*.

[8] Lynch, *Narrative*, 396–397.

[9] Ibid., 400.

[10] Ibid., 403; *New York Herald*, July 29, 1848, 1.

[11] *Appleton's Cyclopedia*; Meehan, "Henry James Anderson, M.D., L.L.D.," 112–118.

[12] Kirk and Allibone, *Allibone's*, 591.

[13] Lynch, *Narrative*, 405; *New York Herald*, July 29, 1848, 1.

[14] Lynch, *Narrative*, 419–420.

[15] Ibid., 434.

[16] Ibid., 434–435.

[17] Ibid., 439–440.

[18] Kark, *American Consuls*, 103.

[19] Lynch, 449.

[20] Lynch to Pennock, Jaffa, May 25, 1848, T829, Roll 438.

[21] Lynch to Pennock, Beirut, July 29, 1848, T829, Roll 438.

[22] Camden, New Jersey Phoenix, September 27, 1848, 2; John Young Mason Papers #1546, Ser. B.

[23] Mason to Mary Ann Mason, Washington, July 19, 1848, John Young Mason Papers #1546, B.

[24] Lynch, *Narrative*, 459–460.

[25] Ibid., 463.

[26] Ibid., 467.

[27] Ibid., 477.

[28] Ibid.

[29] Ibid., 485–486.

[30] Lynch identified the malady from which they suffered, and which killed Dale, as a "low, nervous fever": Lynch to Mason, Beirut, July 29, 1848, T829, Roll 438.

[31] Lynch, *Narrative*, 503–504.

[32] Ibid., 505.

[33] Lynch to Mason, Beirut, July 6, 1848, T829, Roll 438.

[34] Lynch to Mason, Beirut, July 14, 1848, T829, Roll 438.

[35] Lynch, *Narrative*, 505–506; Lynch to Mason, Beirut, July 18, 1848. T829, Roll 438.

[36] *National Intelligencer*, quoted in *Trenton State Gazette*, July 19, 1849, 2.

[37] Lynch, *Narrative*, 507.

[38] *Bibliotheca Sacra* 5 (November 1848): 770; *Keene* (New Hampshire) *Sentinel*, September 28, 1848, 3.

[39] Lynch to Mason, Beirut, July 29, 1848, T829, Roll 438.

[40] Ibid; Lynch, *Narrative*, 507–508.

[41] *Bibliotheca Sacra* 5 (November 1848): 770.

[42] Ibid.; Lynch to Mason, Malta, September 10, 1848, T829, Roll 438.

[43] *New York Herald*, September 11, 1848, 3.

[44] Ibid.; Lynch to Mason, Marseilles, September 30, 1848, T829, Roll 438; John Mason, Jr., to Lewis Mason, At Sea, July 26, 1848, John Mason, Jr., to mother, At Sea, August 31, 1848, John Young Mason Papers #1546.

[45] Cooper and Woolsey, *Lives of Distinguished American Naval Officers* (1846).

[46] *New York Herald*, September 11, 1848, 4.

[47] M .F. Maury to Ann Maury, Washington, August 9, 1848. MP, Box 3, LOC; John Thompson to MFM, Richmond, September 7, 1848. U.S. Naval Observatory, RG 78, Letters Received 1838–1884, 7:4, NARA; *Southern Literary Messenger* (September 1848).

[48] Thompson to Maury, Richmond, September 7, 1848, U.S. Naval Observatory—Letters Received 1838–884, 7:4, NARA; Minor, *Southern Literary Messenger*, 1834–1864, 165.

[49] Virginia Lynch to MFM, Louisville, October 16, 1848. U.S. Naval Observatory— Letters Received 1838–1884, 7, NARA.

[50] *New York Herald*, September 11, 1848, 4; *Bibliotheca Sacra* 5 (November 1848): 764–770.

[51] Lynch to MFM, Off Gibraltar, October 20, 1848, MP, Letters Received 1838–1884, RG78, U.S. Naval Observatory, NARA.

[52] Lynch, *Narrative*, 508.

Chapter Fourteen

[1] Mason to Sloat, Washington, D.C., December 9 and 12, 1848, 4; Mason to Lynch, Washington, D.C., January 9, 1849, M325, Reel 4.

[2] *Washington Globe*, December 16, 1848, p. 3; *Trenton State Gazette*, December 16, 1848, 2.

[3] John Mason, Jr., to Mason, Gilbraltar, October 20, 1848, John Young Mason Papers.

[4] *Trenton State Gazette*, January 5, 1849, 2; Aulick death notice: *New York Herald*, June 11, 1868, 1. Buried at Congressional Cemetery in Washington, he was reburied at Oak Hill in 1897.

[5] Lynch to Preston, Baltimore, February 7, 1850, M335, Roll 189; Pre-

ston to Lynch, Washington, D.C., February 13, 1850, M325, Roll 45.

[6] Mason to Lynch, Washington, January 9, 1849, Mason to Sloat, Washington, D.C., January 18, 1849, M325, Roll 44; Lynch to Mason, Baltimore, January 15, 1849, M335, Roll 188; *Trenton State Gazette*, January 5, 1849, 2.

[7] Lynch to Mason, Washington, D.C., February 3, 1849, T829, Roll, 438; *Sen. Journal*, February 26, 27, 1849.

[8] *New York Herald*, September 11, 1848, 4.

[9] Lynch to Mason, Washington, D.C., January 12, 1849, February 3, 1849, Philadelphia, February 22, 1849, M335, Roll 188; Mason to Lynch, Washington, D.C., February 10, 1849, M325, Roll 44.

[10] *New York Weekly Herald*, February 24, 1849, p. 64.

[11] Lynch to Mason, Philadelphia, February 22, 1849, M335, Roll 188; Mason to Lynch, Washington, D.C., February 27, 1849, M325, Roll 44.

[12] Maury to Blackford, Washington, D.C., March 12, 1849, MP, Box 3, LOC.

[13] *Nautical Magazine and Naval Chronicle*, vol. 20, part 1 (1851), 13.

[14] Woodward to Lynch, Washington, D.C., April 21, 1849, Lynch to Preston, Philadelphia, April 23, 1849, M335, Roll 189; Preston to Lynch, Washington, D.C., April 24, 1849, M325, Roll 45.

[15] Montague, *Narrative of the Late Expedition*, ix; *Trenton* (New Jersey) *State Gazette*, March 26, 1849, 4.

[16] *Savannah Republican*, May 24, 1849, 2, *Columbus State Journal*, May 30, 1849, 4, *Barre Patriot*, June 1, 1849, 4.

[17] Lynch to Preston, Philadelphia, May 9, 1849, M335, Roll 189; Warrington to Lynch, Washington, D.C., May 10, 1849, M325, Roll 45.

[18] Lynch to Mason, Philadelphia, June 7, 1849, John Young Mason Papers, #1546, Ser. A.

[19] *Baltimore Sun*, June 14, 1849, 1.

[20] *New York Commercial Advertiser* and *New York Tribune*, quoted in *Littell's Living Age* (October 6, 1849): 1–48.

[21] *Savannah Republican*, June 14, 1849, 2; *Missouri Republican*, July 21, 1849, 2; *Merchants' Magazine & Commercial Review* 43: 140.

[22] *New Hampshire Patriot*, June 14, 1849, 3.

[23] *Boston Daily Atlas*, July 26, 1849, 1. The Whig *Atlas* also reprinted the highly favorable view of the unbound sheets from the *Philadelphia Inquirer*, on June 9, 1849, 2, perhaps another message of "let bygones be bygones."

[24] *Sharpe's London Journal*, July 1849, 66; *North British Review*, August 1849, 494; *Chambers' Edinburgh Journal*, August 1849, 103; *Literary Gazette*, July 1849, 498.

[25] *Baltimore Sun*, July 22, 1851, 1.

[26] Author correspondence with John Lynch and John Lynch II, June and September 2010.

[27] *U.S. Federal Census 1850*, District 1, Baltimore, MD, Family no. 2334, Roll M432-280, 390a, image 385; *U.S. Federal Census Mortality Schedules*, 1850–1885, Roll T755-6, 130, line 34, E. D. Lynch, widowed, born Virginia about 1820, died May 1880 of epilepsy in Washington, D.C. She was a resident of the Louise Home, an imposing retirement home established by art philanthropist W. W. Corcoran for genteel yet impoverished ladies; many residents were Confederate widows: Paul K. Williams, "Scenes From the Past," *Washington InTowner* (April 2009); 8. Burial: Lot and Interment Cards, William F. Lynch, Green Mount Cemetery, Baltimore, MD.

[28] *Baltimore Sun*, November 27, 1849; Lynch to Beale, Baltimore, January 11, 1850, Maury to Beale, Washington, February 28, 1850, in Bonsal, *Edward Fitzgerald Beale*, 56–58.

[29] *Proceedings of the American Philosophical Society*, vol. 5, 307. Both Lynch and Maury were expelled from the society for joining the Confederacy, in the meeting of March 21, 1862: *Proceedings*, vol. 27, 162–163.

[30] *New York Herald*, March 24, 1858, 2, April 3, 1858, 1, 5.

[31] *New York Herald*, December 8, 1859, 1.

[32] Doubleday, *Reminiscences of Forts Sumter*, 144.

[33] Record and Pension Office, War Department, *The War of the Rebellion: A Compilation of the Official Records of the Union and Confederate Armies*, Series 3 (Washington, D.C. 1902), vol. 1, 22.

[34] William S. Dudley, "Going South," 13 and table 3, "Proportions of Officers 'Going South,' " 18–19.

[35] *Nautical Gazette*, May 1940; Wells, *Confederate Navy*, 58–61, 64.

[36] Frances L. Williams, *Matthew Fontaine Maury*; Hearn, *Tracks in the Sea*; Corbin, *Life*.

[37] William Francis Lynch, *ZB Biography* (U.S. Navy Chronology), compiled March 22, 1935; Wells, *Confederate Navy*, op. cit., 15, 142–143; Presidential document, handwritten: "*Executive Pardon, Case of W. F. Lynch, Formerly of the U.S. Navy, late in the Rebel Service: Application for Special Pardon: Respectfully referred to the Hon. Attorney General. Let the pardon applied*

for issue in this case. Andrew Johnson, President U.S. No. 99, Pardoned June 11, 1865."

[38] *Baltimore Sun*, October 18, 1865, 1; *Philadelphia Inquirer*, October 19, 1865, 1; *Washington Constitution Union*, October 18, 1865, 1; *Baltimore Sun*, October 20, 1865, 1.

Bibliography

PRIMARY SOURCES—Books, Periodicals, and Articles

Abbott, Jacob. "Memoirs of the Holy Land." *Harper's New Monthly Magazine* 5 (June–November 1852): 289–303, 433–450, 577–596, 721–738.

Adams, Charles Francis (ed.). *Memoirs of John Quincy Adams*. Philadelphia: J. P. Lippincott, 1875.

Allen, William. *The Dead Sea, A New Route to India: With Other Fragments and Gleamings in the East*. London: Longmans, Brown, Green, and Longmans, 1855.

American Geographical and Statistical Society Bulletin 1 (1853): 84.

Ammen, Daniel. *The Old Navy and the New. Personal Reminiscences*. Philadelphia: J. B. Lippincott, 1891.

Baltimore Sun

Barre Patriot

Bedlow, Henry. *War and Worship: A Poem*. New York: Truth Seeker, 1902.

———. *The White Tsar and Other Poems*. New York: J. S. Tait, 1895.

Boston Daily Atlas

Boston Journal

Bronson's Quarterly Review

Conder, Claude Reignier, *Heth and Moab: Explorations in Syria in 1881 and 1882*. London: A.P. Watt, 1892.

Congressional Globe, 1836–1861.

"Critical Notices." *Southern Quarterly Review* 16 (October 1849): 233.

"The Dead Sea, Sodom and Gommorah." *Harper's New Monthly Magazine 10* (December 1854–May 1855): 187–193.

Doubleday, Abner, *Reminiscences of Forts Sumter and Moultrie in 1860 and '61.* New York: Harper, 1876.

Hayden, Ferdinand V. "United States Government Surveys." *American Journal of Science and Arts* 2, no. 34 (New Haven, CT, 1862): 98–101.

Josephus. *Works of Josephus*. Trans. William Whiston. Peabody, MA: Hendrickson, 1987.

Irby, Charles and Mangles, James, *Travels in Egypt and Nubia, Syria, and the Holy Land.* London: John Murray, 1844.

Littell's Living Age 15 (October, November, December 1847): 606; 22 (July, August, September 1849): 160; 40 (February 1854): 303; 48 (January, February, March 1856): 227–301; 675–676; 63 (October, November, December 1859): 308–312.

Lynch, William F., Lieut. *Bericht Uber die Expedition der und dem Todten Staaten nach dem Jordan Meer.* Leipzig: 1859.

———. *Commerce and the Holy Land: A Lecture Delivered Before the N.Y. Kane Monument Association.* Philadelphia: King and Baird, 1860.

———. *Narrative of the United States Expedition to the River Jordan and the Dead Sea.* Philadelphia: Lea and Blanchard, 1849.

———. *Narrative of the United States Expedition to the River Jordan and the Dead Sea, A New and Condensed Edition.* Philadelphia: Lea and Blanchard, 1850.

———. *Naval Life; or, Observations Afloat and on Shore.* New York: Scribner, 1851.

———. *Official Report of the United States Expedition to Explore the Dead Sea and the River Jordan by Lieut. W. F. Lynch, USN.* Published at the National Observatory by Lieutenant M. F. Maury, USN, Superintendent, by the authority of the Hon. William A. Graham, Secretary of the Navy. Baltimore: J. Murphy, 1852.

———. *Report of Commander W. F. Lynch, in relation to his mission to the coast of Africa.* Washington, D.C., 1853.

Maundrell, H.A., *A Journey from Aleppo to Jerusalem at Easter, A.D. 1697.* Boston: Simpkins, 1836.

Maury, Matthew. *Astronomical Observations: Made Under the Direction of M. F. Maury, Lieut. U.S. Navy, during the year 1845, at the U.S. Naval Observatory*. Washington, D.C., 1846.

———. "The Dead Sea Expedition." *Southern Literary Messenger* (September 1848).

———. *A New Theoretical and Practical Treatise on Navigation*. 3rd ed. Philadelphia: Biddle, 1845.

———. "On the Navigation of Cape Horn." *American Journal of Science* 36, no. 5 (July 1834).

———. *The Physical Geography of the Sea*. New York: Harper and Brothers, 1856.

———. *Wind and Current Chart of the North Atlantic*. Washington, D.C.: U.S. Hydrographical Office, 1847–1852.

———. *Wind and Current Chart of the South Atlantic*. Washington, D.C.: U.S. Hydrographical Office, 1852.

McClean, John (ed.), *Reports of Cases Argued in the Circuit Court of the United States for the Seventh Circuit*, 2. Cincinnati: E. Morgan, 1840–1856.

Melville, Herman. *Journal of a Visit to Europe and the Levant, October 11, 1856–May 6, 1857*. Ed. Howard C. Horsford. Princeton, NJ: Princeton University Press, 1955.

Merchant's Magazine and Commercial Review

Molyneux, Thomas. "Expedition to the Jordan and the Dead Sea." *Journal of the Royal Geographic Society of London* 18 (March 28, 1848).

Montague, Edward P. (ed.). *Narrative of the Late Expedition to the Dead Sea From a Diary by One of the Party*. Philadelphia: Carey and Hart, 1849.

Moore, John Bassett (ed.). *The Works of James Buchanan*. Philadelphia: Lippincott, 1908.

National Intelligencer, November 24, 1847; January 1, 3, November 1, 1849.

Nautical Magazine and Naval Chronicle

New Hampshire Patriot

New York Courier & Enquirer

New York Herald, November 30, 1847; December 18, 1848.

New York Review

New York Weekly Herald

Niles Register

Putnam's Monthly

Richmond Enquirer

Richmond Whig and Public Advertiser

Robinson, Edward, and E. Smith. *Biblical Researches in Palestine, and in the Adjacent Regions: A Journal of Travels in the Year 1838* (1856 ed.). Michigan Historical Reprint Series, p.o.d.

———. "Depression of the Dead Sea and of the Jordan Valley." *Journal of the Royal Geographic Society of London* 18 (1848).

Seetzen, Ultich Jasper, *A Brief Account of the countries Adjoining the Lake of Tiberias, the Jordan, and the Dead Sea*. London: Palestine Association, 1810.

Silliman, Benjamin, Sr. "Notice of the Narrative of Lynch's Expedition to the Dead Seas." *American Journal of Science and Arts* 58 (November 1849): 137–138.

Stephens, J. S. *Incidents of Travel in Egypt, Arabia, Petraea, and the Holy Land. By an American*. 10th ed., with additions. 2 vols. New York: Harper and Brothers, 1839.

Theoderich. *Guide to the Holy Land* (1170, 1897). Trans. Aubrey Stewart. 2nd ed. New York: Italica Press, 1986.

Twain, Mark. *The Innocents Abroad* (1872). New York: Signet, 1966.

Washington Constitution Union

Wilkes, Charles. Papers.

Wolcott, Samuel W. Field Notes Compiled by Edward Robinson. "Researches in Palestine," *Bibliotheca Sacra* (February 1, 1843): 54–59.

Wright, Thomas. *Early Travels in Palestine* (1848). New York: Dover, 2003.

PRIMARY SOURCES—Manuscripts

HISTORICAL SOCIETY OF NEW JERSEY

DICKERSON PAPERS

LIBRARY OF CONGRESS

MAURY, MATTHEW FONTAINE, PAPERS, MSS.

NAVAL HISTORICAL FOUNDATION MSS.

MARYLAND STATE ARCHIVES

CHANCERY COURT PAPERS 1845–1846

NATIONAL ARCHIVES

Memo headed *William F. Lynch*, U.S. Navy, March 23, 1833, Office of Early Records Section, Muster Roll of Crew of the U.S. Steamer *Water Witch*, Thomas J. Page, Lieut. and Acting Purser, Old Military Records Division.

Naval History Division, Department of the Navy Records of the Bureau of Naval Personnel, Record Group 24, File No. 148.

Records of the Department of State, Record Group 59, Microcopy, M 83, M 472 (roll 3).

Records of the Naval Observatory, Letters Sent, 1842–62 (Volumes 1–19); Letters Received, 1840–55 (Files 18–29).

Records of the Office of Naval Records and Library, Record Group 45, Microcopy M-88 (rolls 4, 5, 6, 12); M-89 (roll 78); M-25 (rolls 326 368); M-147 (rolls 3467); M-148 (rolls 173–275); M-149 (rolls 41–64); M 517 (rolls 1–17); M 625 (Area 4, rolls 15–16); T-829 (rolls 359–362, 438, 443, 445).

Register of Vessels Arriving at the Port of New York from Foreign Ports, 1789–1919. Washington, D.C.: National Archives and Records Administration.

Selected Pages from *Log of the U.S.S. Supply* (June–September 1848) on microfilm (NNMO73282[685]).

UNIVERSITY OF NORTH CAROLINA AT CHAPEL HILL

John Young Mason Papers, #1546.

Mason, John Young, "Address Before the Alumni Association of the University of North Carolina, June 2, 1847." Washington, D.C.: J. and G. S. Gideon, 1847.

U.S. CONGRESSIONAL DOCUMENTS

30th Cong., 2nd sess. "Report of the Secretary of the Navy, with a Report made by Lieutenant William F. Lynch of an Examination of the Dead Sea. February 26, 1849; Read February 27, referred to the committee on Commerce and Ordered to be printed." *Senate Ex. Doc. No. 34*, 1849.

33rd Cong., 1st sess. "Message from the President of the United States to the Two Houses of Congress." 4, Maps and other illustrations, William Francis Lynch Mission to Africa. Washington. D.C.: Arobert Armstrong, 1853.

House Executive Document No. 147, "Exploring Expedition."

U.S. NAVY DEPARTMENT DOCUMENTS

Annual Reports of the Secretary of the Navy, 1833–1861.

William Francis Lynch Biography, U.S. Navy Library.

SECONDARY SOURCES—Books, Articles, and Dissertations

Abbott, Jacob. "Some Account of Francis's Life-Boats and Life-Cars." *Harper's* (July 1851): 161–171.

Alden, Carroll S., and Westcott, Allan. *The United States Navy, A History*. 2nd ed., rev. Philadelphia: J. B. Lippincott, 1945.

American Journal of Science and Arts.

Americana at the Royal Library Albert I. Brussels: Center for American Studies, 1973.

American National Biography

Appleton's Cyclopedia of American Biography

Army and Navy Chronicle

Bailey, Albert E. *The Gospel in Hymns*. New York: Scribner's, 1950.

Banvard, John, *Description of Banvard's Pilgrimage to Jerusalem and the Holy Land*. New York, n.p., 1853.

Battistini, Lawrence. *The Rise of American Influence in Asia and the Pacific*. Lansing: Michigan State University Press, 1960.

Battle, Kemp P. *A History of the University of North Carolina (1789–1868)*, Vol. 1. Raleigh, NC: Edwards and Broughton, 1907.

Bauer, Karl Jack. *The Mexican War, 1846–1848*. New York: Macmillan, 1974.

Bemis, Samuel Flagg (ed.). *The American Secretaries of State and Their Diplo-*

macy. 17 vols. New York: Pageant Book Co. and Cooper Square Publishers, 1958–1967.

Bennett, Frank M. *The Steam Navy of the United States.* Pittsburgh, PA: Warren, 1896.

Bolander, Louis H. "The Vincennes, World Traveler of the Old Navy." *United States Naval Institute Proceedings* 63 (July 1936): 823–31.

Bonsal, Stephen, *Edward Fitzgerald Beale, A Pioneer on the Path to Empire, 1822 – 1903.* New York: Putnam's, 1912.

Bromley, Geoffrey W., *International Standard Bible Encyclopedia.* Grand Rapids: Eerdmans, 1995.

Catalogue of the Library of the Late Henry James Anderson, Comprising a Fine Collection of Scientific and Mathematical Work, and Many Valuable Manuscripts. New York: G.A. Leavitt, 1879.

Chapelle, Howard I. *The History of the American Sailing Navy.* New York: Norton, 1949.

Church, Ella Rodman. "Lafayette's Last Visit to America." *Magazine of American History* 6, no. 5 (May 1881).

Clark, Arthur H. *The Clipper Ship Era.* New York: G. P. Putnam's Sons, 1911.

Coblentz, Catherine Cate. "Naval Lieutenant Matthew Fontaine Maury—First Citizen of the World." Unpublished biography. Washington, D.C.: Library of Congress (filed with A. F. Maury Collection).

Coker, Robert Ervin. *This Great and Wide Sea.* Rev. ed. Chapel Hill: University of North Carolina Press, 1949.

Coletta, Paolo E. (ed.). *American Secretaries of the Navy 1.* Annapolis, MD: Naval Institute Press, 1980.

Collection of Scientific and Mathematical Works, and Many Valuable Manuscripts. New York: G.A. Leavitt, 1879.

Condor, Claude Reignier. *Heth and Moab: Explorations in Syria in 1881 and 1882.* London: Alexander P. Watt, 1892.

Cooper, James Fenimore. *History of the Navy of the United States of America Abridged in One Volume from the Octavo Edition by J. Fenimore Cooper Continued to 1756 from the Author's Manuscripts and Other Authentic Sources.* New York: Stringer and Townsend, 1856.

Corbin, Diana Fontaine Maury. *A Life of Matthew Fontaine Maury*. London: Silow, Marston, Searle and Rivington, 1888.

DeVoto, Bernard. *The Year of Decision: 1846*. Boston: Houghton Mifflin, 1942, 1943.

Dick, Steven J. *Sky and Ocean Joined: The U.S. Naval Observatory, 1830–2000*. New York: Cambridge University Press, 2002.

Dictionary of American Biography. New York: Scribner, 1928–1989.

Dictionary of American Naval Fighting Ships, Vol. 2. Washington, D.C.: US GPO, 1963.

Dudley, William S. "Going South: U.S. Navy Officer Resignations and Dismissals on the Eve of the Civil War." Washington, D.C.: U.S. Naval Historical Foundation, 1981.

Eisenhower, John S. D. *So Far from God: The U.S. War with Mexico, 1846–1848*. New York: Random House, 1989.

Emmons, George F. *The Navy of the United States from the Commencement, 1775–1853, with a Brief History of each Vessel's Service and Fate as Appears upon Record*. Washington, D.C.: Gideon, 1853.

Factors in Columbia County History, 2. Hudson, NY: Record Printing and Publishing, 1900.

Fasano, Lawrence. *Naval Rank: Its Inception and Development*. New York: Horizon House, 1936.

Field, James A., Jr. *America and the Mediterranean World, 1776–1882*. Princeton, NJ: Princeton University Press, 1969.

Finne, David H. *Pioneers East, the Early American Experience in the Middle East. Harvard Middle Eastern Studies*. Cambridge, MA: Harvard University Press, 1967.

Fulcher of Chartres. *Chronicle of the First Crusade*. Trans. Martha McGinty. Philadelphia: University of Pennsylvania Press, 1941.

Gervase of Tilbury. *Otia Imperialia: Recreation for an Emperor*. Oxford: Clarendon, 2002.

Gil, Moshe. *A History of Palestine, 634–1099*. Trans. Ethel Broido. Cambridge: Cambridge University Press, 1992.

Glueck, Nelson. "The Geography of the Jordan." *National Geographic* (December 1944): 719–744.

Goetzmann, William H. *Exploration and Empire: The Explorer and the Scientist in the Winning of the American West*. New York: Alfred A. Knopf, 1967.

———. *New Lands, New Men: America and the Second Great Age of Discovery*. New York: Viking, 1986.

———. *When the Eagle Screamed: The Romantic Horizon in American Diplomacy, 1800–1860*. New York: Wiley, 1966.

Gould, Benjamin Apthorp, Biographical Notice of James Melville Gilliss. Cambridge: Welsh, Bigelow, 1867.

Guerin, Msgr. Paul, *Les Petits Bollandists: Vies des Saintes*, 14. Paris: Bloud et Barral, 1882.

Haskell, Daniel C. *The U.S. Exploring Expedition: Its Publications 1844–1874: A Bibliography*. New York: New York Public Library, 1942.

Hawthorne, Hildegard. *Matthew Fontaine Maury: Trail Maker of the Seas*. New York: Longmans, Green, 1943.

Hearn, Chester G., *Tracks in the Sea: Matthew Fontaine Maury and the Mapping of the Oceans*. Camden, ME: International Marine, 2002.

Hill, Edwin C. *The Historical Register: A Record of People Places and Events in American History*. New York: Edwin C. Hill, 1920.

Hoskins, Janina W. *Lafayette in America: A Selective List of Reading Materials in English*. Washington, D.C.: Library of Congress, 1983.

Hubbard, Walter, and Richard F. Winter, "North Atlantic Mail Sailings 1840–75." Cleveland, OH: U.S. Philatelic Society, 1988.

"Jordan and the Dead Sea," *Bibliotheca Sacra* 7: 393.

Kark, Ruth. *American Consuls in the Holy Land, 1832–1914*. Detroit, MI: Wayne State University Press, 1994.

Karsten, Peter. *The Naval Aristocracy, The Golden Age of Annapolis and the Emergence of Modern American Navalism*. New York: Free Press, 1972.

Kean, James. *Among the Holy Places: A Pilgrimage Through Palestine*. London: Unwin, 1894.

Kent, Charles Foster. *Biblical Geography and History*. New York: Scribner's, 1911.

Kirk, John Goster, and Allibone, Samuel Foster, *A Supplement to Allibone's Critical Dictionary of English*, 1 (1892). Detroit: Gale Research, 1965.

Krieger, Barbara. *The Dead Sea: Myth, History, and Politics* (1988). Hanover, NH: Brandeis University Press / University Press of New England, 1997.

Lane, Calvin. "The African Squadron: The U.S. Navy and the Slave Trade, 1820–1862." Mystic, CT: Mystic Seaport Library, n.d.

Langley, Harold D. *Social Reform in the United States Navy, 1798–1862.* Urbana: University of Illinois Press, 1967.

Levasseur, A. *Lafayette in America in 1824 and 1825.* Trans. John D. Godman. Philadelphia: Carey and Lea, 1829.

Libbey, William, and Franklin E. Hoskins. *The Jordan Valley and Petra.* New York: Putnam's, 1905.

MacIntire, Jane Bacon. *Lafayette, The Guest of the Nation.* Newton, MA: Anthony J. Simone Press, 1967.

Maclay, Edgar S. *A History of the United States Navy from 1775 to 1901.* 3 vols. New York: D. Appleton, 1901.

Maury, Sarah Mytton, *The Statesmen of America in 1846.* Philadelphia: Carey and Hart, 1847.

Meehan, Thomas F., "Henry James Anderson, M.D., LL.D," *Historical Records and Studies*, 51 (Nov 1907). U.S. Catholic Historical Society, 1907.

Melville, Herman. *Clarel: A Poem and Pilgrimage in the Holy Land* (1876). Ed. Walter E. Bezanson. New York: Hendricks House, 1960.

Minor, Benjamin Blake, *Southern Literary Messenger, 1834 – 1864.* New York: Neale, 1905.

Morison, Samuel Eliot. *"Old Bruin": Commodore Matthew C. Perry.* Boston: Little, Brown, 1967.

National Cyclopedia of American Biography, 1898.

Neeser, Robert W. *Statistical and Chronological History of the United States Navy, 1776–1907.* 2 vols. New York: Macmillan, 1909.

Newman, Rev. John P. *From Dan to Beersheba, or, The Land of Promise as It Now Appears.* New York: Harper and Brothers, 1864.

Olin, Stephen. *Travels in Egypt, Arabia Petraea, and the Holy Land.* New York: Lane and Tippett, 1846.

Orr, James. *International Standard Bible Encyclopedia*. Chicago: Howard-Severance, 1915.

Paullin, Charles Oscar. *American Voyages to the Orient, 1690–1865: A Collection of Articles from the United States Naval Institute Proceedings*. Annapolis, MD: United States Naval Institute, 1971.

———. *Diplomatic Negotiations of American Naval Officers*. Baltimore, MD: Johns Hopkins Press, 1912.

———. *Paullin's History of Naval Administration, 1775–1911—A Collection of Articles from the U.S. Naval Institute Proceedings*. Annapolis, MD: United States Naval Institute, 1968.

Payne, R. *The Dream and the Tomb: A History of the Crusades*. New York: Stein and Day, 1984.

Pelletreau, William S. *Historic Homes and Institutions and Genealogical and Family History of New York*, Vol. 2. New York: Lewis, 1907.

Philbrick, Nathaniel. *Sea of Glory: America's Voyage of Discovery, The U.S. Exploring Expedition*. New York: Viking, 2003.

Pickard, Madge E. "Government and Science in the United States: Historical Backgrounds." *Journal of the History of Medicine 1* (April 1946): 254–289.

Ponko, Vincent, Jr. *Ships, Seas, and Scientists*, Annapolis, MD: Naval Institute Press, 1974.

Porter, David Dixon. *The Naval History of the Civil War*. New York: Sherman, 1886.

Pratt, Fletcher. *The Navy: A History*. New York: Garden City Publishing, 1945.

Reynolds, *Pacific and Indian Oceans*. New York: Harper and Brothers, 1841.

Rook, Robert E. *Manifest Destiny in the Middle East: Lieutenant William Francis Lynch and the Dead Sea Survey Mission, 1848*. Amman, Jordan: American Center of Oriental Research, 1998.

Scharf, J. Thomas. *History of the Confederate States Navy*. New York: Rogers and Sherwood, 1886.

Shanks, Hersel. "Ein Gedi's Archaeological Riches." *Biblical Archaeology Review* (May/June 2008).

Shroeder, John H. *Shaping a Maritime Empire: The Commercial and Diplomatic Role of the American Navy, 1829–1861*. Westport, CT: Greenwood, 1985.

Smith, George Adam. *The Historical Geography of the Holy Land*. New York: Hodder and Stoughton, 1896.

Smith, William. *Smith's Dictionary of the Bible*. New York: Hurd and Houghton, 1872.

Southern Literary Messenger

Sprout, Harold, and Margaret Sprout. *The Rise of American Naval Power, 1776–1918*. 5th Printing. Princeton, NJ: Princeton University Press, 1967.

Stanton, William. *The Great United States Exploring Expedition of 1838–1842*. Berkeley: University of California Press, 1975.

Stevens, William O. and C. Alphonso Smith, "Two Early Proposals for Naval Education." *United States Naval Institute Proceedings* 39, 1 (March 1913). Annapolis: United States Naval Institute.

St. John, Robert. *Roll Jordan Roll: The Life Story of a River and Its People*. New York: Doubleday, 1965.

Thom, J. C. "The American Navy and the Dead Sea." *United States Naval Institute Proceedings* 52, no. 9; Whole No. 283 (September 1926): 1689–1700.

Towle, Edward L. "Science, Commerce, and the Navy on the Seafaring Frontier (1842–1861), The Role of Lieutenant M. F. Maury and the U.S. Naval Hydrographic Office in Naval Exploration, Commercial Expansion, and Oceanography Before the Civil War." Ph.D. diss. Rochester, NY: University of Rochester, 1965.

Tristram, H. B. *The Land of Moab: Travels and Discoveries on the East Side of the Dead Sea and the Jordan*. New York: Harper and Brothers, 1873.

Tyler, David B. *The Wilkes Expedition*. Philadelphia: American Philosophical Society, 1968.

Ussishkin, David. "The Ghassulian Temple in Ein Gedi." *Biblical Archaeologist* 34, no. 1 (February, 1971).

Vogel, Lester I. *To See a Promised Land: Americans and the Holy Land in the Nineteenth Century*. University Park: Pennsylvania State University Press, 1993.

Walker, Franklin. *Irreverent Pilgrims: Melville, Browne, and Mark Twain in the Holy Land*. Seattle: University of Washington Press, 1974.

Walsh M., ed. *Butler's Lives of the Saints*. New York: HarperCollins, 1991.

Ward, Robert D. *An Account of General La Fayette's Visit to Virginia in the Years 1824–25*. Richmond, VA: West, Johnston, 1881.

Weber, Gustavus Adolphus. *The Hydrographic Office, Its History, Activities and Organization*. Service Monograph for the U.S. Govt., No. 42. Baltimore, MD: Johns Hopkins Press; Institute for Government Research, 1926.

———. *The Naval Observatory, Its History, Activities, and Organization*. Service. Monograph for the U.S. Govt., No. 39. Baltimore, MD: Johns Hopkins Press; Institute for Government Research, 1962.

Wells, Tom Henderson. *The Confederate Navy: A Study in Organization*. Tuscaloosa: University of Alabama Press, 1971.

White, Andrew D. *A History of the Warfare of Science with Theology in Christendom* (1895). New York: Braziller, 1955.

Whiting, John D. "Canoeing Down the River Jordan." *National Geographic* (December 1940): 781–808.

Williams, Frances L. *Matthew Fontaine Maury, Scientist of the Sea*. New Brunswick, NJ: Rutgers University Press, 1963.

Wright, John Kirtland. *The Geographical Lore of the Time of the Crusades*. New York: American Geographical Society, 1925.

Yadin, Yigael. *Masada: Herod's Fortress and the Zealot's Last Stand*. Translated from the Hebrew by Moshe Pearlman. New York: Random House, 1966.

Reviews of William Francis Lynch's Publications

American Journal of Science 58 (November 1849): 137–138.

Bibliotheca Sacra 19 (August 1848): 397–409; 20 (November 1848): 764–770; 7 (April 1850): 393–397.

Chamber's Edinburgh Journal 12 (1849): 103–105.

Harper's

Hogg's Instructor (London) 3 (1849): 387–405.

Ladies' Repository 10 (August 1850): 275.

Littell's Living Age 22 (July 1849): 157–162; 23 (October 6, 1849): 1–16.

Merchants' Magazine & Commercial Review 43, Vol 21 (July 1849): 140.

Methodist Quarterly 9 (October 1849): 633–653.

New Englander and Yale Review 7 (August 1849): 443–469.

The North British Review 11, no. 8 (August 1849): 494–527.

Sharpe's London Journal 10 (1849): 65–73.

Southern Literary Messenger 14 (1848): 547.

Southern Quarterly Review 16, no. 1 (October 1850): 233–235.

Theological and Literary Journal 2 (New York, July 1849): 288.

Index